# HOW THE LAW THINKS ABOUT CHILDREN

K

OC

# How the Law Thinks
# About Children

## Second Edition

Michael King
Christine Piper
*Co-Directors, Centre for the Study*
*of Law, the Child and the Family*
*Law Department*
*Brunel University*

*arena*

Published by
Arena
Ashgate Publishing Limited
Gower House
Croft Road
Aldershot
Hants GU11 3HR
England

Ashgate Publishing Company
Old Post Road
Brookfield
Vermont 05036
USA

**British Library Cataloguing in Publication Data**

King, Michael
  How the Law Thinks About Children –
  2 Rev. ed
  I. Title II. Piper, Christine
  344.204327950269
ISBN 1 85742 226 0

**Library of Congress Catalog Card Number**: 94-72893

Phototypeset in 10/12 Palatino by Photoprint, Torquay, Devon and printed in Great Britain by Hartnoll's Ltd, Bodmin, Cornwall

# Contents

# Acknowledgements

We should like to thank Alex Stein and Stewart Asquith who read and commented helpfully on draft chapters of the first edition of this book stages during its period of gestation. We are especially grateful to David Nelken, Brad Sherman and, of course, Gunther Teubner whose advice and encouragement were invaluable at a time when we were wrestling with the complexities of autopoietic theory. A word of thanks, also, to those members of the Tavistock Clinic whose interest and concern over the way that the legal system in England and Wales deals with child welfare issues proved to be the starting point for some of the ideas which we have developed in this book. Finally, a word of appreciation to all those who commented on the first edition and whose comments have resulted in improvements and corrections to this second edition.

*Michael King and Christine Piper, Uxbridge, April 1995*

# Preface to second edition

When the first edition of *How the Law Thinks About Children* appeared in late 1990 (King and Piper, 1990), very few people in English-speaking countries had heard of autopoietic theory. Indeed, for many academic law or social policy teachers, our book, or the article in the *Journal of Law and Society* which was based on the first two chapters of the book (King, 1991a), represented their first exposure to the ideas of Gunther Teubner or Niklas Luhmann. Much has changed since then. Firstly, there has been a rapid growth of interest in Luhmann's ideas among socio-legal scholars. Even if some of the ways that Luhmann is presented in Anglo-Saxon intellectual discourse hardly begin to do justice to the complexity and modesty of his concepts, people are beginning to take seriously his original, if rather inaccessible, contribution to twentieth-century thought. Secondly, Gunther Teubner's book, *Law as an Autopoietic System*, has been published in an excellent translation by Anne Bankowska and the late Ruth Adler, edited by Zenon Bankowski (Teubner, 1993), while Teubner himself has been appointed to a chair in the Law Department of the London School of Economics. In the UK, therefore, an increasing number of law students are being exposed to this unfamiliar but thought-provoking way of under-standing the relationship between social systems and their environments.

While none of this affects directly the second edition of our book, we are very conscious that we now have to address our ideas about the application of autopoiesis to legal decision-making about children to a more knowledgeable and theoretically sophisticated audience than was the case four years ago. This in turn has provoked us into re-examining some of the applications of the theory set out in the book, and, where necessary, to adjust these in order to clarify the text or to rectify our own misunderstandings or partial understandings of the original theory.

A second important development since the publication of the first edition of *How the Law Thinks About Children* has been the 'globalization' of children's rights through the medium of the United Nations Convention on the Rights of the Child.[1] This convention has the effect of transforming children's rights into international law. The response of lawyers and politicians to the endorsement of the convention by the United Nations and its subsequent ratification by so many of the world's nations (with some notable exceptions) has tended to brand as faint-hearted or a rights-sceptic anyone who responds to the appearance of the convention on the global arena in anything other than euphoric terms. Yet, what we wrote four years ago in Chapter 4 about children's rights applies as much to the international situation as it does to individual state jurisdictions.

We would also suggest that analytical accounts of international rights for children would do well to consider legal rights as communication,[2] as messages sent to society from the legal system which not only construct children, parents, governments and nation states as 'semantic artifacts' of law,[3] but also project a particular identity, a self-image of law. In its communications on children's rights the legal system offers society an image of itself as capable of protecting children and promoting their welfare all over the globe simply by declaring unlawful any acts which harm or are likely to harm children or exclude them from having a say in decisions concerning their lives. The particular vision provided by the United Nations in its Convention on the Rights of the Child is one of a three-tiered hierarchy of international law, state law and national institutions, agencies and organizations. The image of a direct line of command (or at least influence) from United Nations to nation state to citizen is conveyed through the convention's exhortations to the world's national governments that they should 'assure', 'promote', 'encourage', 'undertake', 'provide', 'respect', 'use their best efforts', and 'take all appropriate legislative, social and educational measures'. It is further strengthened by the impressive tally of governments that have formally ratified the convention and accepted these exhortations as binding international law.

This image, unfortunately, bears little relation to any realities except those created by law itself. Readers of our book may, we suggest, wish to arrive at a more cautious, less idealistic and, above all, more complex version of law's potential for promoting unmitigated good for the children of the world. At the same time, however, they will be aware that the very exercise of conceptualizing the global suffering and impotence of children as unlawful breaches of human rights may itself be of value as a way of bringing attention to a wide range of activities which are potentially harmful to children's present and future lives.

Since we wrote the first edition, most of the much-celebrated Children Act 1989 has come into force, within England and Wales. As any subscriber to autopoietic theory would have anticipated, its provisions have been reconstructed within the legal system, in ways which are amenable to law's understanding of its external environment. Despite the Act's attempts to introduce an inquisitorial approach to the court proceedings, lawyers still talk of 'winning' and 'losing' their child abuse cases. Despite the Act's declaration that parental rights will give way to parental duties and responsibilities, lawyers still fight to assert the rights of parents over their children. The removal of a child from the family, even for a short period, and even where the parents are allowed to keep in close contact with their child, is still treated as a gross infringement of parental rights, and so subject to the close scrutiny of the courts. Despite the new emphasis on partnership and co-operation between social workers and families, the obtaining of sufficiently reliable and admissible evidence to convince a court of law still appears to be the crucial factor in determining whether social workers will intervene to protect a child from abuse (Wattam, 1992).

Where children who commit crimes are concerned, it appeared in 1990 that the welfare/justice dichotomy concentrating on punishment, treatment and the courts, which we discussed in Chapter 1 of the first edition, had yielded to a management approach designed to avoid courts and sentencing.[4] The need for politics to claim that it is able to control 'the crime problem' has, however, more recently led to a resurrection of the old dichotomy, with one side demanding that children should be prosecuted and, 'where appropriate', punished, if 'necessary' by custodial sentences,[5] with the other side arguing that this will lead only to an increase in juvenile criminality and demanding instead more treatment and preventative schemes. Once again it is the political debate which is setting the agenda for an inadequate and largely untheoretical academic analysis. The only additional factor to emerge in recent years is the emphasis by researchers on the injustices inflicted by the criminal justice system on ethnic minorities, but even here it is political considerations which are dictating the terms of the debate among criminologists and legal academics.

The period since 1990 has also seen a change in the nature of the debates on the use of mediation to settle conflicts about arrangements for children when parents separate. There is now an apparent consensus that family mediation is 'a good thing', with debate concentrated on whether or not non-child issues should be mediated, or whether lawyers can and should be involved in mediating. In the UK, a recent Consultation Paper[6] seemed to herald a rapid movement towards mediation as the preferred course of action for divorcing couples, with its proposed self-denying ordinance on the involvement of lawyers acting as lawyers in the divorce process. At the same time as these developments have been occurring, feminists have been arguing that mediation is unsuitable for resolving conflicts in families where domestic violence has occurred because it cannot safeguard or promote the welfare of mother and child, and may in fact make them more vulnerable to violence. Both developments, therefore, provide us with a different context for our analysis of how law responds to communications from outside the legal system.

Finally, we have made some changes in the second edition of the book as a direct response to criticisms. Some of the critical comments that the first edition of the book attracted were often the result of reviewers' unfamiliarity with and, therefore, incomplete understanding of autopoietic theory. One critic, for example, took us to task for not exploring sufficiently law's power.[7] The systems theory approach of autopoiesis, however, deliberately avoids the representation of power as some ubiquitous and universally recognizable object which is seized by some group and then used to dominate and subdue all resistance. For autopoietic theory, power analyses are necessarily analyses from within a political perspective, and one of the objects of the book was to rescue discussions concerning the welfare of children away from a theoretical perspective which sees political ideology at the root of everything that happens in society.[8] In a similar vein, we regard criticisms which interpret our application of Teubner's notion of 'enslavement' as a description of the total domination by lawyers of child welfare professionals[9] as a misunderstanding of our intentions, based again on the employment of inappropriate notions of power and subordination. What we are referring to, rather, is something much more complex and reciprocal, captured in the notion of 'structural coupling',[10] but with law's communications gaining acceptance in the prevailing social environment to a much greater degree than those of 'child welfare science'.

On a theoretical level, the criticism that has caused us the greatest concern relates to our identification of 'child welfare science'. How, we are frequently asked, can you possibly make the assertion that social work decisions concerning children are 'scientific'? Up to a point we anticipated that criticism in Chapter 3 (pp.36–42), but we would be the first to admit that difficulties still remain as to what we mean by 'science' in this context. From the sociological perspective from which we view this issue, it does not worry us that scientists themselves have drawn up criteria to determine whether something is or is not *scientific*. The 'science police' are entitled to engage in this exercise of ruling what is and what is not science, but this does not oblige everyone to abide by their decisions. We are concerned, rather, with science as a system of communications which has become functional for society as the ultimate determiner of truth and falsehood such that, in contemporary society, scientists may be wrong, but science can never be wrong; or put another way: if it is false, it cannot be science. In the world of communications, what is 'scientific' depends upon what society accepts as science – that is, capable of providing true/false answers to questions which science itself selects as scientific questions.

While some physical scientists may wish to exclude psychoanalysis or even psychology from the scientific community, there is little doubt that these two systems observe the environment in a scientific manner in so far as they rely upon some supposedly objective notions of truth and falsehood in their coding of the social world, rather than, for example, faith, legality, profit or love. It seems to us quite legitimate, therefore, to write of *child welfare science* or *child welfare sciences*. The only problem we have is in describing the practices of social work as 'scientific'. In some instances they are, in others they are not. At times the communications of social work come much closer to medicine than to science, with children's present and future wellbeing and the state of families being discussed very much in terms of healthy/unhealthy, normal/pathological. At times also, and increasingly in those Western countries which have largely abandoned – or have never experienced – the welfare state, social work communications are conducted on the economic basis of profit and loss, with measurable achievement or performance indicators being set off against financial cost. Alternatively, the discourse may be in the political terms of racial discrimination and 'political correctness'. All these are possible modes of communication within social work practice. Yet where social work and law encounter one another at the institutional level, social work communication almost invariably takes on a scientific or medical mode, for it is essentially scientific predictions and medical prognoses that the law seeks from social work in order to construct a lawful decision.

To criticize our use of the term 'science' on scientific grounds would, therefore, appear to miss the point. We would feel it necessary to destroy our invention of 'child welfare science' only if empirical evidence existed to the effect that social workers communicated in ways which did not assume the possibility of establishing scientifically the causes for child abuse and, on the basis of these causes, making predictions as to the future welfare of children. Having said that, our tendency today, if pressed, would probably be to suggest that *child welfare* is developing in modern post-industrial societies as a functionally differentiated system in its own right, within which the external environment is coded in terms of good for children/bad for children, and the social function of which is to avoid the need continually to assess and reassess not only the needs and progress of each individual child but also the very criteria against which such needs and progress are being judged – the function, in other words, of giving the impression of certainty as to what is good or bad for children at a time when such certainty is no longer generated through the traditional manner of communications between generations within the same family. This

emerging communicative system, including the social institutions developing around it, reconstruct those other discourses that we have already
mentioned in ways that answer questions of good or bad for children. The
recent criticisms by mediators, psychotherapists and psychologists of law's
damaging effects on children, through its insensitive procedures and
simplistic categorizations, may thus be seen as child welfare reconstructing
law very much on its own terms.

One final criticism concerns the recommendations in Chapter 8 of the
first edition. This relates to the apparent paradox in the concept of 'child-
responsive law'. If law, in Luhmann's scheme, is able to 'think about' its
environment only through coding or selectivity of lawful/unlawful, its only
way of becoming child-responsive is through its own operations: that is,
through law. Yet we all know that to code children and the complexity of
their activities, needs, wishes and sensitivities in terms of lawfulness/
unlawfulness hardly fulfills the criteria for child-responsiveness. Indeed, it
is likely to have just the opposite effect. One is left, therefore, with a way
forward which seems, on the face of things, impossible to pursue, for the
more that one tries to make law more responsive through law, the further
one moves away from a formal legal system which is adapted to children
and their needs, as defined by child welfare science.

In order to extricate ourselves from this apparent paradox, certain
distinctions have to be made. Notably, we need to distinguish between law
as a functional system of communication and the formal legal system,
consisting of courts, judges and the like, which give authority to decisions
about what is and what is not good for children. While the latter clearly
institutionalizes the former, it is not defined by it. In other words, although
courts produce legal decisions and only legal decisions, what happens in
courts is not necessarily all contained within the coding lawful/unlawful.
Judges may, for example, deliberately make no decision, but rather
attempt to create the conditions for decisions to be made within other
communicative systems, such as economics or science. Such 'settlements'
may subsequently be endorsed by the court, but no one would pretend
that they have been reached through legal operations.

Therefore, the idea that courts may provide the physical locus for people
to communicate in non-legal terms is not in itself paradoxical. Admittedly,
in the context of Anglo-American, lawyer-dominated court systems, it may
be extremely difficult for reasons that we describe in our book. Nevertheless, we advocate child-responsiveness, including the active encouragement of non-legal 'settlement' or the postponement of legal decisions, as
an ideal to be pursued by courts.

Such a solution would appear to avoid the social evil of *de-differentiation*
against which Luhmann is constantly warning us. This merging or
hybridization of social communication systems occurs, not through the

simultaneous performance of their operations in one locus, but through the reconstitution within one communicative system of the operations of another. When law uses its operations to discover what is best for the welfare of the child, there is *de-differentiation* and social confusion. When law leaves other systems to answer such questions, but lends legal authority to their decisions or agreements not to decide, the results may be criticized for other reasons, such as the lack of procedural protection, but not for having committed the Luhmannian sin. Such a solution would involve a clear distinction within the court setting of what is legal and law, and what is legal and child welfare. The so-called 'system' of family courts which operates in England and Wales does not, unfortunately, even begin to make such a distinction. Even the North American or Australian creation of family courts, having their own separate staff and courthouse, fails to separate law from child welfare science in a way that avoids de-differentiation. Given the problems of the lawyer-driven Anglo-American courts systems, the solution in those countries is probably, wherever possible, to remove from the courts decisions aimed at promoting children's welfare.

# Notes

1   See Alston et al. (1992), Freeman and Veerman (1992) and King (1994).
2   See King (1994).
3   See Chapters 2 and 4.
4   As we describe in Chapter 6.
5   See the Public Order and Criminal Justice Bill 1993.
6   Lord Chancellor's Department (1993).
7   Bill Hebenton, in *Social and Legal Studies* (1992, Vol.1, No.1, pp.115-17).
8   See, for example, Frost and Stein (1989), Parton (1985), Parton (1991) and Smart (1989).
9   See James (1992), James and Hay (1993) and Michael Freeman's review in the *British Journal of Criminology* (1993, pp.110–11).
10  See Chapter 2.

# 1 The limits of welfare/justice

The phrase 'thinks about children' in the title of a book tends to suggest a psychological approach to understanding children – parents or perhaps teachers interpreting their behaviour and responding to their needs. Yet to include 'law' in the title is confusing. The law is not an individual; it cannot think, at least not in the usual sense of the term. Is this title, then, no more than a rather silly conundrum – a way, perhaps, of catching the browser's eye to disguise yet another legal textbook on child law or another research study about the decision-making of the courts in children's cases? No and yes. No, it is not a conundrum – the law, as we shall explain, does think; and yes, this is a book at least partly about the courts.

However, our purpose in writing this book is not merely to add to the growing list of publications about the failures of courts and social work agencies to protect children against abuse by adults. Nor is it to offer any simple proposals for changes in the law itself which would result in more children being saved from death, serious injury or sexual exploitation at the hands of those who are supposed to be ensuring their welfare. Our goal is, rather, to examine recent perspectives on the law as a social institution capable of 'thinking' – of generating knowledge about children, what they are, who should look after them, and, above all, what is good or bad for them. In the course of 'thinking', law must encounter other social institutions which also 'think about children', often in different ways to those in which law thinks. We want to see first of all whether this unfamiliar approach can throw light on current concerns over children's issues in the courts and, secondly, what happens when 'law's thoughts' conflict with those of other social organizations.

1

# I Child welfare in law

The problems faced by the law when deciding issues concerning children have received more than their fair share of attention in the press and media over recent years. The scandals of child battering, and later child sexual abuse, the scourge of juvenile delinquency and the heartache of children separated from a parent through divorce or state intervention have pointed the laser beam of public concern in two directions, highlighting firstly, the courts and their decisions, and secondly the 'caring professions': the doctors, social workers, psychiatrists, psychologists and psychotherapists who are increasingly involved in identifying the abuse and suffering of children and in protecting them from harm. This focus on children (and adolescents) and the dangers that lie in wait for them has become a major cause of concern in all Western industrialized countries.

Despite political rhetoric about family and parental responsibility, it is clear that the autonomy of families, the power to educate and bring up their children as they please without pressure or interference from agents of the state, has long since passed. One only has to open the newspaper and read of proposals to outlaw the smacking of children[1] to realize just how far matters have progressed towards the acceptance of external influence in the parent–child relationship. The question today is not 'Should the state intervene?', but, as a French writer expressed it:

> Which social classes, which sub-cultures, which professions or institutions, or which combination of these are going effectively to insert their social, moral and psychological values into the process of determining the child's best interests? (Stender, 1979)

We have now arrived at the point when many thousands of people throughout North America, Australasia and Western Europe, after undergoing specialist training which often lasts several years, spend all or much of their professional lives assessing children at risk and making recommendations and decisions about their future. It is clear, therefore, that the debate which raged in the 1950s/60s over the rights and wrongs of state intervention in the family has been won by the child protection lobby.

There are many factors, beyond the scope of this book, that have contributed to the present firm and deep commitment of state institutions to such protection. Some sociologists would point to the 'depoliticization' and 'technicalization' of social problems,[2] whereby major issues are 'taken over' by professional groups who thereafter claim a proprietary interest in these problems and their solutions. Others would identify such factors as cultural and moral pluralism,[3] the fragility of the traditional family,[4] the diversity of parenting arrangements and changes in gender roles,[5] to list but a few.

Whatever the causes, it is clear that the debate has moved on from the subject of family versus state power to that of how to make the exercise of state power effective in its protection of children, yet, at the same time, responsive to the rights and needs of children and the rights and responsibilities of parents. In addition to claiming proprietary interests in those social problems concerning children, state institutions have tended to 'internalize' the family versus state debate. It has been transformed into a balancing act where the rights of parents and families are weighed by the institutions themselves against what is perceived to be the welfare of the child and what are seen to be society's interests in protecting children and reinforcing norms of conduct towards children. The debate, in other words, progresses using formulae selected and developed by those very social institutions which are engaged in the process of promoting child welfare and justice for children.

As long as social problems remain at the level of general public concern and debate over principles, there can be much common ground between different countries and different legal jurisdictions facing similar social phenomena. The problems of drugs, the physical and sexual abuse of children, marital breakdown and youth disaffection and unemployment have, in these times of rapid communication, passed like virulent epidemics from one country to another and from one continent to another. As a result, the problems posed by children and young people are almost identical in all Western post-industrial countries, while the ultimate objectives of child protection and delinquency prevention and reduction are also broadly similar. However, the form that the internalization of the family versus state issue takes has varied in line with historical and cultural differences.

Such differences have been magnified by the fact that, in most countries, it is the formal legal system – traditionally the principal state institution for balancing conflicting interests – which has taken over responsibility for providing a firm but sensitive response where measures to protect children are seen necessary. Within the legal system, much that is common between different jurisdictions is lost beneath a mass of rules and procedures which occupy the minds of professional participants and convince them that their problems are specific to the country, city or even the particular court in which they practise. These legal concerns, in all their different varieties, tend increasingly to submerge policy objectives beneath a mass of codes, statutes, cases and procedures, to be learnt and absorbed by students and practitioners alike. Not only do they obscure the normative processes at work within the law, but they also make comparisons between policies and practices in different jurisdictions ever more difficult. The result is a highly confused situation. Moreover, these differences are increasing as legal structures develop in ever more complex ways.

As if this were not enough, anyone wishing to indulge in generalizations about children and the law is faced with the great divide between common law and civil law, between the public and the private, between the accusatorial system of Anglo-American law practised in English-speaking countries and the inquisitorial system operating on the continent of Europe. Once child welfare issues, which are common to almost all post-industrialized nations, become 'juridified' within the different legal systems they are transformed into concepts which necessarily classify and contain them within narrow cultural and geographical boundaries.

## II    The welfare/justice clash

There is one theoretical paradigm, however, which appears to have been universally accepted by lawyers and legal commentators as being common to those children's issues coming before the courts. This paradigm sees policies and decisions in such cases as subject to two opposing ideologies, welfare and justice.[6] They are most starkly opposed in the area of criminal justice, where welfare represents the desire of the courts to diagnose the underlying problems of children who commit crimes, and to treat these problems in some therapeutic way, and justice represents the traditional concerns of the law to punish wrongdoers according to the seriousness of their offence, to promote procedural fairness in order to protect the innocent against wrong decisions or the arbitrary use of power. One researcher of the US lower courts sees the problem as follows:

> The modern theory of juvenile justice argues for individualized justice tailored to treat a wide range of factors as relevant to respond to the 'whole person'. It de-emphasizes the strictly 'legal' proceedings, and purposefully expands its inquiry beyond and away from the provoking incident in order to determine the root of the child's trouble and consider appropriate alternative responses . . . *the central problem of the court* . . . is entrenched in the official's aspirations to do good, in the impulse for flexibility and substantive justice which give rise to competing conceptions of justice. (Feeley, 1979, pp.284–6, our emphasis)

This dichotomy has particular repercussions for criminal trials of young offenders, where the formal legal rationality tends to be rigid and inflexible. According to another US writer,

> Within such a framework of individualized justice, emphasis is placed upon information and perspectives which are inconsistent with formal legal rationality

and adversarial due process. This information may include psychological 'evidence', therapeutic diagnosis and social history of the family . . . (Sibley, 1981, p.23)

In order to make sense of this apparent paradox, the debate among lawyers and criminologists over juvenile justice has been couched in terms of a clash between these distinct approaches of welfare and justice. In other areas of the law, although the analysis has taken a somewhat different form, the issues are still presented in terms of this clash between different ideologies.[7] In child protection cases, for instance, the intervention of social workers is seen as presenting a serious problem for civil liberty, and so for justice. According to this view, the law must require any case for removing a child from its family or cutting off contacts between the child and its birth parent(s) to be based on evidence that has been tried and tested in a court of law according to legal criteria. This, however, may not necessarily be compatible with the efforts of social workers and child care experts to support the family and promote the child's welfare through therapy or preventative measures of intervention. So the law, which in liberal Western countries has traditionally protected the rights of citizens from interference by the state, is seen as being set against the very different philosophy of welfare – that of therapeutic intervention for the benefit of a child at risk – in which parental objections and refusal to co-operate are regarded as problems to be 'worked through', rather than issues of rights and freedom from state coercion requiring legal resolution.

The form the ideological battle has taken in child protection cases nevertheless varies from jurisdiction to jurisdiction. In England and Wales, for example, campaigns for rights for parents and children have repeatedly clashed with the child-protection lobby.[8] Dominant issues in this battle have been the provision of lawyers to 'defend' parents and their children against social work intervention, and the right of appeal to the courts in cases where parental access to the child is denied. In England and Wales the Children Act 1989 was presented to Parliament as an attempt to balance the rights of families and the duty of the state to intervene and protect children in the different areas where conflict arises between these two approaches.[9] In keeping with current legal beliefs, it places much emphasis on parental rights and the use of the courts for the determination of disputes between parents and those engaged to protect children, while at the same time restating the principle that parents are the best people, under normal circumstances, to determine what is in the interests of their children.

A third area where justice and welfare have been seen as opposing forces is that of disputes over children when marriages or cohabitation arrangements break down. Here the ideological clash takes the form of a conflict between the traditional role of the courts as arbiter between two opposing parties[10] and the desire to minimize the harm caused to the children by the separation and divorce of their parents. Traditionally, lawyers have been people whose training and professional orientation leads them to do all in their power to secure the best outcome for their client, with the result that the interests of children often disappear from view. Worse still, it may lead to the children being used as ammunition in the courtroom battle. The welfare approach, on the other hand, claims to make the child's interests the dominant concern. According to this view, whilst courts should have an important role to play in protecting the children of divorced couples and promoting their welfare, parents should be discouraged from using the courts to resolve differences between them and encouraged through mediation and conciliation to come to some sensible, mutually acceptable child-centred arrangements.[11] Where courts are used, the balance between welfare and justice may be seen to be achieved by using court welfare officers, both to promote parental co-operation over their children's future and, where they are unable to agree, to act as 'experts' in recommending to the judge which parent is best fitted to have care of the child.

The problems that arise from these attempts by law to respond to current demands for just but sensitive decision-making have tended to be portrayed again in terms of different ideologies and the conflicts and imbalances between them. Typically, complaints against the operation of the courts argue, on the one hand, that too little credence is being given to social workers and child welfare experts or, on the other hand, that too little account is being taken of individual rights, or that the testing of evidence is inadequate. All will be well if only the right balance can be found.

Justice and welfare have therefore become concepts with a dual function. They are used to explain the complexity and confusion of court decision-making in the main areas concerning children: juvenile justice, child protection and matrimonial disputes. They also serve as ideological rallying points in those campaigns which seek to promote one or the other as the preferred way of dealing with children's issues in the courts or, alternatively, they combine to serve as the ideal of 'welfare going with justice', the firmness of law with humane care and understanding, to be pursued by all legal policy- and decision-makers.

## III   Policies for reform

If we take juvenile justice as our archetype of the ideological stage on which welfare and justice perform, the performance takes the two different modes set out above – the one where justice and welfare are locked in conflict, the other where they work together in harmony. In its conflictual form, the frequent complaint from commentators, including two of those we quoted earlier, is that the courts are less than ideal institutions for dispensing welfare or, in Feeley's terms, 'individualized justice' (see page 4). The factors associated with individualized justice are, according to Sibley, 'uncomfortably out of place when they are tailored to the requirements of legal evidence, proof of guilt and considerations of legal responsibility' (Sibley, 1981, p.23). The result is that, 'ironically, the impulse to provide justice seems to foster a sense of injustice' (Feeley, 1979, pp.284–5).

It is not surprising that Morris and Giller (1987), in their authoritative book on the juvenile courts, point out that those who are critical of welfare as an objective for law see the juvenile justice system to be 'an ineffective mechanism for defining welfare needs and for delivering welfare services'.[12] Instead, the advocates of justice wish to restrict and simplify the basis of the operation of the juvenile court to dealing solely with the juvenile's offence (p.251).

At other times, and in different jurisdictions, the deficiencies of the juvenile justice system have been portrayed in terms of its failure to deal with offending as a family problem or as individual pathology. Indeed, in the 1960s in both the United Kingdom and the United States, much of the debate concerned ways of identifying and remedying these problems using the courts as a diagnostic and therapeutic process. The offence or pattern of offending would be seen as symptomatic of some deeper underlying problem which needed to be addressed if the family and child were to be restored to health and normality.[13] One solution to the conflict between justice and welfare would therefore be achieved by the complete elimination of either justice or welfare, or through the imposition of legal rules and procedures to give precedence to one of these ideologies and restrict the operation of the other.

The other main solution within juvenile justice tries to achieve harmony between the two. This may be presented by introducing reforms that effectively promote justice and welfare within the same institution, or by linking different institutions, such as court and clinic.[14] These may either bring together the two distinct philosophies in a way that allows young offenders to be moved easily between one and the other, according to their needs and the needs of the community,[15] or they may combine them by interweaving them in every decision that is made about the best way to deal with children who commit crimes. The mechanism for achieving this might be, for example, the separate processing of those cases where 'offence is both the ground and basis of legal intervention rather than [merely] an indicator of possible need for intervention' (Adler, 1985, p.137). Harris (1985), on the other hand, argues for a different kind of integration of justice and welfare by ensuring that the amount of welfare applicable in each case is proportionnate to the offence charged.

Ironically, within the field of juvenile justice the 'Return to Justice' movement, which for a time strongly influenced policies in the United States in the mid-1970s and in the United Kingdom in the early 1980s, and is even now experiencing a revival among the ranks of right-wing politicians, ultimately promoted co-operation and harmony rather than conflict between welfare and justice. In its initial, conflictual form, 'Return to Justice' was able to score gains, such as the introduction of determinate sentences for juvenile offenders on both sides of the Atlantic, the abolition of some status offences, and the proliferation of lawyers appearing in children's cases. These justice-promoters had to contend, however, with a powerful lobby of vested interests in the form of probation officers, welfare officers, social workers and other child care professionals who were, and for many years had been, engaged in promoting welfare within the confines of the courthouse. These welfare professionals argued strongly for the influence of a humanizing ideology in a legal world where the strict application of rules, precedents and tariffs takes little account of the needs of children. The legislation for England and Wales is fairly typical of recent trends in all post-industrial Western countries in increasing the scope of this humanizing role by requiring that the courts request welfare professionals to supply them with the 'facts' necessary to consider all the circumstances and all possible alternatives, before passing a custodial sentence upon a young offender.[16]

Therefore, instead of the separation of welfare and justice, what has occurred in practice over the past decade has been the co-existence of both these very different philosophies towards the court's role with regard to young offenders, each associated with different professional agencies involved in the management of juvenile crime, and each associated with different political tendencies. It is hardly surprising, therefore, that the policies of the courts have tended to be portrayed by academic commentators as a pendulum swinging back and forth between these two opposing ideologies.

At the same time, on the level of practice, however, a succession of pragmatic compromises could also be interpreted in terms of welfare and justice, by pointing to the ways in which it was possible for the two philosophies to complement one another. This has clearly been true of juvenile justice (as Chapter 6 will illustrate in some detail), with the invention of schemes to divert young offenders from the courts and from custody. The same kind of development has occurred within the area of matrimonial disputes, where Family Courts, or a 'Family Justice System'[17] have been widely promoted as the means of providing clearly delineated, but combined, justice and welfare services. In post-separation disputes between parents over the care of and contact with children, there has been a proliferation of schemes in almost all English-speaking countries designed to help parents reach agreement without resorting to a full legal hearing of their dispute. Many of these schemes involve conciliation or mediation appointments (or some similar title)[18] on the court premises, with the parties' legal representatives present under the eye of the judge or registrar.[19] Mediation using solicitors and social workers or counsellors as co-mediators has also developed in recent years.[20]

In the area of child protection there have been moves towards reducing the workload of the courts by filtering out those cases which are not seen as needing the heavy hand of judicial intervention. Terry Carney, the Chair of the Victorian Child Welfare Practice and Legislation Review, denies that he and his fellow review members are arguing for 'an orderly withdrawal on the part of the law'. Instead, their central thesis is rather that: 'overreliance on adjudicative styles of legal intervention should be redressed by way of the substitution of facilitative laws. This new bond between welfare and justice is embodied in the proposals' (1989, p.37).

In the state of Victoria the proposed bond between welfare and justice also involves the introduction of a Family Court, a 'semi-inquisitorial and more expert body' (Carney, 1989, p.35). Its expertise is to be augmented by 'court liaison officers', whose task it is 'to advise on the provision of necessary services and reports'. Although England and Wales still await the introduction of Family Courts, the practical bond between welfare and justice within the courtroom has in recent years been cemented by the arrival in care proceedings of the guardian *ad litem* (an independent social worker representing the child's interests) to advise courts.

Much discussion has occurred, but the result in terms of greater clarity of analysis and actual institutional change is tantalizingly small. Even from this brief account of recent attempts to 'improve' the legal system it is clear that, despite the changes that have been introduced, 'the vast edifice of the courts', as Davis (1988b, p.12) has called it, remains virtually untouched. The same is true of the legal profession. Despite the development in several countries, including the UK, the United States and Holland, of training programmes which aim to provide such lawyers with a wide range of knowledge and skills to enable them to become specialist child advocates, most lawyers continue to ply their traditional trades of advocate and negotiator, although perhaps with a greater appreciation of the complexities involved in relationships within families.

# IV   Fundamental flaws

What is evident in this brief survey is that the problems of decision-making in children's cases and the ways of solving these problems have been constructed largely in terms of ideal and idealized notions of 'justice' – the rallying cry for lawyers, police and right-wing politicians – and 'welfare' – the goal of the caring professions and politicians of the left. Our interest at this stage is not, however, in the fact that these ideals in their pure form have never been fully realized and should probably now be recognized as unrealizable. Nor are we concerned here with explaining why changes to the balance between welfare and justice seem often to have made very little difference to the manner in which courts, lawyers and court welfare professionals actually conduct their business. What does require some explanation is the way that almost all those involved in the process of legal decision-making about children continue to use these categories of welfare and justice to describe the operation of the system, to explain how ideally it ought to work and to account for failures in its operation.

Where failures do occur in the compromise solutions between the two ideologies, responsibility is often attributed not to the inadequacy of justice and welfare as analytical concepts on which to base policies, but to such remediable factors as inadequate resources[21] or the lack of co-operation and communication between professionals.[22] According to this view, given the right working conditions, these professionals are quite capable of achieving the collaborative ideal. This gives rise to the belief that it is only stressful working conditions, poor communications and perhaps the lack of good will on both sides that cause things to go wrong. Typically, the response is to demand more resources and better structures which will give the appearance that compromise solutions can indeed work to provide a more favourable environment for the two ideologies and the professions which claim to embody them.

At one level this demand is constantly being met by the production of new laws, regulations, codes of practice, guidelines and directions, all designed to eliminate ambiguity and confusion and to provide a framework for clear decisions and precise action in every situation where children are at risk, a danger to others or out of parental control.[23] At a higher level, new court structures are invented. As we have already noted, the Family Court in New Zealand, Australia and some North American jurisdictions,[24] has been heralded as a monument to the successful marriage between welfare and justice, and the UK family courts system since the Children Act 1989 is seen as incorporating all the elements required for just and sensitive decision-making in children's cases.

Similarly, the solution of merging professional ideologies in the person of one functionary who is supposed to incorporate the best of both welfare and justice has been taken further. For example, the French *juges des enfants* are drawn from the ranks of the judiciary, but are encouraged to temper the insensitive and impersonal nature of legal rationality with the caring compassion of welfare. Within the realm of welfare, a similar spirit of co-operation and integration has been responsible for the introduction of law-like concepts from the legal process.[25] These supposedly offer protection for the rights of the citizen, be they parents or children, against the arbitrary power of experts to identify harm and remove children from families. Welfare agents are to consult with representatives of the law, both in the selection of those children who are to go before the courts and in the decisions as to what should happen to them. In Holland, for example, the Child Protection Councils, incorporating social workers and lawyers, work together in teams on cases of child abuse. More critical writers, we should add, reject this general belief that failures to provide justice and welfare for children can be eliminated by giving more resources to professionals, improving laws and the operation of legal institutions. Rather, they attribute the failures of society to realize the ideals expressed in the welfare and justice models to confusions and contradictions within the conceptual framework which sustains these models. For example, Harris and Webb, drawing upon the theoretical writings of Michel Foucault[26] and Jacques Donzelot,[27] write:

> Historically welfare has emerged to fill a vacuum which is itself the product of a series of conflicts, confusions, compromises; it is a strategy of power, a means of investigating families, of controlling non-delinquent children, an acceptable means of expanding the power of the state. (Harris and Webb, 1987, p.168)

They also maintain that the logic of justice is flawed, first, in its claim that treating 'like cases alike' is clear and unproblematic, and secondly, in the vagueness and ambiguity of the very idea of justice. 'Of itself', they argue, 'justice means very little' (1987, p.168). For those who offer radical, post-structural critiques of the existing social order and its historical antecedents, however, the debate between welfare and justice is no more or less than a device designed to legitimize a reductionist, dualistic ordering of experience. They point to inherent contradictions and illogicalities in the very notions of welfare and justice, and to the confusion of ideologies and objectives that abound wherever attempts at co-operation or merging occur. They prefer analyses which identify power relations based on wealth, class, gender or race, by which the state, the rich, the ruling class or white males exercise and retain control over families.[28]

Yet there are serious difficulties with an analysis which sees the issues purely in terms of power, for it misses the fundamental point that the ideals of welfare and justice are not just smokescreens to conceal or legitimize the domination of the weak by the strong. They have significance for all those involved in decision-making about children, and the meanings that these decision-makers attribute to the concepts of welfare and justice inform and guide their practice and policies. To talk in simple terms of power, discrimination and domination ignores the precise forms that power takes in practice, and the meanings and understandings by which power is generated and sustained. We would wish to add two refinements. The first is that the concepts of justice and welfare are 'real' in the sense that people working within those social systems involved in generating decisions about children behave as if they were real. The second is that both welfare and justice are seen very differently from the perspective of different social systems, be they politics, economics, medicine, science, etc. What has been overlooked is that current debates about the right way to deal with delinquent, abused or neglected children or with the antagonism and confusion that may result from family break-up are not only about law; they are also formed by law. The very terms used in the debate – 'justice' and 'welfare' – have specific and unique meanings which have been constructed by the operations of law itself.

As a legal concept, justice is construed narrowly, firstly in terms of procedural justice,[29] and secondly as justice to individuals based on the idea of a just 'return' for the amount of individual responsibility and rights deemed relevant. Justice, in the wider sense of the term, is found only in the sentencing of offenders, where the outcome can be influenced by the concept of justice to a society wronged by the individual offender. This is, however, simply a symbolic justification for what is done to an individual[30] according to a principle of 'just deserts' for a legally constructed amount of personal culpability. By contrast, outside the law, justice is not always constructed in such individualistic terms. The concept of social justice, which suggests the influencing of a more equitable balance of both legal rights and social welfare in society generally, is very different from the narrowly defined idea of legal justice.

This is no novel idea. The most widely quoted expression of this 'gap' is probably the argument that the rule of law, and therefore legal justice, is simply an ideology to mask the existence and consolidation of social *in*justice.[31] As Stewart Asquith remarks:

> Policies which ignore the social and economic realities in which children find themselves, while promoting greater equality and justice within formal systems of control, may not only ignore, but may compound the structural and material inequalities which have been historically associated with criminal behaviour. (Asquith, 1983, p.17)

# V   Law's version of welfare

Where welfare is concerned, what has been neglected by commentators is the corresponding gulf between the concepts of welfare constructed within and outside the law. Just as legal justice is not the same as social justice, the welfare offered by social workers operating within and around the law is not the same as social welfare.[32] This concept of welfare is one which claimed to be able to deliver social justice to the point that welfare became a shorthand term for a particular type of social policy aimed at greater and more equal social provision in terms of education, housing, health care and economic rewards.[33] ' "Welfare state" has been used as a way of defining "welfare" itself.'[34] Used in opposition to justice, however, 'welfare' appears to mean something much narrower. The focus of attention becomes not social policy, but the individual, and relationships between individuals.[35]

How such a narrow concept of welfare has been constructed within the legal discourse is a question which will be addressed in more detail in Chapter 3. The point we wish to make here is that there are limits to 'welfare in law' because there are limits to law's effective action set by the intrinsic nature of law and by law's own concept of its role.[36] Law's *raison d'être* is as a body which conceptualizes the world into rights, duties and responsibilities on which it can adjudicate, and which swings into action when an individual, personal or corporate, wishes to activate a right, impose a duty or identify a responsibility.[37] The courts' actions are largely reactive. They are determined by the nature of rights, duties and responsibilities embodied in the legal rules which, in civil law jurisdictions and increasingly in common law jurisdictions, are made by external agencies, notably the legislature. Therefore, if the legislation (or case law) does not provide a parent with the right to 'satisfactory accommodation' for rearing children, then the courts will rightly assume that they are not authorized to make that provision.[38] Under the Children Act 1989, for example, the courts may, instead, find themselves having to make choices between a parent who has failed in his or her responsibility to provide a home for his or her children and a local authority social services department which is able to offer the children a home away from their parents.[39] Similarly, the law cannot find employment for a parent or improve the education provided by schools,[40] it can only respond when what might be a relevant right, duty or responsibility is brought to its attention[41] and recognized as requiring judicial action. This is stating the obvious in order to draw the distinction between constraints imposed by law's own processes and procedures and those which arise from external sources – political, economic or whatever. Law's self-identity is one of an independent 'institution', free from political constraints and, conversely, without any desire to usurp the functions of a democratically elected legislature or an administration which is simply following the laws laid down by that legislature.[42]

The communications of academic and practising lawyers construct and uphold this concept of neutral insularity. So, for example, in the Anglo-

American common law system, the 'rules' of statutory interpretation, self-imposed via judicial *dicta*, allow the use of the 'mischief rule' (whereby the intentions of the legislature are sought and, if necessary, gaps in the law filled) only if the 'literal rule' is argued to be inapplicable. This reveals a constraint imposed by the need to think about and communicate decisions in these terms. The rules of legal precedent in these jurisdictions have been similarly formulated as rules within the law. Cases are decided on past cases, precedents, and policy implications can be made an explicit influence on decision-making only if judges argue that precedents are sufficiently in conflict, unclear or lacking.[43] Needless to say, both these sets of internally constructed rules make innovation more difficult than conservatism, but this self-referential nature of legal argument also has other important repercussions, as we shall describe later.

This depoliticization and individualization by the law of a wide range of issues covering children and their families has led, therefore, to the establishment of a relatively narrow concept of 'the welfare of the child'.[44] It is easy to compile from the case law and statutory provisions the 'items' which are deemed necessary for consideration of the child's welfare. Indeed, some jurisdictions have issued guidelines as to how these items should be evaluated, as in the US states of Alabama, California, Georgia, Kansas, Louisiana and Texas. In other jurisdictions these guidelines have become rules of law as, for example, in Latin American countries, whereas some legal systems have guidelines operating only as presumptions.[45] However, the significant point is not the different attitudes to issues like maternal preference and blood ties expressed in these guidelines, but the type of issues addressed. Because of the essential nature of law's role, these are heavily slanted towards choice of parent (for example, 'psychological' or natural), evaluation of which adult has the 'better' claim to care for the child, and the weighing of parental duties and parental rights (for example, religious principles not permitting consent to blood transfusions).

This definition of what welfare means within family and child law is confirmed by an analysis of the 'checklists' enacted in some jurisdictions to 'control' the matters that the court takes into account when pronouncing on the welfare of the child. For example, the following section of the Australian Family Law Act, as amended by the Family Law Amendment Act 1983, asks judges to consider these matters:[46]

  (i)   the nature of the relationship of the child with each of the parents of the child and with other persons;
 (ii)   the effect on the child of any separation from – (a) either parent of the child; or (b) any child, or other person, with whom the child has been living;

(iii)  the desirability of, and the effect of, any change in the existing arrangements for the care of the child;

(iv)  the attitude of the child, and to the responsibilities and duties of parenthood, demonstrated by each parent of the child;

(v)  the capacity of each parent or of any other person, to provide adequately for the needs of the child, including the emotional and intellectual needs of the child;

(vi)  any other fact or circumstance (including the education and upbringing of the child) that, in the opinion of the court, the welfare of the child requires to be taken into account.

This concept of welfare is in sharp contrast with those wider concepts of social welfare in social policy as, for example, set out in the United Nation's Convention on the Rights of the Child or the often-quoted definition of child welfare from a New Zealand custody case: 'material welfare both in the sense of an adequacy of resources to provide a pleasant home and a comfortable standard of living and in the sense of adequacy of care to ensure that good health and due personal pride are maintained'.[47] Neither do these concepts bear much resemblance to social scientific notions of social welfare as defined, for example, in the work of Richard Titmuss.[48] This is the very antithesis of law's individualistic approach in its criticism of egoism and economic market values and in its promotion of the idea of a socially administered society with integrative welfare policies.[49] While welfare, as interpreted by social welfare organizations, is a much narrower concept than the socialist version of social welfare,[50] it nevertheless includes all those services provided by 'welfare' generally, including a wide variety of forms of practical, financial and emotional support for the old, children, handicapped and poor. Even the narrower version of 'social' welfare offered by the social service organizations is very different from that of welfare-within-law.

Indeed, it could be argued that 'legal welfare', like 'legal justice', may also compound structural and material inequalities, in that the individualized brand of welfare dispensed by the courts, dealing with juvenile delinquency and failures in child care as if they were personal or interpersonal problems, also ignores wider social and economic factors. The practical expression of this restriction of the meaning of 'welfare' by the courts is described in a critical account of the work of the Probation Service:

Criminal acts are viewed purely as a particular aspect of an individual's behaviour and not as a more widespread social phenomenon with social, economic and political causes. Probation officers operate within that *individualized system of criminal justice* and maintain that perspective. They must remain within the limits of relevance set by the court . . . the poor housing situation of an individual offender can be described and may evoke sympathy but comment about the way in which market forces systematically disadvantage certain groups would be unacceptable. (Walker and Beaumont, 1981, p.23, our emphasis)

It would therefore appear that those who advocate a welfare approach within the legal system cannot in practice deliver welfare as conceptualized by those outside the law. At the same time, those who call for justice are unable to provide a legal system dealing with children's issues which, in practice, either operates according to strict principles of law or admits any notion of 'social justice'. Those who have helped to create and now sustain co-operative ventures in which welfare and justice go hand in hand (such as Family Courts and juvenile bureaux), understandably perceive and present issues in terms of the idealized values of their respective disciplines. Only by believing in the values expressed in the justice and welfare models is it possible to contemplate their merger or the existence of professionals who incorporate the values of both models. From this perspective the problem is fairly simple – how to reconcile different views about the best institutional methods to control delinquent children, problem families or the conflict generated by family breakdown. As we have seen, the resulting tensions that arise between the lawyers on the one hand and the child care professionals on the other tend to be seen as teething problems to be overcome by even greater co-operation. It is not surprising, therefore, that much of the mainstream analysis of these issues gives either explicit or implicit recognition to the existence of these two seemingly coherent set of values.

So where do we, as authors of this book, stand on the theoretical map? If pressed, we would locate ourselves somewhere close to the radical critics. On the other hand, when we enter the world of these radicals, we very soon find ourselves being tossed about without a rudder in a seemingly endless sea of fragmented beliefs concerning gender, race, class power, hegemonic state power, bureaucratic power, etc., which are a challenge to even the most skilful intellectual traveller. It was in the search for a new paradigm which, while offering a radical critique of the taken-for-granted assumptions of judges, lawyers, social workers and 'psy-experts', at the same time offers a visibility clear enough to navigate and seas calm enough to proceed in one direction at a time that we encountered the theoretical approach set out in Chapter 2.

# Notes

1   In Sweden the physical punishment of children is already outlawed. In England and Wales corporal punishment is illegal in state schools. An organization called EPOCH (End Physical Punishment of Children) is at present campaigning to achieve its objective through *inter alia* legal reforms.

2   See Haines (1979) and Manning (1985).
3   See, for example, McIntyre (1964) and Rorty (1982).
4   See, for example, Cooper (1971) and Badinter (1981).
5   See, for example, Barker and Allen (1976), Lamb (1981) and New and David (1985).
6   These are not necessarily the terms used by all authors in all countries at all times. The same concepts have been variously defined as legalism, legal rationality and due process on the one hand, and paternalism, responsive justice, and individualized justice on the other. This list is by no means exhaustive.
7   See King (1981).
8   See Taylor et al. (1979), Morris et al. (1980) and Geach and Schwed (1983).
9   See Parton (1991), Ch.6.
10  Where divorce and civil disputes are concerned, this applies equally to inquisitorial and adversarial jurisdictions.
11  See generally Davis (1988a and 1988b). This retreat of law in favour of parental autonomy is only partial. It is the courts, rather than parents, child welfare experts or mediators, which remain the final arbiters of what is best for the child. See the discussion on this issue in O'Donovan (1993, p.95). See also the Consultation Paper on divorce reform (Lord Chancellor's Department, 1993) which promotes the use of mediation rather than lawyer negotiations or court adjudication.
12  Francis Allen, in *The Borderland of Criminal Justice* (1964), was one of the first critics of the use of juvenile courts to dispense welfare.
13  See the UK government's White Paper, *The Child, the Family and the Young Offender* (HMSO, 1965); cf. Sutton (1981). This was very much the approach of the French *juges des enfants* throughout the 1970s and 1980s.
14  See Emerson (1969).
15  See the discussion of the Scottish Children Panels in Chapter 6.
16  Criminal Justice Act 1982, section 1(4) as amended by the Criminal Justice Act 1988, section 123 and repealed by Schedule 13 of the Criminal Justice Act 1991. Juveniles are now subject to the same criteria for the imposition of a custodial disposal as are adults: see ss.1 and 2 of the Criminal Justice Act 1991.
17  For proposals for different forms of Family Court see, e.g., The Finer Report (1974), Graham-Hall (1973) and Murch (1980). See also Murch and Hooper (1992).
18  For example, the principal registry in London now diverts all applications for contact and residence under s.8 of the Children Act 1989 to in-court mediation. The term 'mediation' is now increasingly being used rather than 'conciliation': in the UK the National Family Conciliation Council changed its name to National Family Mediation in 1993, for example.
19  See Davis (1988b, p.12).
20  For example, in the UK, National Family Mediation has been piloting schemes which involve lawyer input in mediation, and the Family Mediators Association trains lawyers as mediators.
21  See Holman (1978 and 1988).
22  See, for example, Mitchell (1983) and Waterhouse (1989).
23  The Children Act 1989, implemented in 1991 in the UK, has so far been accompanied by two sets of rules, eleven statutory instruments and a series of volumes of 'Guidance and Regulation' issued by the Department of Health.

24   In France the Chambre de la Famille introduced in the early 1980s in some courts has a similar role.

25   See Nelken's (1988a) study of the use of 'contracts' within social work.

26   See Foucault (1977 and 1979).

27   Donzelot (1980).

28   For analyses based on power, see Frost and Stein (1989), Parton (1985) and Parton (1991). The inherently racist nature of the criminal justice system in England and Wales is described in NACRO (1986). For a feminist challenge to the male-dominated orthodoxy, see McLoed and Saraga (1988).

29   So that, for example, evidence cannot be admitted unless certain procedural rules have been followed in their collection and presentation.

30   In only a small minority of cases does sentencing involve 'justice' to the victim, victim groups or communities. See Silby and Merry (1988) and Wright and Galaway (1989) (for details of UK and US reparation schemes).

31   See the writings of Marxist and conflict theorists of law – for example, Beirne and Quinney (1982), Fine et al. (1979).

32   For a general discussion of these issues in relation to juvenile justice, see Harris and Webb (1987).

33   See Reisman (1977) for a critical analysis of the concept of welfare in the writings of Titmuss.

34   See Brandt (1976).

35   Garapon's (1989) use of the term 'paternalist' to describe the French system of child care is probably a more accurate way of describing the nature of welfare in the UK child care system. It implies the role of the court as a good father, operating within a context limited to significant adults in the child's life, making decisions which promote the physical and emotional, educational and economic wellbeing of the child in question by altering (or reinforcing) the arrangements between these significant adults.

36   See Pound (1916) and, with particular reference to children's cases in the courts, King and Trowell (1992) and Allen (1964).

37   The law may be involved in a partly proactive process, as when it activates a duty imposed on itself. Examples would include the pre-Children Act procedure whereby courts had a duty to consider the future arrangements for the child's welfare (section 41, Matrimonial Causes Act 1973) and the Children Act provisions allowing the courts to make section 8 orders even though no application has been made by the parties to the proceedings. (section 10(1)(b), Children Act 1989).

38   See, for example, *R* v. *Inner London Education Authority, ex parte Ali and Another, The Times Law Report,* 21 February 1990.

39   See King and Trowell (1992), Ch.1.

40   Legislation has, of course, provided parents with rights to choose and monitor schools with the aim of bringing market forces to bear on the quality of education. This does not mean that legislation offers any direct mechanism to improve the education of a particular school (see Piper, 1994a).

41   See, for example, *Re T* [1970] All ER 865.

42   See, for example, *A* v. *Liverpool City Council and Another* [1981] 2 All ER 385.

43   See, for example, Zander (1985), Twining and Miers (1985).

44   See, for example, the preamble to *The European Convention on Recognition and Enforcement of Decisions Concerning Custody of Children and on Restoration of Custody of Children* (20 May 1980).

45  As several states in the USA have, for example, expressed a preference for joint custody and for the natural parent over other claimants for child custody. See Kaganas and Piper (1994a).
46  See also Children Act 1989 checklist set out in section 1(3)(a)–(f).
47  Hardy Boys J in *Walker* v. *Walker and Harrison*, noted in [1981] NZ Recent Law 257, quoted in the English Law Commission's Working Paper *Family Law Review of Child Law: Custody* (Law Commission, 1986).
48  This includes an international dimension also. See Titmuss (1970).
49  See Titmuss (1950).
50  Marshall (1976, p.51) noted this distinction when he wrote: 'Let me say first, by way of definition, that I am using the word "welfare" in the broad sense given to it in the term "welfare state" and not in the more specialized meaning of the services provided by Welfare Departments.'

# 2 Law as a self-referential system

We hope that with experience we are better equipped to exercise our wide discretion more correctly in the best interest of the children with whom we have to deal but we are not professional doctors, psychologists or social workers . . . Our duty is to evaluate the evidence before us and the greater the exchange of views between those involved in child care the greater is the hope that correct, or at least the best, solutions will be found. (The Hon. Mr Justice Waterhouse, 1989, p.17)

Interference of the law and other social discourses does not mean that they merge into a multidimensional super-discourse, nor does it imply that information is 'exchanged' among them. Rather, information is constituted anew in each discourse and interference adds nothing but the simultaneity of two communicative events. (Gunther Teubner 1989, p.745)

Both these positions, the one advocating dialogue and co-operation, the other claiming that no real dialogue is possible, in a sense move away from the welfare/justice conflict mentioned in the last chapter. Of course, they are made at very different levels. The first is by a practitioner writing about the day-to-day relationship between lawyers and child care experts. The second comes from an article by a German theoretician who is concerned in a general way to define the nature of law and what he calls 'the legal discourse'. For the practitioner, the way to bridge the gulf between welfare and justice is to bring the two sides closer together and, by doing so, arrive at 'the correct' or 'the best' solution. For Gunther Teubner, the nature of the legal discourse is such that attempts to merge it with other social discourses can result only in 'interference' between the two. All that results are simultaneous statements about the child and its problems, which, like parallel lines, never meet, but continue along their own path. Instead of joint or co-operative decision-making, therefore, information about the child is 'constituted anew' within the legal and within the social work or child care discourse.

While Mr Justice Waterhouse's pleas for more co-operation and understanding between the legal system and child care experts restate the hope expressed by many different judges and lawyers over many years,[1] Teubner's ideas about the way the law 'thinks' are new. For this reason we have devoted this chapter to an account of his theoretical model. In doing so, we are not, it must be emphasized, embarking upon some fruitless academic exercise with no practical application or importance for people who have to live their lives in the real world. If Teubner is right, or even half right, the implications for law and the relationship between law and other disciplines are considerable. Much of what we have taken for granted, including the high hopes of Mr Justice Waterhouse, will have to be abandoned, at least for the time being, while the very nature of law's role in a wide range of children's cases is re-examined and re-evaluated within the context of a different theoretical framework.

# I   Constructing the truth

## 1   The nature of social reality

The starting point for this theoretical framework is the proposition that reality exists but is not directly accessible; in other words, there is a 'world out there', but the way that the limitations of our senses and cognitive processes operate makes it possible for us to 'know' that world only in a limited, reductionist way. What results, therefore, are different versions of reality. What is accepted as reality by an individual or group depends upon a variety of factors, including pre-existing beliefs and values, cognitive style, and present motivation for accepting one version of reality rather than another.[2] This applies equally to 'realities' about social institutions, such as the legal system itself, as it does to truths about those people and situations presented to lawyers and the courts for legal decision-making.

What, then, determines whether one statement is accepted as 'true' and another rejected? Habermas's discourse theory suggests a consensus theory that it is the 'potential consensus of all participants' which operates as the criterion for truth. According to Teubner, Habermas emphasizes the importance of formal and procedural characteristics for determining the validity of the consensus upon which truth is based (Habermas, 1985):

> It is this proceduralization of the truth criterion which has rendered Habermas's discourse theory so important for law. It makes the theoretical-empirical dis-

course of the sciences directly comparable to the practical normative discourse in politics, morals and the law. (Teubner, 1989, p.733)

Each discourse or communicative network, according to Teubner, therefore, has its own procedures for generating and assessing the truthfulness of any statement. The criteria for establishing truth are a product of this proceduralization process. Accordingly, different versions of truth or reality may co-exist, each supported and sustained by adherents to particular methods and procedures for arriving at 'truth'.

To summarize, Teubner sees knowledge about the world, including people and social situations, as relative, not absolute. Disciplines, professions and formal social institutions, through their reliance on different communicative systems, have their own procedures for determining the truthfulness of any statement and for generating knowledge about the world. Statements which have been generated by the approved procedures have the potential for acceptance as truth, but only within a communicative network which shares the same procedural criteria. Other communication networks using different networks may validly reject this particular version of reality.

## 2  How organizations think

An essential feature of Teubner's theory lies in the proposition that social organizations and institutions think, and that this thinking is different to, and independent of, the thinking of its individual members. For all social psychological theorists and most sociological theorists this represents a radical departure from traditional ways of conceiving the social world. Berger and Luckmann (1967), for example, were concerned with the way individuals construct reality, while G.H. Mead (1934) sought to explain how awareness of the self and others developed through the internalization of the social world. For these writers, it was individuals who both created social reality and internalized that reality in a way that enabled them to locate themselves in society. All economic and many social theories assume rationality or at least intention in such individuals, so that all collective social phenomena may be reduced to the intentional actions of human individuals (Teubner, 1989, p.730).[3]

To understand Teubner's account of the nature of law in contemporary society one must first accept this seemingly unlikely proposition that the law, along with other social organizations, does in fact 'think'. To support him in the exposition of this concept, Teubner again cites Jürgen Habermas, who, having recognized that cognition is basically a communicative process, then proceeds to identify intersubjectivity within the communicative community, and not the autonomous individual, as the authority which determines what passes for truth and knowledge (Habermas, 1984, Ch.3).

Teubner then invokes Michel Foucault's widely celebrated ideas on discourse and power (Foucault, 1972, 1974 and 1982). Foucault's major contribution to a social epistemology, according to Teubner, has been 'to liberate the core concept of "discourse" from any transcendental [that is, universal and timeless] foundation and any "psychic" [that is, the internal mental activity of individuals] foundation' (Teubner, 1989, p.734). For Foucault, Teubner tells us, 'it is not the individual consciousness of the subject that constitutes reality' (p.734), nor is it Habermas's intersubject-ivity; 'Rather it is *discourse*, an anonymous, impersonal, intention-free chain of linguistic events . . . The human subject is no longer the author of the discourse. Just the opposite: the discourse produces the human subject as a semantic artifact' (p.735).

Yet Teubner is quick to point out that this is not a structuralist position for discourse in Foucault's account is social practice, not social structure, meaning that it emerges from what people do and say, rather than being predetermined by the existence of institutions and organizations which impose their discourses upon people. 'It is *énoncés*, that is the social usage of language, that constructs reality' (1989, p.735). The *épistème* (the framework for generating truth and knowledge and for understanding about the world) for any particular historical epoch is determined by this social practice of discourse.

Teubner, however, finds the theoretical approaches of both Habermas and Foucault problematic in one fundamental aspect – their self-referentiality. Put at its simplest, the dilemma lies in how to explain the way in which discourses which construct truth, knowledge and reality obtain the knowledge of procedures for evaluating truth, knowledge and reality, except by referring back to themselves. One is left with the circularity whereby the procedures of discourse can be justified only by discourse, whose procedures in turn have to be justified by discourse. Habermas brings into play the concept of communicative transcendental-ism to escape from this circularity. Foucault, on the other hand, invokes the ubiquity of power in order to externalize self-referentiality. Power, it seems, can transcend prevailing *épistèmes*, but does not explain how this is supposed to happen. Neither of these theoretical accounts, according to Teubner, is satisfactory. He turns, therefore, to a third contemporary theorist, Niklas Luhmann, to resolve this problem.

## 3   Luhmann and the theory of autopoiesis

Autopoietic systems are, in the language of the biologists Maturana and Varela (1980), systems that recursively produce their own elements from the network of their own elements (Teubner, 1989, p.736).[4] By applying the notion of autopoiesis to social systems, Luhmann succeeds in resolving the paradox and tautology of self-reference, simply by stating that self-referentiality, far from being a problem, is an essential characteristic of organizational discourses:

> As autopoietic systems, discourses cannot but find justification in their own circularity and cannot but produce regularities that regulate themselves and that govern the transformation of their own regularities. (Teubner, 1989, p.736)

What Teubner sees as emerging from Luhmann's resolution of the problem of self-referentiality is, therefore, a far more radical approach than had ever been conceived by previous reality construction theorists. Not merely is all knowledge, whether of a scientific, political, moral or legal nature, seen as purely an internal production of individuals or organizations, but:

> any cognitive activity – be it theory or empirical research – is nothing but an internal construction by the cognizing unit; and every testing procedure that pretends to examine the validity of internal constructions against outside reality is only an internal comparison of different world constructions. (Teubner, 1989, p.737)

In other words, within each system of communication one can only judge the validity of cognitions – statements about the world – by referring back to the internal procedures of the system which determine the validity of a particular piece of knowledge, whether they are the hypothetico-deductive methods of normal science[5] or the rules of procedure and evidence of the legal system.

*Psychic and social autopoiesis*   Luhmann's notion of social autopoiesis is exclusively based on communication – that is, 'the synthesis of utterance, information and understanding'. As Teubner puts it, Luhmann (1984 and 1986), unlike Habermas in his concept of 'intersubjectivity', makes a clear distinction between social constructions of reality and psychic constructions; the former concerns relations between social systems, while the latter pertains exclusively to the internal mental activities of individuals. Teubner sees psychic processes as forming a 'closed reproductive network of their own – psychic autopoiesis' (Teubner, 1989, p.737).[6] Individuals operating within a social system will, therefore, reconstruct reality according to their own internal procedures, separate and distinct from the organizational or systems thinking, which exist in closed autopoietic systems of their own. Social systems, on the other hand, 'think' through their communications. These, as we shall see, express their coding of the external environment.

This separation of social and psychic systems means that the two are in no way able to relate directly to one another. As Teubner puts it,

> Psychic and social processes do co-exist, they are 'coupled' by synchronization and co-evolution, but there is no overlap in their operations . . . psychic processes produce mental constructs of society, and social processes produce communicative constructs of the psyche. (Teubner, 1989, p.737)

We shall return to the distinction between psychic and social communications when we come to discuss the nature of legal discourse (see pages 29–31)

*Plurality and fragmentation*   Teubner identifies another important concept that Luhmann has developed from earlier theorists concerning the historical nature of discourses. While Foucault, as we have mentioned (see page 24) sees each historical epoch as characterized by an all-pervasive, society-wide *épistème* (and views the modern epoch as governed by a 'subjectivist' *épistème*), according to Teubner, Luhmann interprets modernity as the:

> fragmentation of society into a plurality of autonomous discourses. The crucial feature of modern society is the loss of a unifying mode of cognition. Society is seen as fragmented into a multiplicity of closed communicative networks. (Teubner, 1989, p.738)

Each of these communicative networks constructs its own version of reality according to its own rules of procedure, and each of these reality constructions is in principle incompatible with the reality constructions of other communicative networks.[7]

Teubner sees this notion of fragmentation as 'one of the strongest points' in Luhmann's theories, but, at the same time, he expresses doubts about a theory which sees each social system as closed and quite unable to relate to other social systems except by reconstructing them within the framework of another *épistème* (Teubner, 1989, p.738). What is important to Teubner and also for our specific purposes is to arrive at some understanding of how the law, both as a communicative system and as a formal institution, relates to other systems of communication.

# II   How the law thinks

## 1   Law as an autopoietic system

Only if law is seen as a system of communications does its self-reproductive or autopoietic nature become apparent. Legal communications 'are related to each other in a network of communications that produces nothing but communications' (Teubner, 1989, p.740). In other words, 'law as a communicative network produces legal communications' (Teubner, 1989, p.740). This means that the law cannot deal directly with 'the outside world'; as we have already mentioned, it can only reconstruct that world in forms that are acceptable as legal communications accessible to other legal communications in the network of legal communications.

This approach is likely to raise all manner of objections from all those who operate in and comment on the law and legal system. They would undoubtedly maintain that the law is constantly dealing with real people. It takes into account the motives and behaviour of litigants, police, judges and legislators. The law refers constantly to people's mental states, such as *mens rea* or malice aforethought. It also deals with their behaviour in its utterances – negligence, parental control and abuse of power are but a few examples. According to Teubner, however, this is an illusion. The 'persons' that the law deals with 'are not real flesh-and-blood people, are not human beings with brains and minds . . . they are mere constructs, semantic artifacts produced by the legal discourse itself' (Teubner, 1989, p.741).

This proposition may not be so outrageous as it first seems. Clearly there are certain legal constructs or fictions that even the most traditional lawyer would accept as artifacts, such as 'the reasonable man' or 'the guilty party' in divorce cases. If pressed, the traditional lawyer might also accept that there are states of mind and aspects of behaviour that exist only as legal constructs – the law imposing sense and order on untidy social situations in order to do justice or resolve disputes. These might include 'provoca-tion' in murder trials, 'contributory negligence', 'consent' in rape cases, 'intentionally homeless', or 'the intention of Parliament' in statutory interpretation. Teubner, however, would not single out such examples as exceptional. Rather, they typify the need of law as a social process to attribute communication to actors in order to continue its self-reproduction (Teubner, 1989, p.741). The construction process is not, therefore, confined to what lawyers recognize as 'fictions'. It extends to all those persons, be they individual or corporate, who become involved in legal communica-tions, whether as litigants, witnesses, judges, legislators, limited com-panies, parents, children, local authorities or the state. They all become 'role-bundles, character-masks, internal products of legal communication', existing only in the 'autopoietic reproduction of the social life of law in which human actors are not elements but constructed social realities' (Teubner, 1988, pp.133ff. and 1989, p.741 ).

## 2   Law as a second-order autopoiesis

Society, meaning the sum total of all existing communicative possibilities, is a closed communicative system in its relation to nature (the transcendental) and mind (the psychic), but is not a discourse in the sense that it reconstructs the environment in the ways that we have described earlier. In this sense, therefore, it operates as a 'first-order autopoiesis'. Within modern society a number of functional discourses or subsystems have emerged, such as religion, art, economy, politics, education and law. Each of these has its specific way of coding – that is, making sense of – the external environment. There remain, however, diffuse communications, similar to Habermas's (1985) life-world, which are not part of any functional discourse or subsystem, although there is always the possibility that they will in the future become so. When, therefore, *A* meets *B* in the street and remarks on the unpleasant weather and *B* agrees that the weather is indeed unpleasant for the time of year, this exchange takes place within society, but not within any specific discourse or subsystem of society. It is possible, however, in the future, that the state of the weather may become so important to society that major institutions emerge which have the function of monitoring and attempting to control the weather. At this point one would be able to identify an autopoietic discourse subsystem called 'weather', where the coding of the external environment might be in terms of favourable/unfavourable for society or the planet. At this point the discourse on the weather will become autonomous from general or diffuse social communication.

If we now turn to the legal discourse, this, along with other discourses, has become autonomous in modern society, developing its own communicative network. 'It develops into a closed communicative network that produces not only legal acts as its elements and legal rules as its structures, but legal constructions of reality as well' (Teubner, 1989, p.742), and it is this fragmentation of society which, according to Teubner, has resulted in legal operations functioning as a second-order autopoiesis. Fragmentation implies here an increasing autonomization of specialist social discourses, 'in which reality constructions of general social communication are increasingly replaced by reality constructions of the specialist discourse . . .' (Teubner, 1989, p.742).

Even basic social concepts, such as 'child' or 'parent', are redefined by the law and thus given a legal meaning. The same thing happens to more complex concepts, such as 'harm', 'responsibility' and 'reasonable parent'. As Teubner points out, 'legal discourse increasingly modifies the meaning of everyday world constructions and in case of conflict replaces them by legal constructions' (1989, p.743). It is this inability to deal directly with the social world as perceived and experienced, the commonsense world, that relegates law to a 'second-order autopoiesis'. At the same time, the autonomous or autopoietic nature of the legal discourse makes it, in Cotterrell's words, 'largely impervious to serious challenge from other knowledge fields', be they scientific, economic or the commonsense, practical reasoning of diffuse or non-specific communication (1986, p.3).

What Luhmann and Teubner tell us, therefore, is that the truths generated by law as an autopoietic system cannot be influenced directly by the truths produced by subsystem discourses outside the law or by direct communications from society. Their influence can operate on law only in a refracted manner, through their reconstruction by law as valid legal communications.

# III   The nature of legal discourse

Teubner may insist that 'law is communication and nothing but communication', and that communications consist of 'utterances, information and understanding'. He says little, however, about the content of such legal communications other than their concern with legal rules, norms, doctrines and procedures (Teubner, 1993, Ch.3). For elucidation as to the nature of law we must turn to his compatriot, Niklas Luhmann. Yet to embark upon a detailed examination of Luhmann's rich and complex ideas would lead us far away from the subject of this book and deep into the jungle of abstract, philosophical debate from which we should probably never emerge. While we are fully aware of the all-or-nothing nature of the theory of autopoiesis, we have quite deliberately chosen to extract a number of key concepts from Luhmann's total vision of law's function in maintaining social order. In doing so we are aware that not only are we probably guilty of distorting and oversimplifying some of Luhmann's ideas, but that in departing from his total vision we are moving towards a rather different model of law and its relations with other social discourses.

Firstly, Luhmann defines law's function in terms of its 'stabilizing of congruent expectations' (1982 and 1985), its provision of certainty and continuity, offering people the possiblity of not learning from experience. Although people may experience daily illegal behaviour, this experience does not teach them that the behaviour has now become legal. It remains illegal until the law declares it legal. Law offers society a version of social reality, which substitutes normative expectations for those derived from experience. In doing so, law not only simplifies and reduces social issues, but it also absorbs and neutralizes them. As David Nelken explains:

> For Luhmann, law is the great concealer, hiding the fact of violence at the basis of social order, handling irreconcilable political and moral choices in a world without either consensus or absolutes. Teaching people not to learn from their disappointed expectations . . . (1988a, p.203)[8]

Law's social role includes tasks which it performs for other social institutions – not merely the obvious task of resolving disputes, but also dealing with politically contentious problems, preventing too close an interdependence between institutions and reminding other social organizations, such as politics and administration, of the existence of an environment external to their own operations, an environment in which normative legal expectations prevail. (Nelken, 1988a, p.201).

All this is possible only if law is able to maintain and to reproduce its way of seeing the world in terms of legality and illegality, to distinguish between the legal and the illegal. Like all other social communication systems, it necessarily reduces the complexities of the environment to manageable proportions by imposing simple (and simplistic) concepts. From this flows, for example, the tendency for the law to reduce behaviour to rights, duties and responsibilities, or to culpable and innocent conduct – those normative, moral judgments that, where they are not made explicit, lie just below the surface of formal legal pronouncements. From this we can also see clearly why the law necessarily concentrates attention on offences, illegal acts or upon the degree of individual responsibility, and why it is driven to identify and even seek out villains and victims. In this way law maintains and reproduces its own autonomy from society and from other social communication systems and asserts the validity of its truths independently of the truths produced by these other systems.

Teubner takes matters a stage further by identifying the methods by which law achieves this functional objective as the restructuring of external realities within the legal system, using legal procedures for constructing reality to generate statements which are acceptable to the law and unassailable on moral or political grounds. 'The law autonomously processes information, creates worlds of meaning, sets goals and purposes, produces reality constructions and defines normative expectations . . .' (Teubner, 1989, p.739). An illustration might be the issue of prison overcrowding. Economic and political discourses might construct this phenomenon as resulting from a number of factors, such as underfunding of the prison building programme and/or the closing of mental hospitals, combined with the failure to provide adequate hostel accommodation and community care for the mentally unstable. For the law to accept such analyses would be to leave open the possibility of judicial decisions being attacked on moral or political grounds, or of law having to face the empirical consequences of its pronouncements. Within legal communications, however, the problem of prison overcrowding simply does not exist. Judges and magistrates impose terms of emprisonment where this is legally the 'right' sentence for the crime committed. The law does not 'know' about the conditions in prisons, but only about the correctness or otherwise of the sentence.

# IV   The epistemic trap

Law faces a special problem in that it is obliged by the roles it plays in modern society – stabilizing, imposing order, resolving disputes – to confront and deal with other discourses or communicative systems. Yet, at the same time, it must produce statements for consumption by society and other social subsystems within society which promote and reinforce its own claim to regulate and control these subsystems and, indeed, much of what happens within society. Thus it is caught in an irreconcilable conflict between the maintenance of its own autonomy and its dependence for its legitimacy upon 'a multiplicity of competing *épistèmes*' (Teubner, 1989, p.743).

We must distinguish here between the world of non-legal communication and that of legal communication. Outside legal institutions, such as the courts, barristers' chambers or lawyers' offices, whenever legal constructs conflict directly with or sit uneasily alongside those produced by other discourses, 'inevitably legal constructs lose in the epistemological competition' (Teubner, 1989, p.745). The reality constructions produced by science, politics and economics prevail over those generated by law. However, within formal legal institutions, legal discourse claims to be entitled to 'enslave' other cognitive operations according to its own normative context and institutional purpose. One example is the way in which psychiatric experts give evidence on the mental state of an offender at the time of the crime. This evidence is then reconstructed by the law to answer the question: 'Was (s)he responsible at the time?' Yet any notion of responsibility is quite foreign to the psychiatric diagnosis and treatment of mental illness.

To perceive the relationship between law and other disciplines as one of exploitation is not new. A number of writers had drawn attention to the legitimization role that experts play within the context of legal decision-making. Teubner, however, goes much further than that. He maintains that the institutional context of the legal process produces an internal contradiction:

> While it requires idiosyncratic reality constructions through legal communication, it forces legal communication to reconstruct the scientific constructs of reality and to expose – even within the law's empire – juridical constructs to the 'higher' authority of science in cognitive questions. (1989, p.745)

Because law inevitably has to deal with issues of conflict, it is obliged to examine any new piece of knowledge produced outside the law, where such knowledge is relevant to the operations of law. Both legal and scientific scholars[9] have been quick to criticize lawyers and legislators for the naïve, prescientific models of human behaviour which inform the law's

procedural and evidential rules and to propose scientific alternatives. For
Luhmann this naïvity or reductionism, far from being a failure of the law,
is essential to its successful social functioning. Law's role is indeed to
reduce complexity to manageable proportions in order that its normative
communications may be acceptable to society.

Yet, for Teubner it is the need for law as an autopoietic discourse to win
social approval by subjecting its procedures and reality constructions to the
higher authority of other discourses that leads to a loss of legal authority. It
places law in what he calls 'the epistemic trap', in that 'law is forced to
produce an autonomous legal reality and cannot at the same time
immunize itself against realities produced by other discourses in society'
(1989, p.745). This may lead to situations where law has literally no way of
coping with the reality constructions of other discourses, except by
invoking more non-legal reality constructions and so entering still further
into the epistemic trap, with the confusion and ambiguity that this entails.

# V   Escape routes from the epistemic trap

## 1   Renouncing epistemic authority

For Niklas Luhmann, the way out of the trap is to discharge the law from
re-examining everyday interpretations and scientific constructs. Questions
over which the law at present exerts its authority could be 'turned aside or
referred to philosophy' (Luhmann, 1988a, p.340). Teubner, however points
out that it might not be possible for the law, when faced with controversial
or politically 'hot issues', simply to 'turn them aside or refer them to
philosophy'. 'In the day-to-day practice of legal decisionmaking, law is
constantly forced to decide autonomously on cognitive questions which
are supposedly within the competence of scientific enquiry or of common
sense' (Teubner, 1989, p.746).

Such adjudications are necessary even if the issues they address cannot
be resolved scientifically, and even where the legal adjudication makes
little sense outside the confines of the law and serves further to isolate the
law from other discourses, thus confirming its autopoietic nature. Even if
the law in the short term might be able to renounce its authority, in the
longer term, scientific or commonsense issues will inevitably find their way
back to the law for adjudication.

## 2   The integration of law and social sciences – the production of hybrids

In this second of the principal escape routes, the law, instead of separating
juridical knowledge from social scientific knowledge, is supposed 'to

incorporate social knowledge into its world constructions and permanently revise legal models of social reality according to the accumulation of knowledge in the social sciences' (Teubner, 1989, p.747). Teubner here distinguishes between two types of overlap of law and other discourses: 'diffusion' and 'interference'. Diffusion occurs where 'legal discourse is part of a diffuse social discourse and is not differentiated.'[10] This can only happen, therefore, in those situations where law is not autopoietic in nature, for example in pre-modern societies or informal groups. It cannot occur in modern post-industrial conditions, characterized as they are by the functional differentiation of social discourses. We are left then with 'interference', that is, with 'communications that apparently bridge both discourses [but which] are in reality separate pieces of information in each discourse and are coupled only by their synchronization and coevolution'.[11]

Far from making law more responsive to the demands of other discourses, bringing it closer to the taken-for-granted world which is widely accepted as 'social reality', these attempts to incorporate 'social knowledge' within law have tended to produce 'hybrid artifacts with ambiguous epistemic status' (Teubner, 1989, p.747). What, he claims, happens in practice is not 'that they merge into a multidimensional super-discourse, nor does it imply that information is "exchanged" among them. Rather, information is constituted anew in each discourse' (Teubner 1989, p.745). This means that those constructs which started out, for example, in the social sciences cannot be simply transferred unchanged into the legal discourse:

> They are not imported into the law bearing the label 'made in science', but are reconstructed within the closed operational network of legal communications that gives them a meaning quite different from that of the social sciences. (Teubner, 1989, p.749)

Teubner goes on to insist that it is not simply a matter of the same thing being looked at from different angles or in ways appropriate to the methods and needs of different disciplinary interests. This interpretation rests on the assumption of some underlying reality, and therefore the possibility of unification between different disciplines, and the resolution of conflicts arising from differences of approach. For autopoietic theory, 'these differences are to be found in the realities' which the different discourses produce, so there is no possibility for unification or reconciliation. It is clear that 'what happens to [social scientific] constructs once they enter the legal scene is no longer in the hands of the social sciences' (Teubner, 1989, pp.749–50).

Other discourses cannot merge with the law because the autopoietic nature of law demands that it 'recursively produce its own elements from the network of its own elements', and not from the elements of other discourses or communicative systems. For Teubner, law has its own, unique procedures for determining what constitutes reality and valid knowledge. Knowledge and reality constructions produced outside the law must, therefore, be transformed and reconstructed if they are to become accepted as legal truth and legal knowledge.

One obvious objection to this analysis is the apparent evidence of everyday experience. Lawyers and others are constantly subjecting the law, its procedures and its processes to critical scrutiny, seeking to improve it so that it can indeed deal more effectively with current social problems. Moreover, contrary to Teubner's assertions, new forms of, and criteria for, legal decision-making do appear to emerge from communications between representatives of law and other discourses. At the level of individual and professional action, there can be no argument with the fact that lawyers and representatives from other disciplines do indeed work together in the production of solutions.[12] Yet this is somewhat different from the 'merging' or the direct 'exchange of information' that Teubner refers to. The possibility of co-operation between individuals from different disciplines or discourses is in no way denied by his theory. The question is rather whether such joint enterprises do indeed involve a genuine merging of different discourses, whether they remain in essence separate and distinct from one another, or whether one discourse in practice reconstructs in its own terms the communications of the other or others. According to Teubner, true merging or diffusion of different discourses is not possible in modern societies, where functional differentiation operates as an unsurmountable obstacle to such fusion.

At the epistemological level, while the same statement may appear simultaneously in the legal discourse and, for example, in the psychiatric discourse, it will, according to Teubner, have a very different meaning depending upon its institutional and epistemological context.[13] Although there may be co-operation between professionals, therefore, there can be no real meeting of minds, no real communication between lawyers and psychiatrists, as long as each remain within their own discourse. It is always possible, however, for either of them to speak and act in ways appropriate to the discourse of the other, while still calling themselves 'a lawyer' or 'a psychiatrist'.[14] Teubner describes this as 'role-interference', that is, 'the overlapping membership of persons' (1993, p.90).

The phenomenon of interference, giving the impression of genuine fusion and direct communication in law's relations with other discourses, may also occur at the structural level. This arises in two different situations. The first is within the legal domain, where law, in its attempt to be responsive to the demands created by contentious moral or political issues, imports concepts from other discourses and in doing so necessarily reconstructs them in ways which advance its own social functions of simplification, dispute resolution, depoliticization and the upholding of the moral order. This results in what Teubner calls the 'over-legalization of society'.[15] Here, legal 'regulatory programs obey a functional logic and follow criteria of rationality which are poorly suited to the internal social structures of the regulated spheres of life' (Teubner, 1985, p.311). The succeeding pages of this book give many examples of this process at work in the area of children's issues.

A similar, but less destructive process may occur within domains outside the law, where concepts drawn from the legal discourse are imported, supposedly to bring legal rationality to activities which appear to lack any clear direction. An example here would be 'social work contracts', where, according to David Nelken (1987 and 1988a), the borrowing of legal concepts may create confusion and distort the essential nature of both legal and social work communications. This process is discussed in some detail in Chapter 6.

The second situation is that of the 'over-socialization of law'. In its attempts to be responsive to societal demands and merge its operations with other subsystems, law may, in effect, 'surrender' to those other subsystems of society at the cost of its own self-reproduction. Teubner writes, for example, of law being 'captured' by politics or economics (1985, p.311). This is not, we would argue, a major problem in the regulatory field of parent–child relationships, although others, such as James (1992; and James and Hay, 1993), argue that the influence of welfare officers on court decisions should be seen as a retreat of law rather than a legal colonization or 'enslavement' of child welfare. We would argue that a far clearer example of legal operations being 'captured' by the child welfare system would be the French *juges des enfants* (Chapters 6 and 8). If one seeks an illustration of politics 'capturing' law, one need look no further than juvenile justice in the UK throughout the 1980s and early 1990s, when the operation of courts for young offenders was constantly being changed to meet political demands.[16]

## 3 'Reflexive law' as a solution

Teubner (1989) identifies a third possible solution to the problem of the epistemic trap – 'a kind of middle path between the two escape routes', where the law neither takes over full epistemic authority nor totally delegates it to another social discourse. In his article 'Substantive and Reflexive Elements in Modern Law' (1983) he introduces the idea of 'reflexive law'. Since at the time of writing this article Teubner had not formulated the notion of the epistemic trap, he was not in a position to propose reflexivity as a solution to the problem of law's loss of authority in relation to other social discourses which it is forced to confront. Rather, reflexivity is offered as an answer to the crisis caused by the failure of legal rationality under modern conditions to provide law with the necessary tool to restore consensual moral and political values.

Reflexive law is Teubner's response to the 'colonization' or inappropriate imposition of legal rationality upon welfare systems, which 'either turns out to be ineffective or . . . works effectively but at the price of destroying traditional patterns of social life' (1983, p.274). Teubner proposes a 'reflexive' role for the law which, instead of attempting to make law responsive to social problems, seeks opportunities that 'allow legal regulations to cope with social problems without at the same time irreversibly destroying patterns of social life' (Teubner, 1983, p.274). Law, according to this solution, will provide the 'norms of procedure, organization and competencies that aid other social systems', but will not attempt to impose its rationality on those systems:[17]

> reflexive law . . . will neither authoritatively determine the social functions of other subsystems nor regulate their input and output performances, but will foster mechanisms that systematically *further the development of reflexion structures within other social subsystems*. (Teubner, 1983, p.275, original emphasis)

Teubner goes on to give the example of German consumer information law, which does not 'authoritatively decide what constitutes the consumer's interest. It restricts itself to defining competencies of the articulation of consumer interests and to securing their representation' (Teubner, 1983, p.277). Here, the task of the law is not to develop its own purposive programme, nor is it to resolve conflicts between different policies; rather, it is 'to guarantee co-ordination processes and to compel agreement' (Teubner, 1983, p.277). One could easily substitute here 'children's interests' in place of 'consumer interests', so that it would not be the task of the law either to define or to determine what are the best interests of the child, but rather to provide structures within social work and child care systems which would guarantee co-ordination of representations (which could include those of the child's family) and compel them to work towards agreement.

We need to mention at this point that Niklas Luhmann (1992) is extremely sceptical of the notion of reflexive law as a theoretical concept. 'No system', he writes, 'can transcend itself and carry out operations other than its own'. While it may be possible for people, as psychic systems, to project themselves into the thought processes of another individual, this is not a feasible strategy for social systems, since they are able to 'think' only in ways which make sense within their own communicative network. Teubner's proposal leaves law, therefore, facing the strange paradox: 'It must learn to see what it does not see and to regulate what it does not regulate.' This 'leads ultimately to the realization that it does not realize what it does not realize' (Luhmann, 1992, p.411).

These are obviously complex and controversial proposals, which we shall examine in some detail in later chapters of this book. The essential point at this stage is, however, that, for Teubner at least, this 'partial renouncing of authority' by the law offers an escape route from the epistemic trap in that, once it is no longer concerned to impose its own rationality, there is no need for it to create its own reality, 'inspired by the exigencies of conflict resolution' (Teubner, 1983, p.279) and constructed through its own truth-generating procedures. Reflexive law needs to utilize and develop only that knowledge necessary to the control of self-regulatory processes in different contexts (Teubner, 1983, p.281). Even Luhmann, in his critique of this position, goes as far as to recognize that 'the reflexivity of 'reflexive law' [does have some value in that it] could bring home to jurists how little their observation system and that which they define as action corresponds with the operations and self-observations of other autopoietic systems' (Luhmann, 1992, p.400).

## VI   Autopoiesis and social policy

If we are to take Gunther Teubner's ideas seriously, we need also to examine carefully its policy implications. Teubner is not content for his account of the relations between law and other social institutions to remain at a level of abstraction where it can only with enormous difficulty be applied in any direct way to the practical policy concerns of lawyers and legal administrators. His article, 'Substantive and Reflexive Elements in Modern Law' (1983), for example, is clearly directed at policy issues.

However, there are problems in attempting to apply Teubner's ideas. For us the most serious of these is the very concept of the 'autopoietic discourse' which Teubner has developed from his unlikely synthesis of Habermas, Foucault and Luhmann. Teubner implies that pure or whole discourses (Foucault) may be distinguished from hybrid or 'bastard' discourses by their autopoietic nature (Luhmann) and by their unique procedures for validating truth (Habermas). Whole discourses are, it seems, able to operate in a consistent manner within social institutions created around them, producing communications which readily make sense, not only within the particular epistemic community – be they lawyers or scientists – but also for the external social world. Where two or more discourses combine to create a hybrid discourse, on the other hand, the resultant marriage, whether it be in terms of a body of knowledge or a social institution designed to promote the interests of professions or disciplines in which the discourses are joined together, is highly unsatisfactory. Why?

In order to answer this question properly, one needs to go beyond the scope of the present book and examine Luhmann's theoretical account of modern societies as being distinguished by stratification according to functional differentiation. Attempts to combine into hybrids those functionally differentiated subsystems will, in the absence of some overriding authority such as religion or the monarchy, result in the creation of new institutions, but not in new, functionally differentiated communicative systems. The attempt to merge discourses does not result in any new way of knowing the external environment; rather it leads to confusion and identity crises within the institutions – what Luhmann calls 'de-differentiation'. Unless newly-formed institutions follow and flow from the evolution of new ways of knowing or coding the external environment, they are likely to be of short duration only – expedients to meet the most recent demands of societal pressures. In the long term, the discourses which, it is claimed, have merged, are likely to separate again into their component parts.

In his earlier writings, Teubner (1983, 1985 and 1986) did not have to confront the problems created by the synthesis of the three very different theoretical models of Habermas, Foucault and Luhmann. In these works he wrote of 'systems' and 'structures' rather than discourses. These he identified by their self-referential nature, and it was this rather than any intrinsic incompatibility in their truth-validating procedures which he identified as imposing limits on the efforts of substantive or responsive law to regulate the activities of other social subsystems.

In his 'Substantive and Reflexive' article he criticizes those jurists who encourage the development of law as an institution for solving social problems, not for the obvious reasons that judges may be class-bound, gender-bound and race-bound in their interpretation of these problems, but because the law, having developed its own 'rationality' in order to decide social conflicts, then goes on to abstract 'highly selective models of the world thereby neglecting many politically, economically and socially relevant elements' (Teubner, 1983, p.279). This detracts from law's function, which can be defined as 'its capacity to provide congruent generalizations for the whole of society' (Luhmann, 1974).

We find Teubner's theoretical account offers important insights into the relationship between law and other bodies of knowledge which would not have been possible without his telling critique of Nonet and Selznick's (1978) model of responsive law and its unrealistic requirement that law respond to the social demands for regulation by changing its own structures and ensures 'the adequate representation of various interests in the core organization of society' (Teubner, 1983, p.269). For Teubner, law can only act in an autopoietic way, that is by reproducing its own elements. The most that one can hope for is to build into these elements an awareness of the limitations of regulation through law and of the importance of preserving intact the structures of other systems.

## VII　Testing the theory

In 'After Legal Instrumentalism', his contribution to the book *Dilemmas of Law in the Welfare State* (Teubner, 1985), Teubner discusses whether scientific procedures for the testing of hypotheses are an appropriate way to validate the kind of 'strategic model' which he sees himself as constructing. Reflexive law, far from being a scientific theory for the understanding of law's relations to the social environment, is a model 'which incorporates sociological theories of law, but transforms these into legal constructions of social reality' (p.301). Its main function is 'to use the self-identity of law to produce criteria for its own transformation' (p.301), in other words, to make law aware of itself in a way that will lead to changes in its structures, and thus in its relations to other social subsystems. In this sense it is 'strategic'. Teubner accepts, then, that his 'strategic models' are not 'scientific', but refutes categorically the criticism (Blankenberg, 1984) that they are merely unscientific, uncontrolled ideologies. 'Rather', he states:

> they incorporate sociological theories and must be compatible with scientific developments . . . They are 'more or less empirical theories with practical intentions' (Rottleuthner, 1983). In particular, if the models ascribe certain functions to law, they have to deal with sociological theories about the relations of law and society. (Teubner, 1985, p.302)

However, to describe the relation between the models and the social world as 'a contrast between lawyer's ideology and social reality' would be a mistake, because 'there is no direct access to social reality, there are only competing system models of reality. Therefore, one has to see this as a problematic relation between legal and social models of reality; each having its own rightful claims' (Teubner, 1985, p.302). Science should not be used to define authoritatively models of external reality. Where legal models and scientific theories compete, it is as different constructions of the external environment, and the power of any particular theory or model is comparable only in relative terms according to its power to fulfil the goal for which it was constructed.

According to Teubner, the way to test these models is to institutionalize them and expose them 'to the competitive market of scientific discourses and legal doctrinal controversies, conflicts of social movements and to institutional decisions' (1985, p.303). 'Experience', he claims, 'can be gained only in the form of social experiments in which those legal models are tried out' (p.303).

For our own part, as academic authors, it is not possible for us to mount social experiments in the way that Teubner stipulates. However, we are able from our knowledge and expertise in our area of speciality – the welfare of children – to draw upon evidence from existing arrangements between legal and social scientific discourses. This evidence comes from various different legal jurisdictions where different arrangements exist. It includes the results of research, analyses of reported court cases and our own experience.[18] These we present as our contribution to the dissemination of autopoiesis as a radical departure from traditional ways, both legal and sociological, of thinking about law and its role in society. The evidence that we present in this book may also be seen as giving some support to the strategic model of reflexive law that Teubner proposes as a solution to the dilemma of regulation in modern societies. It will be up to others to decide whether our argument is convincing for social scientists and for lawyers, applying the criteria derived from their respective disciplines.

# Notes

1   It has become one of the more predictable recommendations of child abuse inquiries (see Dingwall, 1986) and one of the inevitable elements to be incorporated in proposals for Family Courts.
2   See, for example, Berger and Luckmann (1967).
3   Even exponents of Critical Legal Studies, the most radical of current theories about the law, tend to occupy themselves at a level of analysis where the reasoning of individual judges and the effects on individuals of different styles of dispute resolution are pertinent issues (see, for example, Kennedy, 1986).
4   See Luhmann (1986), King (1993) and King and Schütz (1994).
5   See Kuhn (1962).
6   See also King (1993).
7   See King (1993) and King and Schütz (1994, pp.267–70).
8   See also Rottleuthner (1989) and Zolo (1992) for a general discussion and critique of Niklas Luhmann's theoretical writings on autopoietic law.
9   See, for example, Marshall (1966, p.105), Spencer and Flin (1990) and Stephenson (1992).
10  Teubner (personal communication to the authors).
11  Teubner (personal communication to the authors).
12  See King and Garapon (1987 and 1988).
13  Teubner (personal communication; December 1989).
14  The division of the cognitive world into discrete discourses clearly gives rise to major theoretical problems. Not least among these is the question of how one sets about recognizing 'discourse' in the first place.

15  This leads to what Habermas has identified as 'colonization': the disintegrating effects of legal regulation in different areas of social activity.

16  See, for example, Ball (1992).

17  Another example might be the equitable notion of *the rules of natural justice*, where legal intervention in administrative decisions is concerned only with the basic fairness of the procedures used, and not with the substance of the decision. However, even these rules might go further than Teubner intended in, for example, their requirements concerning representation and cross-examination.

18  One of us has practised as a solicitor advocate in England and has carried out research into the French child protection and juvenile justice systems. The other has undertaken research into mediation procedures in divorce.

# 3  The construction of child welfare science

## I  Child welfare as science

The problems which we identified in Chapter 1 concerning the idealization of welfare and justice into a mode of analysis arise to a large degree from the insistence on seeing both welfare and justice as conflicting ideologies, and therefore inexorably bound up with political debates and developments.[1] What is clear from Teubner's and Luhmann's analysis, however, is that the legal system is much more than the product of political or economic forces. It is a self-referential system with its own communications, its own objectives and its own procedures for determining what constitutes valid knowledge. Yet what of welfare?

While law's procedures are clearly all directed towards the generation of communications in fulfilment of its normative function of distinguishing the legal from the illegal, the same clarity of discursive identity cannot be seen to exist within child welfare. If one takes the whole range of statements made about what is good for children, and the procedures by which such 'truths' are produced, it is extremely difficult to identify the discourse within which such communications are being made. Is it common sense, science, medicine, politics or religion? These waters have been further muddied by the very use of the word 'welfare', which, within the world of politics, has become associated with a socialist ideology which seeks to eradicate the barriers of inequality of opportunity by providing state assistance for disadvantaged sectors of the community.[2] Child welfare as a concept – and those who seek to promote children's welfare – tend to be perceived, particularly at times when right-wing ideologies prevail, as part of the apparatus of the state and little else. This labelling of 'welfare' as representing a particular political ideology also tends to taint people's perception of the knowledge of those social scientists who seek to identify and understand factors affecting the wellbeing of children, be they sociologists, child psychiatrists or developmental psychologists. It is a sad fact, therefore, that the deployment of such knowledge to support campaigns to improve outcomes for children tends to detract from any recognition of child welfare as a distinct body of knowledge whose grounding in the discourse of science is independent of political considerations.[3] It is our contention, however, that only by recognizing child welfare knowledge as ultimately dependent upon a scientific discourse is it possible to analyse adequately the nature of the relationship between this knowledge and the law.

In a broad social context, science has the institutional function of defining what are and what are not 'facts'.[4] It is concerned with identifying causes and effects, which is achieved, wherever possible, through procedures of empirical observation. Both law and science lay claim to discovering 'the truth', but, as David Nelken points out, law's truth may be seen as serving a very different social function to that of science:

> Law is seen as an institution which serves distinctive social functions as compared to science, and therefore develops in different ways. Law's ostensible function of dispute-processing and legitimation of power holders, for example, requires it to offer certainty and reinforce commonsense expectations whereas scientific progress depends on controversy and the undermining of common-sense. (Nelken, 1990, p.21)

When law 'thinks' about science, however, scientific knowledge is not generally perceived as 'depending upon controversy' or as 'undermining common sense'. Rather it is treated as knowledge which is able to legitimize and give weight to law's normative accounts of reality and to decisions based on these accounts. For law, scientific procedures exist as methods which assist in the reinforcement of congruent expectations. Where controversy exists, it is constructed by law as a dichotomy between a right answer and a wrong answer, the choice between one category or another.[5] It is not surprising, therefore, to find legal commentators attempting to classify the value for law of different sciences according to the 'objectivity' of their knowledge – that is, their falsifiability, according to Popper's criteria. Sciences which rely largely upon unfalsifiable statements, namely the social and behavioural sciences, through their insistence upon notions of consequences and causality derived through experience in those very areas of social life where law is seeking to offer congruence and predictability, present a direct challenge to law's normatively-directed version of reality. Law, as a discourse or communicative system, is not interested in actual consequences, but in maintaining expectations that certain consequences will occur, that unlawful behaviour will be condemned as wrong and result in negative consequences for the perpetrator, regardless of, and often in contradiction of, any empirical evidence that may exist.

The procedures for validating child welfare knowledge are concerned almost exclusively with empirical evidence. They rely upon and promote learning through experience, as opposed to law's normative learning.[6] They include, as well as the experimental method of the natural sciences and quantitative social scientific techniques such as social surveys and experimental designs, those more controversial processes such as psychoanalysis and individual case studies. These procedures are concerned with causes and consequences and with identifying these, as far as possible, through empirical procedures. Obviously the interpretive element is likely to be greater in child welfare, as in all the social sciences, than in the natural sciences, but it would be wrong to use this to disqualify child welfare from the scientific community, since interpretative concepts are also an essential feature of physical sciences.[7]

Therefore, while much child welfare knowledge may not be 'scientific' in the manner of the natural sciences, it does fall within the general scientific discourse, for, ultimately, the truths it produces rest upon, and are, validated procedures which empirically examine events in an attempt to identify causes. The disciplines which provide child welfare knowledge go beyond the mere mimicking of scientific procedures or merely clothing themselves in pseudo-scientific language.[8] While both natural scientists and child welfare scientists act out their roles from a script where the dialogue revolves around issues of producing knowledge through empirical methods applied in a systematic manner to events, one difference between them is that the former are concerned with events in the world external to the individual, while for the latter the internal world of the individual, or two or more relating individuals, are often of importance in so far as they throw light on the causes of external past events or allow predictions of future events.

Typical of the controversies that surround the scientific status of child welfare knowledge is that concerning those observational methods derived from psychoanalytic theory. Let us examine more closely these methods and the controversy they generate. In the first place, there are problems of subjectivity associated with the interpretive nature of the statements produced through these procedures. As John Bowlby recognizes:

> What a patient tells us about his childhood and especially what an analyst subsequently reports his patient to have said are probably influenced as much or

more by the analyst's preconceptions as by anything the patient may in fact have said or done. (Bowlby, 1988, p.72)

But this is also a problem which, according to Rosenthal, psychoanalysts share with the rest of the scientific community.[9] Yet Bowlby's solution to the problem of subjectivity serves to highlight the more important problem of child welfare as a scientific discourse. His solution is research – 'systematic study by direct observation of children within different patterns of family care'. Research results, according to this view, are seen as guiding those engaged in observing and analysing in the direction of 'the truth'. If scientifically conducted research studies indicate that failure to bond with the mother at the critical stage in a child's life results in insecurity and clinging behaviour at a later stage, then observations of such behaviour point to the reality of the bonding failure. Yet there are still difficulties. In the first place, scientific studies deal in probabilities, not certainties. Not all children who were not adequately bonded exhibit such abnormal behaviour, and not all children who exhibit such behaviour have been inadequately bonded. Secondly, even if one eliminates the subjective preconceptions of the analyst, the same behaviour may still attract different interpretations depending upon what scientific studies the interpreter has read and given credence to. Some observers, for example, might choose to see insecurity and clinging behaviour as a sign of child sexual abuse or of additives in food, where scientific studies exist indicating that these factors may give rise to such behaviour. How does the social worker choose between the different theories of child development or between research results which draw attention to very different factors for predicting child abuse?

These are very real problems. But while they may affect the reliability of any decisions made for the future welfare of the child, they do not necessarily detract from the scientific nature of the knowledge. It is simply a different kind of scientific knowledge than that produced by quantification and experimentation. Indeed, Farrell (1981, p.44) has argued that this type of knowledge is similar to Newton's theory of cohesion, which was 'not open to [empirical] validation, was unstable and vacuous' and yet played 'a significant role in the subsequent history of scientific enquiry into the nature of chemical reactions and matter'. It would be absurd to suggest that the failure of this theory to meet Popper's criteria of falsifiability should disqualify physics or chemistry from membership of the scientific community.

If it is the methods and procedures that give rise to concern, then one might also question some of the highly interpretive and idiosyncratic methods that have heralded major advances in the natural sciences. Rustin (1989) elaborates on this point when he compares the observational methods of psychoanalytical research into mother–baby relationships with the methods of behavioural psychology. While the former, he argues:

> seek to identify a holistic coherence and recurrent patterns in the evolution of the relationship of mother and baby and in the emergence through this of the individual character of the baby . . . in the larger-scale studies of behavioural psychologists, individual identities and differences of character are subordinated to an atomistic and aggregative method seeking definite findings about specifiable aspects or units of behaviour . . . (p.44)

This, Rustin maintains, does not mean that the observational methods used by psychoanalytically trained researchers outlaws them from the scientific community. If this were the case, one would need also to exile all anthropologists and sociologists who chose to use ethnographic, life-history or case studies as their preferred research method. These methods, Rustin argues:

> can be the original sources of insights which are subsequently formulated as concepts and hypotheses, and tested in more empirically rigorous ways. Alternatively, case study methods can be used to investigate social processes and mechanisms whose existence can be inferred from large-scale statistical studies, which may demonstrate causal connections without offering much explanatory account of them. (Rustin, 1989, p.44)

Child welfare knowledge, even at its most subjective, interpretive and probabilistic then, may be seen as being generated by a scientific discourse derived from science. To define child welfare as nothing more than a collection of subjective, often contradictory, opinions stemming from class and cultural values fails to distinguish procedure from performance. Child welfare decisions may at times be ineffective and its interpretations may have ideological undertones, but this does not affect the scientific nature of the discourse or the knowledge produced within the discourse. Its communications are very different in kind from those in which lawyers or politicians are engaged.

The problem for child welfare which distinguishes it from the physical sciences lies elsewhere. It is to be found in the context in which its knowledge is applied, rather than in the knowledge itself. In order to make its way in the world it has been forced to co-exist in close proximity with other non-scientific discourses, such as law and politics, because, apart from the psychoanalyst's consulting room and the observation psychologist's studio, it has no decision-making forum, no social institution where its procedures control the construction of reality.

When the knowledge of child welfare is applied in practice to a specific social issue or family problem, the results may appear to an outsider anything but scientific, lacking the precision and generalizability of the natural sciences. Yet this lack of precision and absence of general rules arise from the very nature of the phenomena studied, which cannot be reduced to precise predictions or unambiguous interpretations. Nevertheless, the nature of the knowledge is such that its validation or refutation depends upon empirical, scientific procedures and not on religious faith, legal doctrine or political principles. This point is well illustrated by the contents of a talk on relevant knowledge for social workers given at a conference on 'Professional Decision Making in Child Abuse Cases'.[10] The speaker identified four types of relevant knowledge:

> [1] general knowledge of child protection; [2] a particular knowledge of the family in question; [3] a knowledge of the informal, formal and societal systems surrounding both worker and client; and [4] a certain kind of self-knowledge. (Mitchell, 1989, p.11)

The fourth type of knowledge, 'a certain type of self-knowledge', poses some difficulties for, if what is being referred to by the speaker were to be some magical powers or metaphysical endowment – an intuitive sixth sense – or even arising from some religious experience, it would clearly take child welfare out of the scientific domain. However, this does not appear to be the case, for what the speaker is clearly invoking is an understanding of one's own motives, irrational fears, obsessions, etc. specifically in order that these should not interfere with the exercise of distinguishing the factual from the non-factual[11] in questions concerning the future welfare of one's child client.

The same speaker goes on to list in detail the items of knowledge that social workers must grasp under the heading 'general knowledge of child protection':

> normal and abnormal child development (in its physical, psychological and social dimensions); an understanding of the social and psychological aspects of family life; a grasp of the legal framework within which the work must be done (including courtcraft) and, in particular the powers and obligations that exist in order that children may be protected; an awareness of different forms of child abuse, of the circumstances in which it might arise, of the signs by which it might be known and of its consequences; a confidence about different kinds of styles of communication (including the art of communicating with young children) . . . a knowledge of what does and what does not suggest that a child might be left at or returned home; an appreciation of the value of permanence for the child and of the practice requirements entailed in planning for permanence. (Mitchell, 1989, pp.11–12)

In its social work context there clearly are difficulties for child welfare as a scientific discourse, for mixed in with knowledge attainable through scientific procedures are other forms of knowledge which clearly depend upon procedures derived from other discourses. While it is clear that child welfare depends ultimately upon the prospect of scientific validation, it tends to lose its congruence with the general scientific discourse when it becomes one item in the epistemological equipment for practical reasoning of social workers handling child abuse cases. The strategies and processes by which social workers seek to detect child abuse and to protect the child are not necessarily the same as child welfare scientists would use to evaluate and attempt to improve outcomes for an abused child. Further-more, while it may be valid to speak loosely of 'a social work discourse', such a discourse will inevitably include incompatible and even contradic-tory forms of knowledge. What we have is the sort of 'interference' which characterizes Teubner's hybrid or bastard discourses – an untidy bundle of concepts cobbled together for 'practical' purposes which, when subjected to critical scrutiny, disintegrate into their constituent parts.

## II   The 'integration' of law and child welfare

One of the elements in the social worker's epistemological bundle is law. Law 'thinks' about children in fundamentally different ways to the science of child welfare. Take, for example, children's statements. Within the scientific discourse such statements may be constructed as information contributing to truth about the child, his or her personality, and ways of relating to others. For law, by contrast, children's statements are seen as evidence indicating the likelihood of the occurrence of certain past illegal events. A child's fantasies and fabrications may be interpreted within the scientific discourse as windows through which his or her inner represen-tations, hopes, fears and anxieties may be glimpsed. For the law these same fantasies and fabrications may (or may not) be accepted as evidence of unreliability and, in the case of older children, moral depravity. What results, therefore, is 'interference' – 'one and the same statement playing a double role. It is legal information in the legal discourse and scientific information in the scientific discourse.'[12]

A recent book by a child psychiatrist specializing in child abuse highlights how this double role leads to a splitting of 'truths' concerning the same event:

> When a case in which I, as clinician, have clear clinical indications of child sexual abuse is dismissed for legal reasons in court I must not allow my clinical judgement to be devalued by the legal dismissal. A young child who in my clinical judgement has been clearly sexually abused, does not become less sexually abused in my clinical judgement if for particular *legal* reasons of evidence or procedure the court may not wish or may not be able to accept my clinical judgement on the legal level. (Furniss, 1991, p.109, original emphasis)

The psychiatrist goes on to explain how the public declaration of 'legal truth' in such cases of failed prosecutions may, through denial of the occurrence of the abuse and the existence of an abuser in the face of scientific information, provoke further abuse and contribute to a system of 'abuse-promoting child protection' (Furniss, 1991).

The problem for child welfare as science is that, within the legal arena, the information will almost invariably be constructed according to the demands of the legal discourse. The uncertainty and imprecision of statements produced by child welfare both in relation to existing knowledge about children and predictions for their future make both the statements and the statement-makers even more highly vulnerable to 'enslavement' within the legal arena. The law's demand for decisiveness and finality, for winners and losers, for rights and wrongs to be identified and exposed to the public gaze in order to further its normative objectives tend to force legal judgments out of the mouths of child welfare representatives. There is no room in law for suspended judgments.[13]

In general terms the 'enslavement' of the child welfare discourse by law corresponds closely in part to the individualization process identified by several authors.[14] The broad range of factors – genetic, financial, educational environmental and relational – which science would recognize as capable of affecting the welfare of a child are narrowed by law to a small range of issues which fall directly under the influence of the judge, the social workers or the adult parties to the litigation process. Among social problem construction theorists the issue is usually presented in terms of political ideology. By reconstructing the social dimension of any issue concerning the welfare of the child in such matters as housing, education, health care and financial security in ways which emphasize individual responsibility and the failure to accept that responsibility or perform those duties expected of a child carer, law in capitalist societies effectively depoliticizes social problems and reinforces liberal, individualistic ideology to the detriment of socialist notions of collective or governmental responsibility.

Yet the same process may be seen, not in political terms, but as the inevitable consequence of the autopoietic nature of law and its inability to incorporate external discourses except by reconstructing them through the application of its lawful/unlawful coding. Thus the scientific discourse of child welfare in all its richness and complexity is reconstructed as concepts which 'make sense' within law – that is, concepts which further the immediate demands of the law to determine guilt and responsibility, resolve disputes and do justice between litigants and at the same time promote the function of law in modern society – distinguishing the lawful from the unlawful. This reconstruction process necessarily involves reductionism, and simplification as well as a concentration on the behaviour of individuals.[15] In the legal domain welfare becomes 'welfare-within-law' – an enslaved discourse.

Within the English legal system the specific involvement of psychological science in legal decision-making on child welfare issues can be traced to the 1950s, when psychoanalytical ideas were widely disseminated. John Bowlby's major work was abridged and published in paperback in 1953, and in the following five years sold 75,000 copies.[16] This movement, therefore, involved the dissemination and general acceptance of several particular ideas, notable amongst which was the idea of maternal deprivation. As Bowlby said in a BBC broadcast in 1968:

> as time goes by the best solutions will become clearer. Meanwhile we are wise to be wary. Any move that separates young children from their mothers needs scrutiny, for we are dealing here with a deep and ancient part of human nature.[17]

Such particular announcements are crucial to our analysis because it was by these specific precepts that law was able to incorporate, but also reconstruct within its own discourse, the new 'knowledge' being presented to it. The reason for the comparative ease with which this was done was that the law was called upon to deal only with those aspects of the 'new psychology' which by the late 1960s were accepted both by the scientific discourses from which they emerged and also by a wider social discourse.[18]

Therefore, whilst it is true that constructs from 'the new psychology' challenged law's authority to resolve disputes, the discourse which produced them proved relatively easy to enslave in ways which converted psychological notions into quasi-legal principles. The legal reconstructions of this new knowledge were necessarily simplistic because law by its very nature needs clear normative principles. New precepts, focusing on mother–child bonding and stability of relationships were used to justify particular outcomes in particular cases, but such outcomes therefore also became the *ratio* for deciding later cases and guidelines for child protection functions. It is consequently easy to trace the emergence and development of a line of cases dealing with 'mother preference' in custody disputes.[19] Similarly, the work of child psychologists concerning the advantages of stability for the child led to the *'status quo principle'*.[20]

Nevertheless, from the 1950s onwards there are voices within the child psychology camp expressing criticisms of the dominant ideas being purveyed. At first this did not present the law with an insuperable problem.[21] Modifications were made to reality constructions to incorporate new 'facts'. So the idea of 'significant adults' in a child's life was reconstructed into the legal presumption that access was a 'good thing' to be encouraged. As early as 1973, an English judge stated:

Access often results in some upset to the child. Those upsets are usually minor and superficial, they are heavily outweighed by the long term advantages to the child of keeping in touch with the parents concerned so that they do not become strangers.[22]

The mechanism by which law had responded to new child welfare knowledge by the 1970s was therefore that of selective reconstruction of its components. Very simplified conclusions from complex research results had, in practice, become principles within family law.[23] This meant that the law's validating procedures remained untouched; expert evidence had still to be martialled and presented to prove or disprove the relevance of the simplified principles to the family in question. Divorce court welfare officers were employed to acquire such evidence.[24] The result was that the precedents which embodied the child development principles could be dealt with by practitioners in much the same way as precedents are used in other areas of the law. The judge, magistrate or registrar could thereby determine either the 'best' parents within custody disputes or whether a previously absent parent was 'significant' enough to be granted an access order in his/her favour. Law was not, therefore, concerned about the consequences for the child as empirically defined, but sought rather to uphold principles of equality and justice between parents by invoking some normative principle which would avoid the need to learn from experience. Scientific evidence was reconstructed, not as a predictor of consequences, but as a legitimator of normative legal decisions.

The law had succeeded in reconstructing the knowledge of child care experts in such a way that its procedures remained unaltered and unchallenged. The inevitable result was a narrow interpretation of the welfare of the child. In fact there were limits to this reconstruction – limits imposed by law itself; for example, the statement of one judge[25] that:

access is a basic right of the child rather than a basic right in the parents . . . no court should deprive a child of access to either parent unless it is wholly satisfied that it is in the interests of that child that access should cease,

was incorporated into the legal discourse as the principle that access is almost always beneficial. However, since law did not give a child a right to decide whether he or she wished to see the non-custodial parent and could not contemplate giving children such a right, there was no way that the legal system could in practice proceed on that basis. Increasingly, as we shall see in Chapter 5, this 'fiction' was revealed as such by those wishing to expose the law's reconstructions as unworkable and ineffective. Nevertheless, just as for several decades the law had enslaved welfare knowledge, it also succeeded in enslaving the specific knowledge of the welfare expert.

# III Law and the 'welfare expert'

In the same way as it has reconstructed welfare to answer its institutional needs, the law has also constructed the notion of 'welfare expert'. This device allows a privileged status, a mantle of reliability, to be extended to professionals who are not members of the legal fraternity. Being an 'expert' in the eyes of the law, like being a lawyer, carries with it certain privileges which are important in the epistemological game which is played out in the courts. In Anglo-Saxon countries these privileges are of particular significance, for here, experts, unlike ordinary witnesses, may give their opinion on any matter over which their expertise extends.[26] In cases involving children, the law has constructed the notion of expertise in such a way that it covers all members of professional groups part of whose role is the care of children. This may include, social workers, guardians *ad litem* or probation officers acting as court welfare officers, and health visitors, as well as specialized experts such as child psychiatrists and educational psychologists. All are free to give their opinion in court as to the parenting skills displayed by a mother, for example, or the likely effects on a child of seeing its father regularly.

In Continental civil law countries, such as France, the notion of 'expert' is rather more narrowly drawn, since experts are likely to be appointed by the judge or court to act and be treated as judicial assistants.[27] Courts and individual judges have lists of suitably qualified experts to whom they can refer when the occasion arises. Social workers are usually not considered to be experts in this sense, but they may nevertheless enjoy a privileged relationship with the judge which is denied to litigants and ordinary witnesses. In France, for example, it is quite common for a social worker, prior to the hearing of the case, to speak to the children's judge in private on the telephone or in person. Moreover, those social workers who work for the Ministry of Justice as *éducateurs* are based in or close to the court building and are in constant communication with the children's judge.

In French judicial decisions concerning children, the term 'expert' is usually confined to members of the 'psy' professions. One sceptical French commentator recently claimed that the term 'expert' had more to do with the social role that those designated as experts were called upon to play within the legal system than any clear scientific qualifications which united them. He argued that the uncertain contours of the term not only revealed:

> a linguistic convenience, but served also to connote the fact that the term covers different types of required competence, united by the social status of those agents who possess such competencies. It refers to child development professionals having the prefix 'psy' in common (psychiatrists, psychologists, psychoanalysts). Their opinions or beliefs, come with a seal of scientism which

denotes a formal training and/or appropriate experience. It is thus the social legitimation empowering these agents to pronounce some 'psy' knowledge concerning the child which forms the basis of their common classification as experts. (Almodovar, 1988)

This designation by different jurisdictions of certain professionals as child care experts, through the highly dubious construction of the notion of expertise which the law has succeeded in achieving has the added effect of creating 'non-experts' – that is, those who are not permitted to give opinions or whose opinions are accorded little weight.[28] In common law countries, such non-experts may include, for example, the parents or grandparents of the child or even an experienced foster mother in whose home the child has been living. They may describe how the child has been behaving, but they are not allowed to give any opinion as to why the child behaves as he or she does or what will be the best way of dealing with the child's behaviour.

While this clear distinction between expert and non-expert does not exist in the same manner on the continent of Europe, there are other privileges accorded to those designated as 'professionals'. Such privileges concern the way in which knowledge about the child and family is constructed. In France, as we have mentioned, child care professionals may discuss the child and the parents with the *juge des enfants* on the telephone or in the privacy of the judge's room.[29] In Holland, the information that an expert from the Child Protection Council includes in their reports to the juvenile court judge is treated as undisputed fact. Once again, it is not the qualities of the particular person that confer such privileges upon them, but the status which law has granted them in order that it may bring them into the legal arena, both to provide the knowledge required for legal decision-making and to validate that knowledge as genuine, as 'truth'.

There is, however, a high price to pay for the privilege of expertise. Just as the law enslaves the scientific discourse of child welfare, so it may subjugate the welfare expert.[30] Within common law adversary systems, the reliability of welfare experts may be judged, not according to any scientific criteria, but by their performance in court[31] – the confidence with which they give their evidence in court and stand up to cross-examination or confrontation with other experts. In inquisitorial systems, experts may be selected and their opinions heeded according to whether their perspective on child care coincides with that of the judge deciding the case.

This is not to suggest at this stage that the 'truth' that emerges from the scientific analyses of child care professionals is superior in any absolute sense to that constructed by the courts, but rather that each serves particular institutional objectives. To subject one form of truth to the truth-validating procedures of another necessarily results in distortion, because the institutional objectives of these procedures are very different from those of the institution where that particular version of truth or reality was constructed. Likewise, attempts by child welfare scientists to reconcile different discourses so as to achieve desired objectives for the child may, in some cases, require a distortion of scientific truth. To give a concrete example, during a recent research study a child psychiatrist told the interviewer that in those cases before the court where she believed that the child should not be returned to an inadequate parent, but wished contact with that parent to continue, she sometimes felt it necessary to exaggerate the inadequacy of the parent to care for a child. To do otherwise, she believed, would be to risk arguments from that parent's lawyer that the child should return home being accepted by the court.[32]

# IV   The rights of children and parents

The use by law of the 'psy' expert to analyse the parent–child relationship and present the courts with an assessment of what has gone wrong with that relationship and what is likely to happen in the future requires some further comment. To see this arrangement only in terms of increasing the nature and scope of intervention in the family, Donzelot's (1979) tutorship, is to ignore the important differences between the legal and psychological discourses and the relationship between them.

It is hardly surprising that the law's utterances on children's wellbeing concentrate upon the parent–child relationship. The law 'knows' children through the parent or parents. Parents have legal rights, duties and responsibilities.[33] These not merely empower the parents to take decisions about their children's lives, but they are the very threads which the law attaches to people who become legal parents, jerking them into response when things go 'wrong' in the child's life. With very few exceptions, the child's 'wrongness' – its inappropriate, abnormal or illegal behaviour – is seen as the responsibility of its parents. In legal terms, these parents have failed to exercise their rights or perform the duties and responsibilities that have been attached to them through the medium of legal parenthood.[34]

Within a social culture which raises the individuals to the status of prime movers of events and identifies them as the mainspring of causality, it could be argued that all the law is doing in making parents the target of its concern is to reflect accurately external social discourses. This argument gains in strength when it can gather support from 'scientific knowledge'. The individualist approach of Freudian psychology, with its emphasis on the powerful formative effects of the parent–child dynamic, provides just such support. Witness the enormous impact upon law throughout the Western world of Goldstein et al.'s (1973) celebration of 'the psychological parent' in their book *Beyond the Best Interests of the Child*.[35] More recently, the work of Wallerstein and Kelly (1981) has emphasized the importance of continuing parental contact after separation of the spouses. Thus legal duties and responsibilities imposed upon people by the mere fact of becoming legal parents are reinforced by being also 'psychological duties' and responsibilities. A father who fails both to pay child maintenance and to continue to have contact with his child is not only breaking the laws of the land, he is also breaking the 'scientific laws of nature', which may cause the child untold psychological harm.

The impression given by the wealth of literature that now exists in legal publications concerning the psychological effects on children of child care legislation, legal procedures and court decisions is of an increasing rapport between law and psychological expertise on questions of children's welfare. While differences may have existed in the past, and still do occur from time to time, these no longer take the form of a total failure to understand the other's point of view, but are likely to take the form of clashes of beliefs, values and professional ethics. A common complaint among lawyers, for example, is that 'psy' experts tend to resist giving clear answers to direct questions about the likely outcome for the child. The common response from the experts is that in demanding clear-cut answers the law is ignoring the complexities of situations, and demanding certainties where none can exist. Where direct clashes occur between judges and 'psy' experts, they may often be interpreted in terms of differences in ideological values rather than disputes over the likely outcome for the child.

One US case[36] cited by Davis (1987) in her study of the application of the psychological parent theory by the courts concerned the fate of twins who had been placed in foster care following a finding of negligence. This negligence had occurred after repeated violent assaults by the father upon the mother of the children. When some four years later the mother sought the return of the children, the foster agency resisted, stating that it was in the best interests of these children to remain with their foster parents, who had become the psychological parents. A psychologist and a psychiatrist were called to give evidence in support of the psychological parent theory. However, in its decision the court rejected their advice, preferring the view (unsupported by evidence) that the theory did not apply where the child had had contact with the biological mother. It therefore ordered that the children be returned home on trial. Eighteen months later the children appeared to be doing well, so a final order was made.

A triumph for practical reasoning over rigid scientism? Yet one might have expected the court's decision to have been very different if the mother had been the guilty perpetrator of assaults on the children rather than neglecting them involuntarily, being herself the innocent victim of the father's assaults. In other words, cannot the law's 'practical reasoning' be seen as a moral judgement on the mother's past, and thus of her worthiness to be a mother again, rather than an expression of any well-defined notion of what is best for children's welfare? The ideological clash here may be seen as taking place between law's concern for maintaining, wherever possible, congruent normative expectations – that is, that innocent victims do not suffer the further punishment of losing their children – with the concerns of psychiatry and psychology in adhering to the theory of the psychological parent regardless of any moral message that may be conveyed to the outside world. The point is well illustrated by an English case where the court's decision on similar facts may well have caused serious harm to a child.

In this case the social services department was seeking to free a young child for adoption. Here, the young, single mother of a year-old child had shown herself to be incapable of caring adequately for the child's needs and of accepting outside help in the care of her child. The child had suffered from neglect and abuse to the point where a court had decided that he should be placed in the care of the local authority social services department. The mother, who had maintained spasmodic contact with the child, was resisting the freeing order and wanted the child to be returned to her. A psychiatrist, called upon to examine the child and mother and to assess the mother's parenting abilities, concluded that she did have affection for the child and could, given considerable help, develop adequate parenting skills. Shortly before the court hearing, however, the mother had become pregnant, and when the psychiatrist knew of this, he changed his conclusion, and now took the view that the mother would be quite unable to cope with the child and her new-born baby, and that any attempt to rehabilitate the child would be likely to break down shortly after the baby was born.

In the terms of the child welfare professionals, this was a case where their knowledge and experience would predict a very high probability of breakdown if rehabilitation was attempted, and that, if this proved correct, the young child's life would be disrupted three times by changes of care, which would be likely to have an extremely damaging effect on his emotional development, quite apart from the risks of further neglect and abuse that might arise if he were returned to his mother. Their solution was for contact with the mother to be ended and for an adoptive family to be found for the child. This, they claimed, was the solution which was most likely to respond to the child's needs.

The law, however, with its concerns for rights, interpreted the issue as a contest between the child's rights, as defined by the social services department, and those of the mother not to lose contact with her natural child. Since the mother had not acted in such a way as to forfeit her rights by, for example, any serious physical abuse of the child, and could be described as inadequate and incompetent rather than morally wrong, some compromise between the two contestants was appropriate. The judgment was, therefore, for the child to be rehabilitated on a trial basis at a residential centre for parents and children where the mother's parenting skills might be improved and assessed. The matter should return to the court in three months for a review of the situation. According to this logic, delaying the final decision allowed the law to be fair to everyone concerned and not to override the rights of the mother until it could clearly be shown that she had forfeited these rights. For the psychiatrist concerned for the child's welfare, on the other hand, this decision represented not only a rejection of his recommendation, but also increased considerably the risks to the child's wellbeing, for any future separation of the child from the mother would be likely to be interpreted by the child as rejection in favour of the new baby, rather than a carefully planned attempt to provide him with a new and more stable home.

Yet even after his opinion had been rejected, the psychiatrist in this case was prepared to shrug his shoulders and acknowledge that the judge 'was entitled to his view' and had 'accepted responsibility' for the child's future. Could this be interpreted as a clear indication of the advances made in promoting understanding between lawyers and experts?

# V   Fitting science into law

A critical analysis of both these cases might well point to the clash of ideology between lawyers and 'psy' experts. Such an interpretation, as we have noted, holds out the hope that differences might be resolved in future by greater co-operation and understanding between the professionals involved. Indeed, many lawyers and judges would maintain that such co-operation and understanding is essential if the courts are to reach the right decision in cases involving the future welfare of children. Such a cosy vision of interdisciplinary symbiosis would clearly fly in the face of Teubner's theory, for it omits any notion of separate discourses and the divergent reality constructions they produce. Moreover, just as welfare has been constructed within law so as to 'make sense' within the legal discourse, so too has child psychology and child psychiatry. Those psychologists and psychiatrists who regularly give evidence as experts in the courts and who write about legal issues may represent child psychology for the law, but their construction of child psychology may not in any way be representative of the range of theoretical and experimental work across the child welfare and child development fields.[37] One clear example of a psychological version which will not fit easily into law is that of Family Systems Theory. What sense can the law make of explanations of child abuse in terms of 'an organized arrangement of elements which comprise a network of interdependent and co-ordinated parts which function together as a unit',[38] or which assesses families on their capacity to develop adoptive and flexible structures in response to feedback from the environment or from its members. On occasions, systemic child psychiatrists and psychologists have to go to court in order to protect a child client or patient, but, as one such psychiatrist explained:

> It is not possible to talk to the courts about sets of relationships which bring this [abuse] about, which is how one is thinking if one is thinking systemically. What is forced to happen is that out of that context one person is picked . . . The only thing that actually matters is the individual.[39]

This is not to suggest that the dilemma facing this particular psychiatrist – whether to remain faithful to the diffuse notion of causality that systemic theory postulates, or whether, for the purpose of protecting the child, to present her expert evidence in ways that fit the law's expectation to find a responsible (or an irresponsible) individual – in some way epitomizes the relationship between law and psychiatry. What is being proposed here, however, is a further complexity to Teubner's already heavily charged model. It is not enough to state that law and child welfare science are different autopoietic systems, each using their own procedures for constructing reality, for within the domain of child welfare there exist a diversity of discourses which themselves produce different versions of reality, albeit using 'scientific' procedures. From these different versions, law acknowledges and actively promotes those which are compatible with its own autopoietic nature. These are given the status of 'psychology-within-law' or 'psychiatry-within-law'. Law produces, therefore, not only versions of children, childhood, parents and parenthood as epistemic subjects, but also versions of child psychology and child psychiatry. These are but a partial and selective account of these disciplines.[40] Law's version is reinforced by those self-selecting experts whose daily concerns and theoretical orientations (or absence of theoretical orientation) both draw them into law and then trap them within the legal discourse.

# Notes

1   See Morris and Giller (1987, Ch.3).
2   The child welfare reforms put forward in the UK by the Labour Party in the 1950s and 1960s are examples of this conceptual link.

3    We are aware of the view that all science is political in that its concerns reflect power relations which exist in society. It is precisely such simple visions of the nature of science and the scientific discourse that we are arguing against.

4    All this occurs despite radical changes in the philosophy of science which have heralded the abandonment by a significant proportion of the scientific community of the claim that science is capable of identifying absolute truth. This post-positivist movement has also raised serious doubts over attempts to compare or classify, according to reliability, fields of intellectual endeavour because each constructs its own knowledge and experience (see Cotterrell, 1986, p.11 and King, 1986, Ch.3). Today what is meant by the term 'scientific' depends for most scientists, not so much on the application of some external criteria applied to the activities of particular disciplines, as on how members of that discipline define their own activities and the procedures that they apply for validating knowledge (see, for example, Popper, 1965 and Searle, 1984). For a strong case against this post-positivist thinking see Cohen (1977).

5    See Eastman (1992). See also Luhmann (1989) for an account of the binary nature of legal reasoning.

6    See King and Schütz (1994).

7    See Hesse (1980) for an account of those features which distinguish human from natural sciences, and a critique of such distinctions.

8    We are aware of the controversial status of psychoanalytic theory as 'scientific', and in particular of Karl Popper's statement that it has no more claim to scientific status than 'Homer's collected stories from Olympus' but, as we have stated, we do not regard Popper as the final arbiter on what should be considered of scientific status. See also, for example, Feyerabend (1975).

9    See Rosenthal (1963).

10    As written up in the speaker's article (Mitchell, 1989).

11    See Cohen (1977).

12    Teubner: personal communication, 28 November 1989.

13    The very notion that the 'fact-finding' of courts of law involves a large element of interpretation and subjective evaluation is at odds with the legal discourse. Marcus Stone, the Sheriff of Lothian and Borders and the author of a book entitled *Cross-examination in Criminal Trials* (1988) writes, for example, that one sound test of the truthfulness of a witness's evidence is 'its probability or improbability by reference to one's experience of life'. He adds: 'Whether witnesses are lying can usually be decided without difficulty. A crucial factor is that one witness's evidence, though plausible, may be rejected because it is contradicted by another witness whose evidence is accepted as being beyond doubt. This is typical of the adversary system – a total approach in which truth emerges from conflict.' The emphasis is on objective analysis of evidence rather than on a subjective impression of any single witness. See also Stone (1989).

14    See, for example, Ehrlich (1936), Cotterrell (1984, Ch.4).

15    It is also true that certain of the child welfare disciplines (notably developmental psychology and psychoanalysis) individualize the cases of children's 'problems', although there appears to be an increasing awareness of the relationship between events in the external environment and behaviour within the family. See, for example, Bowlby (1988).

16    New methods of popularization were also pioneered. In England, Winicott, who had revised the seminal work of Melanie Klein, made regular wartime broadcasts on the BBC on the subject of child development and management.

17    In a talk entitled 'Security and Anxiety', quoted in Riley (1983, pp.107–8).

18  It had become what Berger and Luckmann termed 'taken for granted' knowledge. An example of this can be found in Backett's work with middle-class parents in the 1970s, which led her to conclude that 'if two words dominated the interviews with this group of parents these were "security" and "stability"' (1982, p.115).

19  *Re S* [1958] 1 WLR 391; *Ives* v. *Ives* (1973) 4 Fam. Law 16, CA.; *Greer* v. *Greer* (1974) 4 Fam. Law 187, CA.; *M* v. *M* (1978) 1 FLR. See also Maidment (1984, pp.182–4).

20  *Re W* [1965] 3 All ER 231; *J* v. *C* [1969] 1 All ER 788; *Re W* (1971) AC 682, 703–4; *O'Connor* v. *A and B* [1971] 2 All ER 1,230.

21  For example, Michael Rutter's work was taken to show that separation from a significant adult was detrimental to the child's development, but that this adult need not be the mother. Initially, the legal system found no difficulty in producing reality constructions which absorbed the qualifications being made because the significant figure was almost invariably still the mother. See Rutter (1972).

22  *M* v. *M* [1973] 2 All ER at p.88, per Latey J.

23  It is fair to point out that the results of this simplification were not always so different from what the popularizers of child psychology had done.

24  In England, fairly simple forms were issued asking for statements of arrangements for children of divorcing parents such that the amount of evidence was strictly limited to what the court could cope with.

25  Wrangham J., in *M* v. *M* (see note 22 above) at p.85.

26  'he may give his opinion on matters calling for expert opinion, even though he has no personal knowledge of the facts. If he does not have such personal knowledge, he may give his opinion on the basis of facts which he has heard given in evidence by other witnesses or on the basis of a hypothetical question, founded on the facts already given in evidence.' (Graham Hall and Martin 1993) For an account of the psychological expert in the USA see Davis (1987).

27  See Damaska (1986, p.54).

28  This practice in child welfare cases runs quite contrary to the formal position in English law, which prefers the application of popular standards to issues in preference to psychiatric standards. See *R.* v. *Turner* [1975] 1 All ER 70.

29  In England and Wales, by way of contrast, a County Court was criticized in the Court of Appeal for communicating in private with a welfare officer. *Re B. (a minor) Independent* Law Report, 4 September 1989.

30  See King (1991b) and King and Trowell (1992).

31  In both common law and civil law countries there are training courses arranged and books written for expert witnesses to prepare them for their courtroom performance. In France, psychologists may obtain a diploma of their proficiency in forensic work.

32  Research carried out in 1989/90 by Michael King at a London psychiatric clinic.

33  For law these terms are almost interchangeable. The English Children Act 1989 (s.3(1)) describes parental responsibilities as: 'all the rights, duties, powers, responsibilities and authority which by law a parent of a child has in relation to the child and his property'. This is almost identical to the definition of parental rights contained in the Children Act 1975 (s.85(1)).

34  It should be noted here that not all biological parents are legal parents. The laws of all Western countries give fathers of non-marital children the status and responsibilities of legal parenthood only if the mother agrees or the court orders it.

35   See Davis (1987) for a general discussion of how the US courts have applied the concept of the psychological parent.
36   *Re M.* Ohio, Misc. 7, 416 NE 2d 669 (Juv. Ct. Div. 1979).
37   See King and Trowell (1992).
38   Barnes (1982, p.140).
39   Extract from research interview carried out by Michael King at a London clinic, 1989/90.
40   Davis (1987) makes a similar point when she criticizes courts for accepting the psychological parent concept without examining its status among child psychological experts.

# 4 The child as semantic artifact

The 'persons' the law as a social process deals with are not real flesh-and-blood people, are not human beings with brains and minds . . . They are mere constructs, semantic artifacts produced by the legal discourse itself. (Teubner, 1989, p.741)

The idea that social statuses are constructions to be negotiated, fought over and eventually changed, rather than being God-given or 'in the natural order of things', has had a profound influence on political thought and action in the twentieth century. Recently several authors, and in particular those from the Critical Legal Studies movement, have begun to trace the contribution made by law to these social constructions. The tendency has been to draw attention to the way in which the law's portrayal of people and organizations and the relationships between them helps to sustain the existing social order with all its inequalities and injustices. These legal constructions are seen as being underpinned by powerful economic and political forces.

Following Philippe Ariès's (1973) 'discovery' that childhood had been invented in Europe sometime during the sixteenth and seventeenth centuries, explanatory accounts of childhood as a social construct assume or actively seek out a prevailing image of 'the child' which supposedly characterizes the attitudes and beliefs about children and childhood for a particular historical epoch. This image and these attitudes and beliefs may then be traced to specific economic or political factors.[1]

Teubner's approach, and that of other radical epistomologists, is somewhat different. As we explained in Chapter 3, Teubner sees the law through its internal communications as producing 'role bundles' or 'character masks' which populate the legal world. The issue of whether law is autonomous on the one hand or influenced by economic and political factors on the other, while of interest to many legal theorists (see, for example, Lempert, 1988), is not a matter of theoretical concern to Teubner and his version of autopoietic theory (Nelken, 1988b). For Teubner, operating at the level of cognitive functioning, the law exists as a self-referential system which knows, thinks and communicates about the world only in ways which distinguish lawful from unlawful. In fulfilling that function it inevitably constructs and operates upon semantic artifacts while at the same time giving the impression in its communications to the external social world that it is dealing with and communicating about 'real' flesh-and-blood human beings, whether they be children or adults.

In the context of legal decisions concerning children, we have applied and developed Teubner's notion of 'semantic artifacts' to concepts of 'the child' that the law constructs. Given that it is both impossible and dys-functional for the law to confront and deal with all the facets and complexities existing within the 'real' child, our interest is in how and why particular semantic artifacts of the child have been constructed. In this chapter we examine four aspects of 'the child'.

The first semantic artifact we discuss is that of the 'child as victim' and, therefore, to be protected without qualification. The second considers 'the child as witness', whereby the child becomes a legal subject, a provider of knowledge and information to the law for its specific legal purposes. The third considers the child as a 'bundle of needs' with adult carers or state agencies disputing the definition of such needs and the ability to provide them. We discuss the confusion that arises when the 'bundle of needs' becomes, at one and the same time, 'the child as victim'. Finally, we examine the child as 'the bearer of rights' and discuss the way in which the concept of children's rights is used by law not only to endow the child with a legal identity separate and independent from that of its parents and family, but also to reduce complex social situations to issues which the law is able to handle. We should add that this is not an exhaustive list of all possible images of children and childhood constructed by the law, but rather draws upon current concerns as illustrations of the law's 'imagina-tion'.

# I   The child as victim

Much of legal reality concerning children has been reconstructed around prevailing societal notions of the child as victim. Indeed, if the child were seen as author of its own misfortunes or as having played a major part in the creation of the distressful or damaging situation in which it finds itself, there would be no justification for the law's intervention to rescue and protect the child. This contrasts with the way law reconstructs women, who can be held morally responsible for rapes and sexual assaults inflicted on them.[2] In child protection the concepts of the willing victim or contributory negligence simply do not arise. Furthermore, it is virtually unknown for child protection orders to arise from situations where the abusers are other children (whether or not within the child victim's family), although it is well-documented that such abuse exists. Children are typically and almost exclusively the victims of adult exploitation, ignorance, neglect or misconduct. Freudian notions of childhood sexuality never enter the law's consciousness. Behind each abused child looms an abusing adult. Adults, by contrast, can rarely be victims of abuse (as opposed to crimes) by children (unless perhaps they are mentally or physically disabled).[3] The law, therefore, casts its epistemic net over the relationship between adults and children, with the child acting as a reflection of, or response to, an adult's or adults' (usually the parent or parents) behaviour. Within the realms of child care and protection proceedings the parent or other adult abuser, as a semantic artifact, closely resembles the offender in criminal proceedings. His or her state of mind is relevant only in so far as it throws some light on the past and future relationship with the child. Just as there is an unstated presumption in criminal trials that the accused is always responsible for his or her crimes, so it is assumed that parents are always responsible for any harm suffered by the child while in their care.

Yet legal rhetoric these days is often couched in terms of identifying risks, preventing harm and providing the care, control and protection that the child needs. This rhetoric, and the related attempts to treat court proceedings in child abuse cases as if they were 'objective enquiries',[4] has all the hallmarks of the external child welfare discourse which the law has reconstructed in order to equip itself to respond to the social problems which are being regularly brought into its arena. The autopoietic nature of the law's discourse means, however, that its utterances, information and understandings will always revert back to the image of the child as victim, and of the parent as the direct or indirect cause of harm.

Why should this be? Why can legal communications not combine with those of child welfare and child development to create a truly interdisciplinary response to child abuse? For a start, child protection proceedings are not and never have been designed to protect children against all possible risks to their healthy mental and physical development. Environmental risks, such as those arising from the proximity of the child's home to a nuclear power station or from polluted water supplies, are not the subject of these proceedings, nor are harms arising from failures of state or private institutions attended by the child, such as inadequate schools or health care services. The law is dealing here rather with harms specific to that particular child, which, because of their specificity, must necessarily involve the child's immediate, intimate environment – namely, the family or family substitute. These harms involve, almost by definition, failures in parenthood, whether they be failures to fulfil legal and moral obligations or failures to act in a manner appropriate to the law's concept of 'good enough' parenting. In child protection proceedings, therefore, the law raises questions specifically about parental behaviour – questions that have to be answered if the parent is not to be condemned as bad or inadequate.

This is in clear contrast to those public enquiries which have become almost obligatory in the UK after the violent death of any child while under the 'protection' of social workers or where allegations of multiple sexual abuse result in children being removed from their home. Here, as the nature of the discourse moves from legal to political, the focus of attention, while still directed to individual responsibility, does not concentrate on the parents and their behaviour but on the failures among those professionals who were supposed to be responsible for protecting the child.[5] Within the legal discourse, past failures in parental care may be interpreted by the law as knowledge, leading to the conclusion that the parents are incapable of looking after the child, while past failures in the standard of care of social work agencies are not seen as evidence of the risks of confiding children to their care.[6]

If one were to widen the scope of an enquiry to include all those factors that could have contributed to a particular case of child abuse or neglect, the list would be endless.[7] One could include as possible causes not only those environmental matters already mentioned, but also a number of factors resulting directly from social policies. These would cover such issues as stress caused by living in overcrowded conditions, homelessness, unemployment and the lack of nursery provision. Yet, once again, these do not enter the law's consciousness in such cases.

As a result, when children are victims in the legal discourse, they are not victims of government policies but of the misconduct or inadequacies of individuals. Some commentators would see this as an example of the depoliticization of social problems,[8] but Teubner's radical constructivist approach would not wish to identify any particular cause or causes as 'true' and others as 'false' or distorted, since all are varying constructions of reality. What is important for our present purposes, however, is the fact that the legal discourse in its construction of the causality of child abuse places stringent limits on what is admissible knowledge for the purposes of the legal enquiry and that what may pass as valid knowledge in the external world is excluded by the law. Indeed, in case after case the questions asked are those identified by King and Garapon as necessary in the court's construction of 'situational reality': 'What type of child do we have here? What type of people are the parents? What has been going on? What have been the results of the child's and parent's behaviour? What is likely to happen if there is no intervention? How can we intervene to prevent this?' (King and Garapon, 1987, p.12).

Given such constraints on what is accepted as relevant, admissible knowledge, to attempt to conduct the case as if it were an 'objective enquiry' is like trying to write a novel using only a quarter of the words in the dictionary. The law inevitably reverts back to the image of the child as victim, and, more specifically, as victim of parental failure or misconduct. Whether the case is conducted in an accusatorial or inquisitorial manner makes little or no difference to the nature of the legal discourse. What is important is the fact that the 'truth' is being determined by lawyers, applying the law within the confines of the legal system.

## II   The child as witness

The courtroom hearing as the principal testing ground for the establishment of legal facts is a central feature of those common law systems of justice operating in Anglo-Saxon countries. The recent 'development' of child sex abuse as a major social problem has meant that the law has been obliged increasingly to confront the issue not only of the child as victim of abuse, but also as witness to abuse. The dilemma for the law, then is, how to reconcile its image of children as victims and, more generally, as vulnerable, unformed, dependent creatures in need of protection[9] with the necessity of extracting 'reliable' information from child witnesses in order to convict an offender or protect the child from further abuse. In criminal trials the law is pursuing a role very much within the traditional legal discourse concerned with establishing that a crime has occurred and identifying and punishing the perpetrator. In such cases the law is not concerned with the child's welfare.[10] Nevertheless, in many cases the law finds that, because the principal witness is a child and law has traditionally treated children as incompetent and unreliable, it is unable to carry out its role effectively simply by invoking its own procedures for constructing truth.

In countries which operate an adversary, day-in-court trial system of criminal law this image of children as unreliable is clearly at variance with the need to bring children into the courtroom to give evidence and face cross-examination just like any other witness.[11] It is not merely that children may be ill-equipped for such a courtroom ordeal and, therefore, fail to give a sufficiently convincing account to convict the perpetrator, but that the very fact of having to participate in the investigative and courtroom procedures may be stressful for the child.

The problem that the law has faced has, therefore, been how to bring the evidence of young children before the court in a form that is likely to result in conviction and how, at the same time, to protect the child from the ill effects of criminal procedures both outside and inside the courtroom which, according to some psychologists, have a more deleterious effect on the child than the abuse itself.[12]

The response of the law to this dilemma has been to seek solutions from discourses and social institutions outside the law, to rush headlong, as Teubner would have it, into the epistemic trap. The results, as Teubner suggests, are 'differences . . . found in the realities themselves that are produced by different discourses and that can neither be unified or reconciled' (Teubner, 1989, p.749). Law, then, tends to sacrifice its own internal logic in order to accommodate concepts and procedures that are incompatible with its own discourse and processes for constructing truth.

In cases of physical abuse this issue of evidence has not created too many problems for children. Medical experts could be called upon to examine the child, report to the court on the child's injuries and offer some explanation, based upon their knowledge and experience, as to how such injuries may have occurred. There is usually no need, therefore, in such cases for the child to appear in court. In the case of sexual abuse, however, much, and at times all, of the evidence will be what the child said happened. The role of the expert in such cases becomes that of developing ways of eliciting from the child a statement in a form acceptable to legal procedures for determining truth. Consequently, social workers, forensic psychologists and child psychiatrists have produced knowledge and procedures from behavioural science to solve these problems. The solutions have taken three forms.

## 1   Reconstructing the image of children as witnesses

Such reconstruction aims at enhancing the perceived reliability of the evidence of children or, at least, removing the assumption that they are unreliable and suggestible as witnesses.[13] This is translated into law in the form of changes in the evidence rules, such as those requiring corroboration of children's evidence,[14] or changing the competency rules so that young children may give evidence in child abuse cases.[15]

## 2   Reducing the ordeal of the child witness

Many different jurisdictions have changed their procedures in ways which protect the child who gives evidence in court from the ordeals of confrontation with the perpetrator and of cross-examination in public. In most European jurisdictions it is not necessary for children to testify in open court; it suffices that the child should have given evidence to the investigating magistrate, which can usually be done in the privacy of the magistrate's room.[16] An example of a different response, in a common law jurisdiction, is Texas, where the Criminal Procedure Code allows the judge, jury and defendant to remain in the courtroom while the child gives evidence in another room before defence and prosecution counsel and any person the child needs to contribute to his or her welfare. The child's evidence is transmitted to those in the courtroom via a closed-circuit television link.[17] Florida has a similar procedure to Texas, available 'where the court finds that there is a substantial likelihood that the child will suffer at least moderate emotional or mental harm if required to testify in open court'. A child for this purpose is anyone under the age of 16.[18] Similarly, in England and Wales recent changes in the law allow for a live video link for child victims under 14 to give evidence in assault and sexual abuse cases, so that the child need not be present in the courtroom.[19]

A somewhat different system, designed to minimize the psychological damage associated with a child's appearance in court, has operated in Israel since 1955,[20] when legislation first provided for the appointment of child mental health professionals as special youth examiners in every case of alleged abuse where the victim is under 14. The youth examiner, usually a social worker, clinical psychologist or child care officer, interviews the child. If she/he believes the child's account, the alleged abuser is prosecuted. In 90 per cent of cases the youth examiner reads out the child's statement to the court and the child is not required to give evidence. The youth examiner may not be questioned on the facts of the incident, but may be examined on his/her reasons for believing the child.[21]

## 3　Training the non-legal professionals

A third solution has been to improve the procedures and techniques employed by those engaged in helping children to disclose the fact that sexual abuse occurred by making them more resistant to attack by lawyers. For example, according to one recent account, 'The clinicians at Great Ormond Street [Children's Hospital] and elsewhere have responded to criticism and have made efforts to eradicate the more objectionable features of the system (such as the use of leading and hypothetical questions).'[22]

It would appear at first sight, therefore, that the collaboration between law and the behavioural sciences has in this instance been successful. Children have been protected from the trauma of giving evidence in court or from having to confront the alleged perpetrator; the rules have been changed so that more weight can be given to the evidence of a child; psychologists and expert child interviewers have been introduced into the legal system without any major upheavals in legal procedures and processes. Teubner's epistemic trap has, it seems, been effectively sprung without any dire consequences.

However, first appearances can be misleading. In altering its procedures to accommodate public concern over child sexual abuse the law has created serious inconsistencies in its construction of children and childhood. Children, it seems, are treated differently depending upon the role they play in legal proceedings. Child victims are seen as different people from child offenders. Whereas the former are considered highly vulnerable, and, therefore, in need of protection from the rigours of courtroom examination, the latter are seen in most jurisdictions as quite competent to give evidence in court and to be examined on that evidence. Of course, very young children are exempt from prosecution, but the protection offered to child witnesses in sex abuse cases extends to children well beyond the minimum age for criminal responsibility. The law, in its internal communications, is able to 'parcel' children according to pre-existing legal categories. In attempting to respond to social demands, the law has cut itself further adrift from external notions of children and childhood.

Another problem arises from the dependency of prosecutions for a successful outcome upon evidence and assistance of forensic psychologists, psychiatrists, social workers or youth examiners. The law's need is for 'facts' – 'truth' constructed from admissible evidence – which will convict or exonerate the alleged perpetrator. Despite the difficulty of obtaining such facts, the public demands the prosecution and conviction of child sex offenders, so the law cannot retreat by renouncing epistemic authority. Applying Teubner's model, therefore, it would appear inevitable that the introduction of 'scientific procedures' to achieve forensic objectives will result, firstly, in the enslavement by law of scientific concepts, and, secondly, it will lead law deep into the epistemic trap through its increasing dependence on procedures external to law for the validation of law's statements. The consequence will be a loss for law of its epistemic authority over what constitutes truth for the purpose of criminal trials.

Furthermore, the introduction of special rules, specialist investigators and special techniques such as video links or previously videoed interviews has created major inconsistencies in the legal discourse. If children as witnesses are to be protected from the rigours of examination in open court, then why not women who have been the victims of rape or sexual assault?[23] If women, why not also witnesses who suffer from a recognized nervous disability which would be likely to prevent them from giving convincing evidence in the witness box? If these witnesses, then why not those witnesses who feel too upset or nervous to give evidence in open court? If these witnesses, then why not defendants, who have so much at stake in a criminal trial and therefore should be entitled to the same protection that is given to nervous witnesses. It is not hard to see how the erosion of a few pebbles could lead eventually to the crumbling of the whole cliff face.

Finally, a different kind of problem arises from the use of 'experts' from other disciplines to carry out fact-finding investigations for the law. It may be that, as individuals, some psychologists and psychiatrists will be quite willing to operate within a legal framework, but the intrusion of law's requirements into therapeutic procedures is likely to cause harm to the therapeutic intentions. The child as witness is not the same semantic artifact as the child as patient or analysand. The objectives of psychiatrists, social workers and psychologists in interviewing child victims of sexual abuse are often very different from those of the law in its determination of the guilt or innocence of the accused. This is particularly so in cases where the expert is also involved in therapeutic work with the child or family. In therapy, 'the truth' may validly be extracted by any technique which enables the patients to confront past events in their lives, yet these techniques may be anathema to lawyers, concerned with finding evidence and testing its reliability in order to determine whether or not the accused committed the offence. The procedure used by clinicians is described in an article from the late 1980s:

> During the course of the interview, use is made of anatomically correct dolls to encourage the child to demonstrate behaviour which she is reluctant or unable to describe in words. Since children are often very reluctant to talk about the matters in issue, the interviewer applies a degree of coaxing and pressure on the child to overcome this reticence. This encouragement to answer may involve leading or hypothetical questions or questions designed to elicit a different answer to one already given. It is felt by the clinic that such pressure is necessary to enable the child finally to make statements against another family member; as one of the clinical staff has put it, it is necessary to match the trauma which the child has suffered throughout the abuse by placing equal pressure on the child to talk about what has occurred . . . *the interviewer starts from the position of wanting to believe the child, not doubting the child's statements*. (Douglas and Willmore, 1987, p.151, our emphasis)

These procedures do not, of course, comply with what law recognizes as acceptable methods of obtaining reliable evidence. Indeed, one lawyer has commented that 'diagnostic interviews . . . may, and sometimes do, flout every convention governing the eliciting of evidence' (Enright, 1989, p.82).[24] This divergence between legal/forensic methods of eliciting evidence and diagnostic/therapeutic procedures for helping patients has led in many cases to virulent cross-examination by lawyers upon the reliability of evidence presented by clinical interviewers to the effect that a child has been sexually abused. These fierce attacks have in turn created a crisis for clinicians, some of whom are, according to Vizard (1987), 'so repelled at having their work attacked in this way in court . . . that they are not prepared to see such children for assessment'. These issues have been addressed recently in the UK, and a Memorandum of Good Practice has been produced by the Home Office in conjunction with the Department of Health (1992). The Memorandum is, in effect, a detailed series of guidelines for conducting and videotaping a single 'medical/legal' interview with the child which could then be introduced as evidence-in-chief. Practitioner comments would suggest, however, that it is not in practice possible to adhere to the guidelines to ensure compliance with legal requirements for admissible evidence at the same time as applying clinical techniques to encourage children to overcome their inhibitions and talk freely about their abusive experiences.[25]

As we shall see, similar conflicts arise in matrimonial and child protection cases, but here the issues are complicated by the fact that the law goes beyond its traditional role and takes on the social responsibility of protecting the child's welfare and determining the child's best interests.

## III   The child as a bundle of needs

In disputes over custody (residence) and access (contact or visitation), the image that critics of legalism frequently invoke is that of children as property. The law, according to this view, encourages parents locked into acrimonious matrimonial disputes to treat their children as spoils to be won, lost and eventually shared. Yet modern law, as we have seen (pages 51–52), is anxious to promote a very different attitude towards children caught up in the divorce or separation of their parents. These children are, rather, the recipients of parental (or adult) responsibilities, the object of parental duties. It is their welfare that must always be given the first and paramount consideration; it is their development that must be safeguarded by the law – always, of course, within the strict limits set by the individualized nature of legal intervention.

However, despite the good intentions of legislators in many different jurisdictions, inequalities between competing adult carers are the inevitable outcome of legal proceedings. The fact that one household has been divided into two, and that, in most cases, it is neither practical nor beneficial for families of more than one child to be divided or for a child's time to be split evenly between its parents, undermines any attempts at equality. The law's new task, therefore, becomes one of persuading parents to accept these inevitable inequalities.[26] This may then take the form of withdrawal by law of epistemic authority, and the encouragement of mediation to resolve conflict (see Chapter 5). Alternatively, law may lay down the details of what is 'in the child's best interests' so that any negotiations between parents must take place in 'the shadow of the law'.[27]

In matrimonial and other kinds of dispute over who should care for or have contact with children (for example, in 'tugs of love' between natural and foster parents) the legal conflicts are shaped by assumptions about children's needs, and resolved by identifying which adult or combination of adults is best able to fulfil those needs. The name of the game is not, as commentators would have us believe, to create a satisfactory environment in which the child may fulfil its potential, but rather to weigh and compare the benefits offered by each of the disputants in response to the child's 'needs'.

In arriving at a result, the child's own views have, until recently, been studiously ignored. The child's needs were what expert opinion projected onto children. There was no need, therefore, to consult with the child, whose preferences were seen as resulting from immaturity or inexperi-ence, and, in some cases, from the influence of adults. Pressure from children's rights activists has now resulted in 'the child's wishes' being added to the list of factors to be weighed up.[28] Yet, it should not be thought that this denotes a movement towards child autonomy. For the most part, children are not being asked to decide the outcome of the dispute, to become in effect the judge of the case. In most instances their views will not even influence the court's decision.[29] Rather, consultation with children so that they can express their wishes and feelings, either directly or indirectly, is treated as yet another 'need', and any parent who denies this is failing to recognize what 'responsible' parenting requires.

As expert opinion on the assumed needs of children has placed greater emphasis on the continuing participation of both parents in the life of the child after the parents cease to live together, the legal disputes have tended to concentrate around those cases where one parent seeks to exclude the other entirely from the child's life. This has led to a marked increase within the legal arena of allegations of extreme deviant behaviour, and particu-larly of child sex abuse, made by one parent seeking to exclude the other. It is no longer sufficient to show that a husband, for example, has been negligent or uncaring to his children in the past, or that he has, through his adulterous behaviour, failed to provide an appropriate model for his children. The only way, it seems, to keep the father out of the child's (and the mother's) life is to prove that he is a monster. The law is a captive of its autopoietic nature. The harder it tries to escape from conflict management, determining who has right on their side, the further it is forced back into this traditional role, and with increasing violence.

There is again a confusion of images, created by the construction of semantic artifacts for different functions, where the child as a bundle of needs confronts the child as victim. The result is a crisis for law of considerable proportions which, in common law, adversary systems, finds expression in dilemmas over the procedural and evidential rules. The cases that give rise to the dilemma typically involve accusations by a mother, made during the course of matrimonial proceedings when the father seeks contact with his daughter after the breakdown of the marriage,[30] that the father has sexually abused his daughter. Just how the imposition of the law's internal rules for validating knowledge is able to transform such parental disputes into something between a Lewis Carroll fantasy and a Kafkaesque nightmare is illustrated by recent cases, which reveal that the first problem the courts had to face was how to deal with a situation that involved both a demand that the allegations against the father be decided one way or the other and the need to protect the child.

Under English law, there are two standards of proof: one for criminal cases – beyond reasonable doubt – and the other for civil cases – the balance of probability. Applications for orders concerning the children in matrimonial proceedings are civil cases. According to the logic of the law, therefore, the test to be applied is the 'balance of probabilities'. However, this makes it possible for fathers to be 'condemned' of sexual abuse on a lower standard of evidence than is required for criminal convictions. The way the judges have resolved this seemingly intractable problem has been to separate the abuse from the abuser. According to one judge, the standard of the level of probability may thus be raised in certain situations:

> A higher degree of probability is required to satisfy the court that the father has been guilty of some misconduct with his daughter than would be needed to justify the conclusion that the child has been the victim of some such behaviour of whatever nature and whoever may have been its perpetrator.[31]

Yet, where the protection of the child is the issue, one can, according to this same judge, abandon the notion of a standard of proof altogether:

> There may also have been circumstances in which the application of 'a standard of proof' as the phrase is commonly understood, is inapt to describe the method by which the court should approach the particular problem; as, for example, where the suspicion of sexual abuse or other wrong-doing, although incapable of formal proof, is such as to lead to the conclusion that it would be an unacceptable risk to the child's welfare to leave him in his previous environment . . .[32]

The logical implication of this is that the law may decide, without recourse to any formal standard of proof, that a child has probably been sexually abused, and therefore needs protection by, for example, not permitting a young girl to stay at her father's house. But this does not mean to say that the father has actually sexually abused the child, since this cannot be proved according to the high standard set by the law. The judge may, according to a later case in the Court of Appeal, 'have sufficient evidence of concern about the past care of the child to be satisfied that the child was in a potentially abusing situation without having sufficient evidence to be satisfied as to the extent of the abuse in the past or the identity of the abuser'.[33]

Perhaps the child was not sexually abused. Perhaps someone else abused her. Who knows? The only reality that the law is acknowledging is that she needs protection against something or someone unspecified. There is an 'unacceptable risk'. Once again the law, in its vain attempt to fulfil a child welfare role, is forced into a position where its reality constructions become increasingly removed from world-as-experienced or commonsense constructions, which do not make these technical distinctions between the standards required for deciding the truth of different statements. Nor do they split consciousness in the way that the law attempts to do in these cases, acknowledging danger, but refusing to state from where or from whom that danger comes.

The other issue that troubles the courts in such cases concerns whether certain evidence should be admitted or excluded. Probably the most notorious example of the exclusion of evidence of child sexual abuse by a father is the US case of *Morgan* v. *Foretich*.[34] In this case, a mother opposing her former husband's application for unsupervised visitation rights to their daughter sought to bring evidence that the father had sexually abused his daughter by a previous marriage. This evidence was held by the trial judge to be irrelevant to the issue before the court, and therefore inadmissible.[35] Commonsense notions of applying information concerning past behaviour in order to predict future conduct, and the scientific knowledge of experts as to the addictive or obsessional nature of much child sexual abuse,[36] seemed in this case to run contrary to the law's concept of valid knowledge. What happened as the result of the court's refusal to accept evidence brought by Dr Morgan that her daughter had been sexually abused by the father is now part of legal history. Elizabeth Morgan hid her daughter first in England and then in New Zealand, while she herself was gaoled for over a year. This is not to suggest that Elizabeth Morgan was right and Eric Foretich had abused his daughter. The issue is rather that the 'commonsense' or 'scientific' ways of establishing truth had been excluded by the legal rules, so increasing Elizabeth Morgan's disillusionment with the courts and the legal system.

In England, a similar controversy has arisen over the admissibility of hearsay evidence in such cases. These typically concern the statements of a child made during the course of therapeutic interviews with social workers or therapists. In the case of young children and children who are unwilling to testify in court, this hearsay evidence is often the only information available to support allegations of sexual abuse by the father.

The problem for the law was succinctly stated by a judge of the Court of Appeal. Because of the difficulties faced by courts in determining where the welfare of the child lies, judges had come to rely on the reports of court welfare officers and information from a wide range of experts, including child psychiatrists and clinical psychologists. As a result, 'the line between primary and secondary evidence has over many years become blurred. Judges have become accustomed to receiving (often voluminous) evidence which by long-established practice is seldom challenged as to admissibility . . . .'[37]

The Appeal Court judge's solution (which she herself admitted was unsatisfactory) was to rely on the doctrine of precedent and to invoke a previously decided case,[38] which drew a distinction between proceedings in the High Court, where hearsay evidence was admissible, and those in the County Court, where it was admissible in interlocutory (interim) proceedings but was not admissible for the hearing of the main application, unless both parties agreed.

In terms of the law's construction of truth, the implications of this judgment appear to be as follows:

1   In its determination of an issue concerning future contact between parent and child, what constitutes valid knowledge will depend upon which court hears the case.
2   If the case is heard in one of the lower courts, statements made to social workers by children claiming that they have been abused do constitute valid knowledge if the case first comes before the courts for decisions of a temporary nature, but not when the issue is brought back to the court for decisions of a more permanent nature. What is considered valid knowledge at one point in the proceedings is, therefore, ruled invalid at another point in the same proceedings.
3   In the hearing for a permanent order these statements may, however, be admitted where the alleged perpetrator of the abuse agrees. The conflicts between commonsense constructions of reality (let alone social science constructions) are so obvious that they hardly need to be spelt out. In the first place, on the general issue of admissibility, the law's rules (applied in the lower courts) as to what is valid knowledge to determine a child's future welfare bear no relation to any non-legal constructions (whether by parents, teachers or child care professionals) about what is good for children. Any suggestion, for example, outside the legal discourse, that a person applying to have unsupervised care of a child should be in a position not merely to contest but effectively to veto the admissibility of allegations of harm he had caused that child in the past would be treated as quite absurd. One does not have to be an expert in child sexual abuse to realize that seeking agreement from a

parent to admit the evidence in these circumstances would be like asking a prisoner to sign his or her own death warrant.

Also, there are contradictions between legal communications and the diffuse communications of those who practise in the courts. According to the latter, it is recognized that the first decision in children's issues frequently sets the scene for the consideration of all subsequent issues concerning the welfare of the child. Moreover, where the issues are disputed, the main hearing may well take place several months after the preliminary order, during which time the child will probably have settled with the residential parent, making any move increasingly difficult to justify. This consideration of likely consequences, as Teubner would have predicted, is unrecognized by the legal discourse, which is concerned with ensuring that congruent expectations are stabilized and the legitimacy of the law is maintained.

The Lord Chancellor, using powers under the Children Act 1989, has now abolished the hearsay rule in cases involving the welfare of children, which may avoid these absurdities and inconsistencies. But the fact that these incongruous rules for constructing reality existed in the first place shows how difficult it is for law to cope with external reality in ways which avoid the imposition of its own idiosyncratic procedures for determining 'the truth'.

## IV   The child as the bearer of rights

Within law, children have come increasingly to be defined by the rights that are attributed to them. The child as a legal construct is not merely a 'thing in need of protection', but also a 'legal person', whose interests must be represented at court hearings and whose views must be sought on issues concerning his or her future welfare. Indeed, the United Nations Convention on the Rights of the Child makes the following stipulations:

> every child alleged as or accused of having infringed the penal law has . . . [the guarantee] . . . to have legal or other appropriate assistance in the preparation and presentation of his or her defence. (Article 40(2))

> [The child shall have] an opportunity to be heard in any judicial or administrative proceedings affecting the child, either directly or through a representative or an appropriate body in a manner consistent with the procedural rules of national law. (Article 12)

The construction of the child as a legal person has in many jurisdictions led to what many would regard as substantial improvements in the process of justice. Children have the right to representation by a lawyer independently of any legal representation for their parents. In some jurisdictions a child welfare specialist may be appointed by the court to 'represent the child's interests', which will include, in the case of older children, informing the court of the child's views.[39] The impression given by those advocating children's rights is that these changes represent a political victory, a recognition of children as citizens in their own right with legal status and views to be respected and, if appropriate, acted upon. While it is not our purpose here to challenge this impression or, indeed, to enter into the debate about the social role and status of children, the use of the concept of children's rights within the legal realm is a matter that concerns us.

From an epistomological viewpoint, what is important is the way in which the 'rights' perspective is used to construct knowledge about the world. Several authors have commented on the way in which the creation of individual legal rights in response to social problems permits governments to construct these problems as conflicts to be resolved between individuals, and to avoid examining their economic and historical causes.[40] To see social relations in terms of 'rights' is also to structure and understand the world in a very different way than to evaluate them, for example, according to the level of love or trust they contain. The value of 'rights' for the law is in its reductionist nature. Not only does the concept of rights allow the law to simplify and reduce complex relations to manageable proportions, but, as King (1987a) has pointed out, it 'has the advantage for lawyers of ignoring almost entirely the context in which decisions take place and the effects of decision both upon those exercising the rights and those affected by their exercise' (p.189).[41]

Provided that one can identify where the rights lie, almost any social situation, however complex, can be constructed into a contest in which the role of the law is to determine whose rights should prevail. In cases concerning the welfare of children, the objects of court hearings may, thanks to the language of rights, be confined, firstly, to identifying the legitimate rights – whether between parents and their children or parents and/or children in relation to state authority – and, secondly, to weighing one set of rights against another.[42]

This has considerable advantages for law when compared to the complex constructions of the child care and child development discourses, for (a) it enables the child's situation to be seen in terms of a contest; (b) it allows the law to revert to its institutional role of dispute management, distinguishing the 'rights' from the 'wrongs' (or the legal from the illegal),[43] and (c) it permits the law to apply principles of fairness and even-handedness where fault or moral blameworthiness are difficult or impossible to identify.

Although these advantages may be more obvious in adversary systems where contests are overt, we would argue that they exist also for inquisitorial systems of law. In these systems, one must distinguish between the form of judicial interventions and their objectives. While the form taken by court hearings in these jurisdictions is usually an enquiry carried out by agents of the law, the ultimate objectives are usually the resolution of disputes and reinforcement of social values through the identification of the 'rights' and the rights infringements in any given situation. An illustration of the way that these concepts may prevail over an expert view of the likely outcome for child and parent is the court's decision in the case set out on pages 57–58 to allow a trial period of rehabilitation rather than providing certainty for the child's future.

The fact that the law often 'needs' a 'psy' expert to identify legitimate rights-bearers underlines the limits of the rights discourse in children's cases. As Davis (1988b) points out, 'the notion of children's rights has limited practical utility. In any child care dispute, the conflict is over *whose conception of the child's needs should prevail*' (p.162, our emphasis). For law, therefore, the problem is not so much one of designing institutions capable of enforcing children's rights (as some authors would have us believe),[44] but of generating universally accepted concepts which are able to take decision-makers beyond the simplicity of the rights discourse. For this exercise, the law must ultimately call upon the help of those child welfare and child development experts whose very presence within the legal forum both enslaves their own discourse and undermines the epistemic authority of the law. While the law's construction of children as bearers of rights may provide a temporary respite from the jaws of the epistemic trap, the relief is short-lived.

# Notes

1   See, for example, Thane (1981, p.22).
2   See Lees (1989, pp.10–13).
3   One notorious example in English law was the rule that a male under 14 years old could not be guilty of rape or attempted rape: see *R* v. *Goombridge* (1936) 7 C and P, 582.
4   See *dicta* of Lord Widgery in *Humberside County Council* v. *DPR (an Infant)* [1977] 1 ALL ER 964. See also Law Commission (1986).
5   See Dingwall (1986), Hallett (1989), Lee (1980) and Reder et al. (1993).
6   See King and Garapon (1987).
7   Seeley (1963) attempts a similar list of the causes of crime which ends with the exhortation to 'Choose your pick.'
8   See Manning (1985).
9   For example: 'Children are especially vulnerable. They have not formed the defences inside themselves which older people have and, therefore, need

especial protection. They are also a country's most valuable asset for the future.' Mr Justice Latey, *Re X* [1975] Fam. Law 47 at 52. See generally Berliner and Barbieri (1984, pp.155–63).

10    Indeed, some experts have argued that the imprisonment for long periods of a parent who has sexually abused his child may well increase the child's problems rather than relieve them. See, for example, Furniss (1991, Ch.5).

11    Article 6(3)(d) of the European Convention on Human Rights requires that everyone charged with a criminal offence have the right 'to examine or have examined witnesses against him'. The Sixth Amendment to the US Constitution gives to an accused person the right to be present at his or her trial and to confront and cross-examine witnesses.

12    Goodman and Jones (1988).

13    See Berliner and Barbieri (1984, pp.155–63); Davies (1988); Davis et al. (1986, pp. 95–103), and Crewdson (1988).

14    In England and Wales the corroboration rule for criminal trials was abolished. Instead the judge has a discretion to warn juries about the dangers of convicting on the uncorroborated evidence of a child (Criminal Justice Act 1988, s.4(2)).

15    See Note, 40 *U. Miami L. Rev.* 245, 257 (1985).

16    These examples were collected by Rosamund Greer as part of the dissertation, 'Child Witness in Court', submitted for the MA in Socio-Legal Studies, Brunel University, and are quoted with her permission.

17    Texas Cri. Proc. Code Ann. 38. 071(3) Supp. 1985.

18    Florida Statutes, para. 92. 54 Supp. 1985.

19    Criminal Justice Act 1988, s.32.

20    Evidence Law, 1955.

21    Reifen (1973).

22    Enright (1989).

23    In fact there have already been demands that women witnesses should be afforded this sort of protection.

24    See King and Trowell (1992) for a general discussion of the problems of using clinicians to obtain unequivocal evidence for the courts of sexual abuse having taken place and of the identity of the abuser.

25    See, for example, King and Trowell (1992), Furniss (1991) and Douglas and Willmore (1987).

26    See King (1987a).

27    See Mnookin and Kornhauser (1979, pp.950–97).

28    See, for example, the Children Act 1989, s.1(3)(a), by which the court, in certain circumstances, must have regard to 'the ascertainable wishes and feelings of the child concerned (considered in the light of his age and understanding)'.

29    See, for example, *Re DN (a Minor) (Custody)* (1984) 14 Fam. Law 17; *M* v. *M* [1987] 1 WLR 404. Cf. *Elder* v. *Elder* [1986] 1 FLR where the Court of Appeal overruled the trial judge's decision and allowed a 12-year-old child to stay with her father, not because of any recognition of her entitlement to choose, but because of her violent reaction to the original decision and the risk of trauma.

The Court of Appeal declared that a 16-year-old anorexic's decision to refuse medical treatment could be overruled by her parents and doctors in life and death situations. *(Re J (a Minor) Medical Treatment*, Court of Appeal, 10 July 1992, *Independent* Law Report, 14 July 1992).

In *Re C (a Minor) (Leave to seek section 8 orders)* [1994] 1 FLR a 15-year-old girl was unhappy at home and her parents agreed that she could stay with a friend and her family during the holidays. At the end of the period she refused to return home. Social Services became involved and suggested that the girl should seek legal representation. She applied for leave for a residence order to remain away from her parents, and for a specific issue order that she should be allowed to go on holiday with her friend's family to Bulgaria. The parents opposed the application. The court decided that there was no identifiable advantage in making a residence order at this stage, and indeed there were possible disadvantages in that it could impede the situation which should be resolved by discussion between the girl and her parents. The holiday in Bulgaria was not the kind of issue that Parliament had envisaged as being litigated. It should be reserved for matters of importance. Leave would not be in the child's best interests. She might interpret this as having given her some advantage over her parents in a situation where she should be dealing directly with them.

30  For example, *Re G (a Minor)* [1987] 1 WLR 1,461; *C v. C: Child Abuse: Evidence* [1987] FLR 323–31; *Re H, Re K*, Court of Appeal, 25 May 1988.

31  Sheldon J, in *Re G (a Minor)* [1987] 1 WLR 1,461.

32  *Ibid.*

33  Butler-Sloss LJ, in *Re H, Re K*, Court of Appeal, 25 May 1988.

34  546 A 2d 407, 408 (DC 1988) cert. denied, 109 S. Ct. 790 (1989).

35  In a separate action for damages brought by the mother in a different court, the same evidence was admitted (*Morgan v. Foretich*, 846 F.2d 941, 944 (4th Cir. 1988). For a general discussion of the issues arising from *Morgan v. Foretich*, see Apel (1989).

36  See, for example, Furniss (1991).

37  Butler-Sloss LJ, in *Re H, Re K* (see note 33).

38  *Rossage v. Rossage* [1960] 1 WLR 249.

39  In England and Wales this role is performed by the guardian *ad litem* in child care cases and by the official solicitor in High Court wardship or divorce cases. In Scotland it is undertaken in some cases by the 'safeguarder'.

40  See, for example, Freeman (1984, p.55).

41  See also King (1994a).

42  The confused legal judgments of the English law lords in the case of *Gillick v. West Norfolk and Wisbech Area Health Authority* [1985] 2 WLR 830 HL illustrate what happens when the law abandons the safety of a rights discourse.

43  Luhmann (1988b, pp.16 and 25) sees all the operations of the legal system as oriented by the binary code of right/wrong, legal/illegal or lawful/unlawful.

44  See, for example, Dingwall and Eekelaar (1984).

# 5 The child in mediation and divorce

We have traced in Chapter 3 the increasing dependence of law on child welfare science where issues of children's needs and the quality of parenting are brought to the courts for determination. Law's identity as resolver of conflicts for society rests in such cases on the fragile premise that 'the welfare of the child' is a relatively stable and consensual notion. The absence of either stability or consensuality leaves law struggling to formulate normative principles from constantly shifting information about what is good and bad for children. Law, therefore, needs some author-itative concept of child's welfare, or at least an authoritative source of knowledge where unstable concepts may be given the stamp of scientific or medical respectability, which it can then apply to its own communications. Yet law itself, including legal processes and the practices of lawyers, may become an object of concern within discourses concerning children's needs and welfare. There is a serious risk, therefore, that its reliance on external authority (from science and medicine) will result in law having to construct within its own communications an image of itself which may cast serious doubt on its ability in practice to resolve conflicts in ways which promote children's welfare. This chapter examines law's problem as it has evolved in the context of divorce and the massive increase in the numbers of children who are affected by the separation of their parents.[1]

## I  A new perspective on the family

In 1978 Lerner and Spanier referred to 'an emerging synthesis in social science of sociologists, psychologists and physicians', within which the dominant themes were 'the reciprocity of effects between developing individuals and developing families',[2] the idea that the family must be viewed and treated as an interacting unit and the belief that the relationship between the parents affects the whole of the family unit. This dynamic, interactionist view of child and family relations presented potentially greater problems for law than had previous non-law constructions of the family, because of the conjunction of a broad knowledge base within the scientific discourse and an increasingly persuasive political ideology. Three important principles can be abstracted from this new synthesis which now threatens law's authority to make decisions about children whose parents separate:

## 1   An emphasis on the family functioning as a unit rather than on the individuals within the family functioning as individuals

This crucial element originated in two scientific discourses: first, from sociology of the family came ideas about the socialization of the child and, specifically, the effect of an interactionist perspective on the functioning of a family; and, secondly, from psychiatry a similar emphasis on 'the unit' led to an interest, in both social work and psychiatry, in group dynamics and group therapy, beginning in the 1950s.[3] It led specifically in the 1970s to a growing popularity, amongst members of child care professions, of a family systems approach.[4]

## 2   A thesis that parental conflict is potentially the most detrimental event in a child's development

This truth is not only a logical extension of the above principle, but is also supported by psychoanalytic research studies of children conducted by child psychologists.[5] The most influential study, that of the US researchers Wallerstein and Kelly (1981), extended the parental conflict thesis beyond the separation of the child's parents. Whilst their research reached different conclusions about how to manage parental contact from that of an earlier and also well-publicized book (Goldstein et al., 1973), both laid great stress on the child's need for healthy relationships with both parents. They also both argued that healthy parent–child relationships are not possible if parents are in conflict. So, whilst the results of some studies[6] showed that the splitting of families is less harmful to the children than their continuing in a conflictual situation, other research stressed the possibility of the conflict continuing after divorce, with similarly detrimental effects on the children. Indeed, one research study concluded that 'the family relationships that emerge after divorce affect children as much or more than the divorce itself' (Hess and Comara, 1979, p.94).[7]

Whilst early research supporting this new perspective on family conflict and child welfare was largely from the USA (Richards and Dyson, 1982, p.10), the 1980s saw the production of a vast quantity of research into the implications of the perspective in several common law jurisdictions. In the UK, for example, several studies were completed,[8] drawing on non-medical and retrospective statistical data, as well as clinical accounts of the effects of various separation situations. A particular strand of research in Europe and North America focused on the detrimental effects on children of parents' attitudes towards their ex-partners – for example, in terms of the relationship of parental stress to child adjustment (Woody et al.,1984). Another study, of the indirect effects of one parent's absence, concluded that the father's support for the mother has a beneficial effect on the child's wellbeing, even when the father is not present, and that the mother's representations of the father's absence influence the father–child relationship (Lewis and Feiring, 1978). The work of Wallerstein and Kelly (1981) is crucial to this body of knowledge, because it drew the significant conclusion that open communication between an individual parent and child is impossible if the parents are in conflict. More recently, longitudinal research has focused on the possible long-term effects of parental divorce and conflict, particularly in relation to education, behaviour and employment.[9] Therefore, on both sides of the Atlantic, several components of a broad 'psy' discourse (developmental psychology, child psychiatry and psychoanalysis) were, by the 1980s, providing society with remarkably similar versions of the effects of parental conflict and separation upon children.

### 3   A political discourse emphasizing individual and parental responsibility

The emergence of the above 'truths' about child welfare from socio-medical and educational discourses coincided with an increasing reference by politicians to notions of personal and parental responsibility. These then became incorporated in political manifestos and legislation,[10] and, through the reconstruction of political communications by other systems, were reinterpreted as, for example, the notion that children 'need' parents who accept responsibility and who exercise firm control over them.[11]

## II   The law as harmful to children

There is, therefore, a large measure of consensus within and between non-legal discourses that children suffer if parents are in conflict and that this is potentially more detrimental than most other factors in child development. Indeed, a recent Consultation Paper issued in the UK claims that 'when conflict continues through a separation and divorce, the effects on children can be very damaging', and goes on to point out that research 'not only confirms what we already know – namely the awful trauma children suffer when their parents are in conflict' – but that a 'major factor' in alleviating the suffering is 'the reduction of conflict between their parents' (Lord Chancellor's Department, 1993, paras 4.4 and 4.5). This is the basis for a further consequential 'truth': that the law and the legal process are themselves a cause of harm to children. The interactionist synthesis constructs the welfare of the child as dependent on the mutual trust, co-operation, communication and joint responsibility of parents whereas the Anglo-American legal system, based on adversarial procedures, is seen as almost invariably creating or fermenting parental discord.[12] From conflicting versions of events law selects, through its unique procedures, the 'truth' or 'the facts' which it then produces as communications for social consumption. Law, through sanctions, ensures that formalities take place on the way to a legal decision, but goals such as encouraging a form of co-operation which goes beyond consultation and establishing a mutual trust which does not rely on legal sanctions are not compatible with law's coding as lawful/unlawful. Law does not think in terms of provisional and changing solutions in response to changing child needs. Its goal is, rather, a 'finding' or a definite decision on what is good or bad for the child.

The interactionist challenge quite clearly places law in an epistemic trap. Whilst law, in the short term, can preserve its autonomy by reconstructing concepts from other discourses in ways that fit into the legal discourse, this strategy, as Teubner predicted, also sows the seeds for the decline of law's epistemic authority. Like the Trojan Horse, the 'psy' discourses, when introduced into the alien camp, eventually confronted it with a 'hostile' reality, in this case a version of social reality which could no longer be incorporated within autonomous legal processes.

This impasse has resulted in the legal system taking the escape route of renouncing, to a greater or lesser extent, epistemic authority. Those areas of adjudication in which law can no longer operate 'efficiently', because of the limits within which change is possible in an autopoietic system, are being 'off-loaded'. What is not yet clear is the extent of this renunciation or the form it is taking. There are several possible developments. Law can retreat from authority and retire gracefully to Teubner's reflexive law stage, where there emerges a new kind of legal structure. This structure no longer seeks to regulate directly the outcome of issues, but 'restricts itself to the installation, correction and redefinition of democratic self-regulatory mechanisms' (Teubner, 1983, p.239). Another possibility is a strategy which may, theoretically, be little different from those it has adopted in the past. The acceptance of interactionist 'truths' may be achieved via the training of legal personnel in the norms and techniques of a relevant non-legal discourse. In that way communications from other systems enter law only through the medium of actors who are able and willing to reconstruct them in ways which are acceptable and understandable by law. This will still result in 'interference with' legal communications and may lead to the 'enslavement' of non-law communications.

An analysis of current developments must also take account of the growing 'competition' between different kinds of communication, notably between those of law and child welfare science. As a self-referential system, child welfare science has itself had to evolve procedures to deal with the family conflict situations presented to it. This has been achieved independently of law, even though the new institutional forms that have emerged may depend upon the 'patronage' of law. One such institutional form which has evolved is mediation or conciliation.[13] This gives the impression of having resolved the epistemic contest because mediation held on court premises or closely linked to the formal legal system allows the courts to retain authority, and yet also allows parental disputes to be resolved in ways designed to increase parental co-operation rather than conflict, and to lead to a focus on the welfare of the participants. Not only does the form of mediation taking place 'in-court' occur within a legal institution so that control can be reasserted over cases where mediation has failed, but the law also retains epistemic authority for adjudication using its own procedures, while at the same time allowing another communication system to operate as part of the legal process. What emerges, therefore, is a supposedly better way for law to resolve child residence and contact disputes.[14]

In order to understand better the emergence of these new forms of conceptualizing and coping with the problems of parental conflict, we need to look in more detail at the epistemic origins of mediation – a generic term covering a multiplicity of procedures and outcomes deemed to count as mediation.[15]

# III   The epistemic status of mediation

An analysis of the nature of mediation is made difficult by the various institutional forms mediation schemes take in different jurisdictions.[16] Indeed, it is difficult to generalize about mediation even within one jurisdiction. However, most schemes can be categorized as either in-court or out-of-court mediation. Both types use a range of professionals: studies of out-of-court mediation reveal varying degrees of involvement by legal or law-related personnel such as solicitors and court welfare officers,[17] by charities concerned with both child protection and marriage counselling, and by a range of individuals from various social work backgrounds.[18] Teubner's and Luhmann's theses are not concerned, however, with differences in the professional origins of mediators: people are seen as part of the environment necessary for the transmission of communications, and, therefore, necessary to the existence and continuation of social systems. What we need to examine, rather, is how law affects the mediation process. Here our analysis faces the difficult task of defining the epistemic status of 'pure' mediation.

The difficulty arises primarily from the existence of the phenomenon of 'interference' – those simultaneous communications whose nature we discussed in Chapter 2. Communications emanating from different discourses which operate within a single institution may give the impression of shared realities and even shared normativity, according to autopoietic theory. Such co-ordination is an illusion. What in practice occurs is interference, the reconstruction by one discourse of the communications of the other according to the terms of the first. For the autopoietic analyst, the problem is to determine which communications are the product of one discourse only, and which are reconstructions. In the latter case the task is to identify which discourse is doing the reconstructing where mediation is concerned. This is a particularly difficult task because economics, in the form of the funding and staffing of mediation services, has, alongside law and child welfare science, influenced claims about what mediation is and what it aims to do. For instance, Walker et al. argue, 'The pioneers of family mediation traditionally worked with a focus on children in their parent professions. In a strategy for gaining acceptance they struck a deal with lawyers to continue this focus in mediation' (1994, p.7). Evidence from the writings of the pioneers of mediation must therefore be assessed with care, but that literature, together with that produced by current analysts of mediation 'styles', indicates that three main social discourses have contributed to the development of mediation:

## 1   Economic

In so far as some early out-of-court mediation schemes used personnel previously involved in industrial relations, negotiation or bargaining procedures were incorporated in the mediation process. Their mode of discourse would seem to be an economic one in which the validated end product is one whereby both parties lose as little as possible in terms of original bargaining positions (Haynes, 1978; Coogler, 1978). If such bargaining takes place within the shadow of the law, then law itself might be imposing its procedures (Mnookin and Kornhauser, 1979).

## 2   Medical (therapeutic)

Therapy as an element in mediation has existed since its inception. This is clear both from the controversies it has stimulated[19] and from the early inclusion of therapeutic concepts in mediation models. Roberts, for example, described a model of 'therapeutic intervention' as a form of mediation in which 'joint decision-making on specific issues is postponed in favour of an examination of the relationships that have broken down within the family' (1988, p.145). To counter arguments that therapy was not an element of mediation, some commentators made an attempt – now largely abandoned – to make a formal distinction between 'mediation' based on negotiation and 'mediation' based on therapy (see Hipgrave et al., 1989). The origins of this psychotherapy-based mediation are in marital and family work – notably family systems theory – and its procedures are those of the 'psy' scientific discourse.

## 3   Medical (child development)

A third element, a child welfare discourse which constructs knowledge about the needs of the child, has also been evident in controversies throughout the 1980s centring on the child protection role of mediation,[20] and, more recently, on the perceived need to 'hear' the voice of the child in mediation.[21] It has been particularly evident in discussions about mediation conducted by divorce court welfare officers in the UK. As Davis wrote of their mediation practices, 'The pendulum swings from child-saving to therapy – and then back again . . . They're all for "conciliation" . . . and yet they want to merge this with their habitual orientation, whether it be therapeutic or child-saving' (1985, p.10). Research on other institutional forms of mediation also reveals communications from a child development discourse being used within the mediation process to encourage awareness of children's needs in pre- and post-divorce agreements (Piper, 1993, pp.137–46) – an element also indicated by recent commentators: 'Mediators can use their particular understanding of child development to help [separating] parents make informed decisions about their families' (Gee, 1992, p.91).

So far, the majority of mediation schemes have offered mediation of issues concerning children only. Even here there is much discussion of the plethora of styles and structures, and mediators are concerned that general comments are not made on the basis of particular practices.[22] It is also clear from mediation literature that mediation as a distinct process is still under development. At the end of the 1980s, existing literature by and about mediators very strongly suggested that the medical scientific element stemming largely from psychotherapy and child psychology was dominant (Fineman, 1988; Bruch, 1988), though the negotiation element was, and still is, influential in some US schemes, as a result of lawyer-controlled mediation of financial and property issues. However, the picture is now a little less clear. In the UK, recent developments would suggest a growing prominence within mediation of economic and legal communications, as evidenced by the availability of 'comprehensive' mediation of all issues, with defined roles for lawyers and social work mediators,[23] and the establishment of the Family Mediators Association to provide training for lawyers who wish to operate as mediators. The interest of the Law Society and the Bar Council in alternative dispute resolution (ADR) generally, and mediation in particular, also reveals a desire to bring traditional negotiating skills to mediating divorce disputes. Mediators are aware that there is now a range of mediation processes available: 'comprehensive mediation [is] a significantly different process from child-focused mediation. They seem to me to be two closely related *yet distinct* creatures in the alternative dispute resolution "family", rather than the same animal' (Parkinson, 1989, p.136, our emphasis).

Whether the communications of science, law or economics are most evident in unreconstructed forms in mediation could be decided by empirical research set up for this purpose. In order to analyse further the nature of the competing discourses within the mediation process we now compare research which has analysed the procedures of independent mediation[24] – that is, out-of-court mediation – with those of in-court mediation. In this way we can see whether, and to what extent, its knowledge is 'enslaved' within legal settings, and to what extent the co-evolution of law and science around the development of mediation has resulted in interference between them.

## IV   Constructing truth in mediation

Conciliators have a clear and unambiguous purpose – in pursuit of the various aims of conciliation its providers seek to deliver a service which is clearly defined in terms of form and function. Its form is defined by the styles and presentation and norms of practice adopted in conciliation meetings. These are differentiated from what a client might encounter in other contexts . . . (Conciliation Project Unit, 1989, p.276)

Despite this claim for uniqueness, mediation therefore appears to be defined by what it is! The basic problem is that mediation is an idea, embracing concepts like trust, civility and responsibility, and portrayed as 'a seemingly wholesome device for the resolution of conflict' (Walker et al., 1994, p.160). As we have seen, it has ambiguous epistemic origins, and there is no one set of agreed procedures and techniques. Nevertheless, research into the process of mediation has shown that, despite differences in methods of working, organizational constraints and professional origins, there has developed a consensus amongst mediators about the values to be promoted in mediation and the procedures by which truth is generated within mediation (Bruch, 1988; Grillo, 1991; Piper, 1988b).

A crucial part of the process by which behavioural norms are introduced by mediators is the process of problem definition. Mediators rarely start from set positions because this is accepting client definitions of the problem. As Roberts has pointed out, all third-party intervention must take some control away from the parties, and, as regards mediation, 'in so far as the mediator succeeds in transforming the disputants' view of the quarrel he comes to share with them control of the outcome' (1983, p.549). Therefore, whilst deriving from psychoanalytical methods, the manipulation of clients has very different objectives, and, in practice, ultimately depends on the mediator asking the 'right' question before and after particular client contributions, or remaining silent after others. Mediators thereby link grievances to emotions, and normalize or reconstruct them by a process of seemingly neutral questions. Thus mediation emphasizes *present* emotions in the parental relationship and renders the *past* irrelevant.

These initial questions set the scene for mediators to query explicitly the definitions of the problem put forward by parents. This more visible process of dispute transformation relies on the construction of a particular concept of parental responsibility which legitimizes the reallocation of responsibility deemed necessary to transform or remove the parental conflict (Piper, 1993, Ch.4). The result is an alternative construction of reality which locates the problem in mutual parental difficulties or faults, or in children who are seen as manipulating both parents.

As a result of this groundwork, the target for any solution which is encouraged or explicitly suggested can only be the parental relationship which has been constituted as the problem or the cause of the children's problem. Mediation therefore focuses on those aspects of the parental relationship which are deemed significant by mediators: communication (especially of feelings), mutual trust and commitment, and the ability to make joint decisions. Solutions are supported by the notion of joint parental responsibility which was constructed in the process of problem definition and further elaborated in solution construction.

All this is a long way from the legal method of reconstructing past behaviours as a basis for present decisions, or, indeed, from the law's encouragement in civil cases of settlement through negotiations over material matters, ignoring almost entirely any considerations of litigants' emotions. Inherent in the mediation process there is, therefore, an implicit refuting of the legal method of constructing truth. There is no attempt to examine conflicting versions of events in such a way that any one version is declared valid. For example, the following excerpt from a mediation appointment shows the mediator responding to a mother's allegation of lying on the part of the father by invoking the notion of relativity in such a way that conflicting memories appear simply as a product of present negative feelings.

> But you know that the truth is always subjective and truth differs according to which angle you look at it and particularly in these kind of circumstances where so many emotions are involved. So I don't think either of you are lying – you just see the same thing from different angles. (Piper, 1988a, p.71)

So specific past incidents are made to appear irrelevant, and the fact of such past incidents is neither challenged nor established, as, for example, when residential parents express concern based on a belief that the non-custodial parent has in the past not cared adequately for the child during access.[25] The assumption, and so constitution, of parents as responsible or capable of responsibility is therefore not only a crucial part of mediation but also a means by which the law's concentration on past events to establish a truth is undermined. However, some parents showed by their comments in mediation and afterwards that they would have preferred legal assessment of blame based on past behaviour, and that they want this allocation to influence decision-making. As one parent said of 'immoral' mediation: 'to try and conciliate between right and wrong isn't necessarily the most moral thing to do.'[26] More recent research has also led to the argument that divorce procedures should allow couples to 'look back' in order 'to face the future in a constructive way' (Corlyon, 1993, p.15). The norms of behaviour that mediation seeks to establish – a 'familial ideology' focusing on a particular form of co-operative parenting, in order to encourage settlement and to promote particular outcomes as settlement – are not yet part of a wider social discourse. As a consequence, parents may perceive that mediation lacks the authority of legal discourse.

# V   Mediation's denigration of law

There can be no certainty that mediation will become the dominant site for managing disputes over residence and contact (visitation) decisions, let alone over matters of finance and housing: it is too recent an addition to those institutions drawing upon a 'psy' scientific discourse, and its procedures lack clarity and social legitimacy. Already, however, mediation has evolved three major strategies to deal with intrusions from law:

# 1   The promotion of mediation as 'science'

Because the process of mediation involves the construction of an alternative version of reality, what the problem 'really is', embodying the truths of child welfare science, then mediator power depends on successfully persuading parents that the knowledge which supports these truths is legitimate. This is done by portraying specialist knowledge as 'scientifically proven' because it is the result of research using the validating procedures of science whereby hypotheses are tested in controlled conditions and/or through the application of statistical methods. Because the 'discoveries' of science are in modern societies given general authority, the specialist knowledge deployed by mediators becomes authoritative.

A small empirical study of English mediation appointments (Piper, 1993) found that the most widely used areas of knowledge were the psychology of children and the psychology of separating parents. The most widely quoted work was that of Wallerstein and Kelly, whose book, *Surviving the Break-up* (1981), became a 'set text' discussed with all parents before mediation begins in some schemes in the USA (Pruhs et al., 1984; McIsaac, 1994, p.56) – an indication of how significant it is that parents should be persuaded that good parent–child relationships are impossible if the parents are in conflict. Indeed, a variety of educational 'pre-mediation orientation' programmes for parents have been established in the USA to provide parents with the necessary knowledge before the mediation session. As the education co-ordinator for Family Court Services in San Francisco has pointed out, 'The overarching goal of premediation education is to make the process more effective for the client and to provide some "normalising" data on how divorce affects children and parents' (Lehner, 1994, p.51). The power of mediators is, therefore, based on a portrayal of themselves as associated with and representing a range of medical and medically-related professions whose pronouncements regarding children are to be regarded as truth. Mediators may simply assert that a particular 'fact' is part of a common professional truth:

> For a child of that age [4] I think time is different. I think long gaps may do him more harm than short periods of access but closer together.
> . . . children who have only one rigid set of rules to abide by become very inflexible adults.
> . . . the thing that you'll absolutely have to do and that is work *together*. (Piper, 1993, pp.116, 122 and 125)[27]

How authoritative such knowledge appears to all those involved is not clear.[28] In addition, some parents may resist the way mediation undermines legal methods of constructing 'truth'. How then does mediation tackle directly the 'shadow of the law'?

## 2   Downgrading the law

Within mediation, the procedures of law[29] are reconstructed in a way which promotes a very particular image of parents and children who avoid the use of legal procedures, as these two statements from mediators working in an English probation-based service show:

> The real answer to it is that those issues are dealt with by the responsible parents not by the courts no matter where the bloody courts are . . . Your problem is you're using a legalistic system to deal with your children, and your children are not pawns in the game.

> Don't you think that actually, that if you look at most situations, most divorces, if adults always behaved in what was the correct way and if they always put the interests of the children first then most of the cases that go to court wouldn't go to court anyway. (Piper, 1993, p.146)

The text of a seminar given as part of a pre-mediation programme in Oregon by the Director of the Family Court Services gives the same message:

> If you go to court it can be very expensive. Some kids will be going to college but it's not going to be your kids. You can spend a lot of money in this courthouse fighting over custody. It's expensive, it's costly, and it can be very damaging. In some instances, it may be necessary – not every situation ought to be mediated but most can be, most parents can co-operate, most parents can work together. (McIsaac, 1994, p.59)

There are clear norms being conveyed: court procedures are unhelpful – if not positively detrimental – and a good parent does not abdicate responsibility by using the courts to make decisions about the children. Mediators therefore seek to keep parents away from the legal system, or, where contact is essential, to give parents a particular explanation of what happens within the legal system so that the medico-scientific discourse of mediation may prove dominant. The following excerpt from a mediation appointment is particularly instructive:

> Because the alternatives are that you rush off and see your solicitors or a solicitor each. You then get somebody to compare what he or she thinks will be your case. It is put into a solicitor's terminology . . . and solicitors have a certain terminology, a certain way and a method of presenting *your* case, in what they believe to be your best interests; which might well cause a great deal of unpleasantness . . . Now all that seems to me to be quite legally proper but I question whether it is proper for children to wake up one morning and find themselves and their future being decided by a person in a court . . . All that, as

I say, makes for contest and conflict, aggression perhaps, and all sorts of things that don't help. (Piper, 1993, pp.126–7)

Such a stance fits neatly into the knowledge of mediation, but it also represents a version of law constructed using mediation's scientific truth-validation procedures. The need for joint parental decision-making becomes, according to this reconstruction, the most important factor for the child's future wellbeing. The way that specialist knowledge about court procedures is conveyed to deter parents from using the courts takes various forms. It may stress the time-consuming nature of court procedures and remedies, the cost of using the legal system, the bitterness generated by the delivery of hostile affidavits, the adversary contest in court, the inflexibility and inconvenience imposed by court orders, and the inadequate knowledge on which courts base their decisions. All of these point out the practical drawbacks for parents of using courts, but they are also linked to images of children. Delay, for instance, is constructed as leading to prolonged tension and indecision which harms the children, and the law's lack of flexibility and lack of knowledge about children are seen as leading to the imposition of solutions which may not be right for the children. As one mediator said, 'That's why this organization is set up to prevent this kind of distress to the children because the law is a very heavy handed thing for this kind of thing' (reported in Piper, 1993, p.147). The courts are therefore portrayed as bad for children, and as places the good parent will not use.

## 3  Institutionalizing non-law links

There is another strategy open to mediation, and that is to cement links between the non-law discourses involved in mediation. The 1989 report of the Conciliation Project Unit in the UK suggested that there should be a combining of current mediation and marriage guidance services to form an agency of general expertise in the area of marriage difficulties and breakdown. This would confirm mediation's epistemic home within those two discourses of psychotherapy and child welfare science that we noted earlier. This might occur in the UK if the proposal of the Lord Chancellor's Department for a 'single first port of call' for divorcing couples, to provide information and to refer them to a range of services, including mediation (1993, para.8.1), were implemented and organized by a new 'independent organisation' (paras 8.10 and 8.11). Evidence from other jurisdictions, however, shows such 'umbrella' organizations to be developing within the ambit of Family Courts, where the legal discourse may either be dominant or a source of interference for scientific discourses.

## VI   Mediation and settlement

Although the law may encourage referral of cases to out-of-court mediation,[30] and although lawyers may be involved in the management of independent mediation schemes and may take part in comprehensive mediation out of court, it would appear, nevertheless, that the law has renounced authority over such forms of mediation. There is no attempt to regulate mediation in the way envisaged by Teubner's concept of reflexive law. In the UK, for example, legal pronouncements have been confined to the question of legal privilege over matters revealed in mediation.[31] However, there is evidence from research about the process of mediation on court premises which suggests that, in this situation, law may have enslaved the communications of mediation. The research of Davis and Bader (1985a and 1985b), based on three in-court schemes in the UK, illustrates how the aim of all professionals involved was one clearly falling within the legal discourse, that of reaching a settlement in a pre-specified amount of time. As one mother said:

> You are under pressure of time and a tremendous pressure to reach a *decision* – which you do, and it's only after that you wonder if it was the *right decision*. And because you're given the impression that it's *your decision* you have to live with your guilt . . . To have to come face-to-face with your ex-husband and to know that people expect you to come to an opinion together on it is asking too much . . . (1985a, p.44, our emphasis).

Furthermore, the research showed that mediation becomes merged with court procedures so that it is dominated by the court setting, with appointments sometimes taking place in the court waiting area, and, more importantly for our analysis, incorporated into traditional 'door of the court' negotiations with 'solicitors and welfare officers dashing to and fro' (1985a, p.43). Davis and Bader therefore make the significant point that, 'If welfare officers are involved *too* closely in the legal process they become identified with it and before you know where you are they are transformed into Action Man, as preoccupied with the search for legal settlement as any lawyer' (1985a, p.45).

The message of their research is clear. Mediators working on court premises find it difficult to operate freely within a scientific discourse because of the constraints imposed by legal norms and procedures:

> Registrars and welfare officers possess different kinds of authority and different vocabularies. Under the present system of mediation appointments there has been *a kind of convergence* which we suspect is unhealthy. It is almost as if these two professional groups were being welded into a kind of settlement-seeking engine on court premises. (Davis and Bader, 1985b, p.86, our emphasis)

According to Teubner, the nature of the convergence cannot be a union of discourses; rather there is here a hybrid, in which the discourse of child welfare science is being enslaved by law. Interference is evident in that both legal and social work personnel communicate in terms, for example, of parental co-operation and communication, and, moreover, downgrade the importance of past events and the allocation of fault. However, the need for a defined and permanent settlement as the end product of the process is what dominates and distorts in-court mediation. As Davis puts it, 'This form of lawyer driven, lawyer dominated conciliation is all about securing settlement' (Davis, 1988b, p.176).

Pronouncements from within both discourses about the aims of mediation reveal the existence of this divergence. For example, an official committee investigating matrimonial procedure argued that mediation should be concerned with the resolution of practical problems rather than emotional ones,[32] a view supported by the family law team of the Law Commission. They appear to want a cheaper, less conflictual substitute for the decision-making stage of the legal process, but, at the same time, want disputes to continue to be constructed according to legal norms, thereby facilitating their return, if necessary, to the formal legal system. On the other hand, the council which co-ordinates independent services in England and Wales has said of mediation that 'the longer term objective is to help both parents (1) maintain their relationship with their children, and (2) to achieve a co-operative plan for their children's welfare':[33] a very different end product than is to be found in the operation of the law. For mediation, 'settlement' is a resolution of disputes involving long-term co-operation and attention to emotional issues. Settlement becomes an agreement to which both parents are committed through acceptance of the 'truths' used in mediation about the welfare of their children.

Law's 'enslavement' of in-court mediation has been difficult to analyse because this key term – settlement – is one used by both law and mediation, yet the term signifies very different meanings in each of the two discourses. The existence of mediation 'has enabled these two groups to employ the same term to describe what are in fact very different approaches and modes of thought' (Davis, 1988b, p.208). Far from indicating a unified or merged super-discourse, it therefore serves as a good example of interference, because, in the legal discourse, 'settlement' is quite different.

Settlement is how the law deals with the majority of civil problems presented to it, and matrimonial cases are no exception (Gypps, 1983). Most disputes about children of divorcing parents are, therefore, settled through the negotiations of lawyers (Eekelaar and Clive, 1977; Priest and Whybrow, 1986), though analysis of mediation in terms of its being an alternative to adjudication obscures this fact. The essence of legal settlement is that it is conducted with explicit knowledge of the shadow of the law, and that the role of the parties is usually confined to that of consenting to the settlement negotiated by their lawyers. As US research has shown (Erlanger et al., 1987; Felstiner and Sarat, 1988), clients' views about 'justice' are overruled by lawyers, 'who produce the deals while the clients are limited to initial instructions and after the fact ratification' (Felstiner and Sarat, 1988, p.28). A family lawyer's settlement will be sold to parents on the basis that it involves the best chance of certain gains and minimum losses given the substantive legal rules operating and the financial costs in legal fees to be incurred by not settling. The law is here using economic communications to promote settlement within the law. To encourage parents to agree, the law may also use knowledge from the child care discourse, but this is distorted to promote settlement. The client is not required to feel less hostile to the other side: a conflict is settled, while a conflictual relationship may or may not be resolved, because this is not within the scope of legal discourse. It is the fact that *consent by parents* to an agreement and *parents in agreement* are not the same which Dingwall and Eekelaar stress is the crucial difference between legal settlement and mediation (1988, p.173).

This analysis has serious implications for any system which designates lawyers as the chief or only architects of mediation in matters concerning children's wellbeing (whether in the private sphere of child residence or the public domain of child protection). For a start, the lawyer's understanding of what the relevant issues are will not result from any systematic identification and examination of all possible factors which might affect the child's future, but will be selected according to the demands of the legal discourse. As Sarat and Felstiner comment in relation to the role of divorce lawyers: 'the lawyer's emphasis on the client's need to separate emotional and instrumental issues may help to construct or reflect a vision of law in which particular parts of the self are valued while others are denied or left for others to validate' (Sarat and Felstiner, 1986, p.132). This same 'vision of law' affects which particular parts of the child's existence are valued and which denied or ignored. Other writers have described how lawyers 'shape the process' of divorce mediation so that the dominant issues become 'those that are largely relevant to a determination in a court' (McEwen et al., 1990).

Secondly, unless a lawyer is appointed and paid specifically to protect the children's interests, there is a serious risk that the interests of adult clients, as defined by the law-derived considerations of fairness and equity, will dominate, while those factors which child welfare professionals would consider important for the child's future welfare, but which are unrelated to the specific adult interests, will gradually be pushed to the side, and eventually lost altogether. By the time a settlement is presented to the court for approval, there is no trace of their existence.

Finally, as McEwen et al. have convincingly demonstrated, the dominance of the legal discourse brought about through the participation of lawyers in divorce mediation frequently leads to the mediation process itself becoming a strategic exercise in the pursuit of goals which have little to do with promoting children's wellbeing, but much to do with the avoidance of formal courtroom adjudication, or with vying for advantage in the anticipated courtroom contest. They found lawyers referring to mediation as 'poor man's discovery' and 'cheap dispositions', with 62 per cent of their lawyer sample acknowledging that mediation served 'often' or 'sometimes' as trial preparation (1990, p.161). One lawyer told the researchers that he nearly always requests mediation 'as soon as possible' after the case is filed, because:

> I want to meet the other side, size them up. I want to see what sort of witness they'd make for the judge. I want a chance to see how they'd hold up under my questioning . . . I want to watch the other lawyer work with the client. I need all that information . . . So I'm a big fan of mediation, but not for all the right reasons! (1990, p.14)

Such data led McEwen et al. to conclude that 'If mediation provides a settlement detour on the road to court, it is a scenic route with a clear view of trial' (1994, p.161). In fact it is another example of Teubner's notion of dual meanings, with lawyers using child welfare concepts from mediation, reconstructed so as to make sense within the legal discourse. The knowledge generated through the mediation process becomes enslaved by law and reconstructed to serve legal rather than child welfare science objectives.

# VII   Conclusions

The insights provided by using Teubner's theoretical model affirm its value for analytical purposes. His hypothesis that law is moving into a new reflexive stage, whereby it encourages the total transfer of decision-making to a non-law body but retains regulatory control, is more difficult to substantiate. In-court mediation clearly does not 'fit' this account, and it is too soon to say whether out-of-court mediation may do so in the future. To renounce authority entirely over out-of-court mediation, law would need to accept the semantic construction by mediation of the courts and adversarial solicitors as a place of last resort for inadequate parents. If legal communications cannot reconstruct this scientific 'truth' then a considerable abdication of authority by law would ensue, and there could arise a politically unacceptable restriction of individual rights to pursue claims in courts of law.

The promotion (through economic sanctions and the use of a persuasive initial interview) of mediation as the 'normal' route for divorcing couples by the Lord Chancellor's Department in the recent Consultation Paper does seem to be based on an acceptance that courts are 'bad' for divorcing parents and children.[34] However, it is difficult to see how law could ever regulate mediation in terms of some universal standards of fairness, given that it can only assess events in terms of lawful or unlawful. The situation is currently both confused and confusing: an analysis of future developments, not only in the UK but in other jurisdictions where mediation is being encouraged institutionally, will provide a crucial test of Teubner's hypothesis.

# Notes

1   For example, in England and Wales in 1954 there were approximately 20,000 children under 16 whose parents obtained divorces (McGregor, 1957, p.5), whereas the total annual figure is now around 200,000, and it is estimated that, if current trends continue, one in five children in England and Wales will experience parental divorce before reaching the age of 16 (Central Statistical Office, 1985).

2   Lewis and Feiring, in Lerner and Spanier (1978).

3   See, for example, Minuchin (1974) for psychiatric theories.

4   For details of the family systems approach, see Walrond-Skinner (1981). For a text which applies this approach to divorce court welfare work, see Howard and Shepherd (1987).

5   See Brophy (1985, pp.107–8).

6   See, for example, Hetherington et al. (1979).

7   For a discussion of other research findings in relation to the welfare of children of divorce, see Piper (1994b).

8   See Mitchell (1983 and 1985), Lund (1984), Walczak and Burns (1984) and McLaughlin and Whitfield (1984).

9   See MacLean and Wadsworth (1988) for a review of longitudinal research relating to the 'life chances' of children, and Elliot and Richards (1991) for a discussion of the British National Child Development Survey data.

10  For example, the Children Act 1989, the Criminal Justice Act 1991 and the Child Support Act 1991.

11  See Piper (1993). This text discusses parental responsibility as it operates in mediation, but shows how, in practice, there is interference between the political and child welfare notions of responsibility.

12  This does not mean that Continental inquisitorial procedures are necessarily any more effective in reducing parental conflict or preventing polarization (see Chapter 8).

13  In the 1980s, 'conciliation' was the term most widely used in the UK, 'mediation' in the USA. However, confusion caused by the existence of two

terms, and, more importantly, caused by the similarity between the terms 'conciliation' and 'reconciliation' – a very different process – is leading to the general adoption of the term 'mediation'.

14   Until the implementation of the Children Act 1989 in 1991 such disputes were referred to as 'custody' and 'access' though, with both parents retaining legal parental responsibility after divorce, these terms are not strictly interchangable.

15   The following is the definition used by the Finer Committee's report, *One Parent Families* (Finer Report, 1974) in the UK: 'By conciliation we mean assisting the parties to deal with the consequences of the established breakdown of their marriage' (para.4.288).

16   North America, Australia and New Zealand set up the first schemes. For example, in the USA, 24 states were providing some form of court-based mediation by 1970, and in Canada, court-related services were established in Alberta, British Columbia and Ontario in the early 1970s. In the UK, growth has been rapid. Within ten years of the first formal mediation service being set up within the court process at Bristol County Court in 1976, court-based mediation schemes came into existence in 83 County Courts. See Parkinson (1986, pp.59–61) for brief histories of mediation in the USA, New Zealand and Canada; Drake (1985) for a discussion of developments in Australia; the Conciliation Project Unit Report (1989) and Walker et al. (1994) for UK statistics and developments.

17   In the UK the procedural form in 36 of the in-court schemes is an appointment before a registrar (lower-level civil judge) working with a mediator (either a court welfare officer, social worker or member of an independent mediation service, who would normally have a social work or counselling background), and in 31 schemes the form is an appointment with a court welfare officer (Conciliation Project Unit, 1989, paras 8.1, 8.5 and 8.9). In New Zealand, the Family Court can order a mediation appointment chaired by a judge, whereas in Australia the mediators are counsellors with qualifications resulting from four years' training in psychology or social work.

18   The funding, as well as staffing, for out-of-court mediation is often from a mixture of sources, including marriage guidance (Relate in the UK), Social Services departments, the Probation Service and national children's charities.

19   See, for example, Davis (1983 and 1985); Francis (1989); Parker and Parkinson (1985); Roberts (1990).

20   A particular concern of mediators has been to devise procedures for use when child abuse is suspected as a result of conversations within mediation.

21   See Simpson (1991) for a review of the arguments for and against the inclusion of children in mediaton. See Fisher (1994) for a summary of the conclusions of a National Family Mediation Working Party on this question.

22   See, for example, Roberts (1992), where the research of Greatbatch and Dingwall (1989) is criticized in great detail.

23   Since the end of 1990, projects incorporating five different models of comprehensive mediation have been piloted in the UK. These projects and research on them were funded by the Rowntree Trust: see Walker et al. (1994), whose data is based on mediation carried out at these projects from June 1991 to September 1992.

24   The Conciliation Project Unit believed that distance from the court and legal system was the most important variable in researching mediation, and therefore their initial data sets were designed on that basis, with four sets

ranging from in-court, through probation-based to independent out-of-court schemes.

25 For example, the following mediator response is after an allegation that the non-custodial new partner does not drive the children in a responsible way on contact visits: 'Can you not let go to the extent that you think she will make good judgments about her children's safety? You see I think you have really got to leave it to her to handle her new partner. I don't doubt if he was driving in a silly way, I think she is going to tell him. Aren't you?' (Piper, 1993, p.95).

26 This comment is taken from the following response: 'I find this whole system [mediation] unsatisfactory. It's almost immoral in my opinion . . . People are sort of actively encouraging the situation to exist where people separate . . . To try and conciliate between right and wrong isn't necessarily the most moral thing to do' (Piper, 1993, p.170).

27 Mediators also use the presence of another mediator to stress their authority: 'But you see we both feel strongly that unless . . .', and 'I mean I think our feeling is that children are much older before they are actually able to make decisions for themselves' (Piper, 1988a, pp.94 and 134). Mediators also frequently refer to their own experience of the issues in dispute, so that the authority is the cumulative knowledge of mediators themselves: 'It just seems to us – we obviously have had experience with quite a lot of other parents with access problems. It does *usually* happen that if you have a fairly set time and fairly regular – that's easy' (Piper, 1993, p.122).

28 A father in a follow-up interview expressed the hope that mediators 'know what they are talking about', having realized that his decision had depended on acceptance of specialist knowledge given by mediators (Piper, 1993, p.144).

29 Mediators refer to both substantive and procedural law. In Piper's research there were an almost equal number of instances in each category, but only a minority of cases had a significant number of instances in both categories, with five cases having no instances of either (Piper, 1988a).

30 For example, a research sample of couples who had been to out-of-court mediation included two cases referred from section 41 hearings. One couple had been granted a satisfaction certificate, and the judge had suggested they attend out-of-court mediation to discuss the details of access. The other couple had been refused a satisfaction certificate (on the grounds that the couple were still living in the same house and had not yet finalized arrangements for the children), and were encouraged to use mediation to agree the details of physical separation (Piper, 1988a).

31 For a summary and discussion of High Court guidance on confidentiality and conciliation, see Fricker and Coates (1989).

32 Report of the Matrimonial Causes Procedures Committee (1985).

33 From paragraph 1 of the Code of Practice (1986), issued by the National Family Conciliation Council (now National Family Mediation) in consultation with the Law Society's Family Law Committee and the Solicitors' Family Law Association.

34 For example, the Consultation Paper suggests that, 'if spouses are relieved of open hostility and conflict caused or exacerbated by the legal process', they might be more likely to reflect on what had 'gone wrong' in their marriage (Lord Chancellor's Department, 1993, para.4.13).

# 6 The child as offender

So far in our analysis of the way law thinks about children we have discussed how the law constructs particular concepts, by reconstituting the social environment, including the concepts of other systems, so as to make them amenable to its own operations. However, across jurisdictions and across time,[1] the formal legal system has separated off, in terms of buildings, personnel, substantive rules and variations of procedure, that section of its adjudicatory workload – the criminal jurisdiction – which carries a particularly heavy normative significance, whether the definition of what is 'criminal' within a particular society is seen as a product of political will or of societal consensus.[2] While, according to Luhmann's theory, the law's general social function is that of stabilizing congruent expectations, that of criminal law may be interpreted as delineating unacceptable moral and social conduct, punishing and stigmatizing perpetrators so that expectations that lawbreaking results in suffering and degradation will be stabilized and the social order maintained.

Law's operations in its criminal mode are, therefore, aimed at providing legal convictions by adjudicating on the issue of 'liability' for past acts and by assessing the weight of any culpability constructed. In so far as law is assessing 'dangerousness', it is also adjudicating on the likelihood that the wrongdoer will break the law in the future, but in the Luhmann/Teubner account, this concern for the future should not be confused with scientific preoccupations, such as the need to relate present decisions to future outcomes. The legal system is not influenced directly by the consequences of its decisions. Empirical evidence, therefore, that prison sentences do not deter individuals from committing further crimes once released, carries no weight in the legal arena. If a legal decision is made on the basis of predictions of future outcomes which do not materialize, this does not make the legal decision legally wrong. Indeed, if the law became concerned with predicted outcomes, its validity would risk being impugned, and with it, its very functioning as an effective social institution.

# I   Constructing the young criminal

When organizing knowledge about offenders (whether adults or minors), the reality-constructing procedures of the criminal law do so in terms of a very limited number of characteristics:

1   whether they are 'offenders' – that is, guilty or innocent of any criminal act;
2   the 'seriousness' or 'dangerousness' of any offences they have committed;
3   the nature and frequency of past acts which the legal system has adjudged to be criminal.

The first two of these characteristics, as in civil cases, construct the wrongdoer as a semantic artifact whose components are only in terms of the existence, nature and extent of the act or acts of wrongdoing which are at issue. An important aspect of criminal law's construction of reality is, therefore, that the offender's culpability is seen as the basis for any outcome imposed on him or her.[3]

The third characteristic, however, refers to law's ability to construct culpability partly in terms of other past actions of the offender, but the offender's past is relevant only or principally in terms of a *criminal* past: law takes account only of a selective personal history. This may appear as self-evident, but if we take a fictitious, and perhaps far-fetched, adult, male offender as an example, it is clear that knowledge can be organized very differently in discourses external to the law. The fact that he may be defined socially as a faithful husband, self-employed, the father of three and a member of the local darts team is of little or no consequence where he has been found guilty of armed robbery and has a record of seven similar offences. Once a person enters the realms of criminal justice as 'the accused', his or her offences – those past and present acts which the law defines as illegal – become the focus of attention. While other matters may not be excluded altogether, law defines them as relevant in marginal cases only, in so far as they throw some light upon the degree of the offender's moral responsibility and 'dangerousness' to society.

Contrast now a child welfare science approach to children and adolescents who engage in anti-social behaviour. This would begin with the collection of information concerning all identifiable factors which might cause such behaviour; these would not be confined to those factors within the immediate control of the young person or the parents, but could include psychological, educational, environmental and dietary factors. In individual cases, the next step would be to assess and analyse the ways in which these factors might impinge upon that young person's behaviour, and then to intervene in ways which might be expected to modify such behaviour. Intervention could range from the infliction of punishment to changing the young person's diet, from a psychoanalytic session to a course of behavioural or social skills therapy. It could equally well include 'preventive' measures designed to provide fulfilling and confidence-enhancing leisure activities in order to absorb or redirect the energies of the young.

The next stage would be to monitor and assess the effects of any intervention upon the young person's behaviour. If it could be established that the intervention was successful, it could be assumed that the cause of the offending behaviour had been successfully identified. If, however, no change of behaviour in the desired direction had been achieved, this would indicate either a failure in the assessment of causality and/or in the form or nature of the intervention. This would necessitate further analysis of the issues, and the application of intervention of a different kind.

This is not to argue that a complete scientific understanding of young people's lawbreaking behaviour is achievable, or that the effects of different forms of intervention are assessable. What interests us here is rather the way in which knowledge is constructed and organized within the social sciences. Simply on this cognitive level we may extract the following organizational principles, which may be contrasted with the principles extracted from the criminal law and criminal justice system with which we began this chapter:

1   Criminal conduct is seen as the result of one or several identifiable causes. These causes are not unique to those who offend, but may be found in a variety of human behaviours.
2   These causes are identifiable through the observation and analysis of young people, either alone or within different social and physical environments.
3   Changes in young people's behaviour are attributable to internal changes taking place within the individuals concerned, or to changes in the external environment, or to an interaction of these two sets of factors.

The child welfare scientific approach does not necessarily assume that criminal behaviour is indicative of some maladjustment or social pathology, or that such maladjustment or pathology may be corrected by judicious application of the 'appropriate treatment'. These assumptions derive from the imposition through the political discourse of ideological interpretations upon scientific reality construction, rather than from anything implicit in scientific procedures. Science as such is incapable of prejudging the causes of delinquent behaviour, either generally or in individual cases. The lack of fulfilling activities for the young could, for example, lay claim as a cause of offending in equal measure with some genetic predisposition to aggressive behaviour, parental separation or 'labelling' through involvement in the criminal justice process. Which of these factors become the subject of scientific investigations is an ideological rather than a scientific choice.

At first sight the distinction between the ways in which law and child welfare science organise knowledge may resemble the ubiquitous welfare versus justice debate. However, to confuse that dichotomy with an analysis using an autopoietic approach is to miss the essential nature of the Teubner/Luhmann scheme. According to their theoretical approach, legal *discourse* is quite distinct from legal *domain* – that is, the courts and lawyers' offices and chambers – in that legal discourse is not confined to geographical or institutional locations. Nor are law and child welfare science to be seen just as political ideologies or philosophical beliefs associated with particular professional groups. They are (according to Teubner) two distinct forms of communication, including totally different ways of constructing reality, and using quite different procedures for validating truth. While welfare versus justice analysts see law as having a clear choice between policies and decisions designed to promote the wellbeing of the child and those associated with the traditional concerns of the criminal justice system, law, according to the Teubner/Luhmann approach, has no such choice. It is obliged, rather, to reproduce itself from its own elements using its own procedures. The merging of the ideals of welfare and justice in, for example, the Children's or Family Court, is seen as an illusion according to this view.

In Teubner's terms, one would expect in the practice of a 'mixed' juvenile justice system to encounter *interference* – that is, the same statement playing a double role; it is legal information in the legal discourse and social scientific information in the scientific discourse.[4] An example might occur when a young person whom the court has referred to a 'treatment' programme, reoffends. If, as frequently occurs, such failure is interpreted by the judge or magistrate as indicating the need for a more severe response from the court, the statement will, in the legal context, have been constructed as information that the treatment tried has not been sufficiently tough to bring home to the offender the seriousness of his or her behaviour. Yet the same reoffending could, in a child welfare science context, receive a very different interpretation. It might, for example, suggest that the treatment was not appropriate to that offender's needs, for reasons which may have little to do with its 'toughness'. It may also indicate inadequacies in the programme itself or in the personnel running the programme. Alternatively, the reoffending may be seen as irrelevant to the success or failure of the treatment, in so far as the programme had indeed changed the young person's behaviour by, for example, giving him or her a more positive self-image, or making him or her more aware of the effects of his or her behaviour upon others.

If we take this example to a more general level, the statement that many young people have reoffended while participating in a particular treatment programme is likely to be interpreted within the legal discourse as indicating that the treatment has not worked.[5] Within a scientific discourse, the use of offending as the independent variable, the sole criterion by which success or failure is to be judged, would cause considerable problems. The reoffending might have little or no causal relationship with the success or failure of the treatment. It might be due to any number of factors, including both general factors – such as an increase in police activity in the area, or a rise in youth unemployment leaving many of the programme participants idle for much of the day – or individual factors – such as parental break-up, or experiencing racial harassment or discrimination.

## II  The child in court: enslavement of child welfare science

In Chapter 4 we discussed four particular concepts of the child which the law constructs in order to deal with children who are part of any adjudicated issue. How then does the law think about young offenders? What is the content of the semantic artifact which encapsulates the child as offender? Firstly, the conceptualization of children's behaviour by the criminal law is somewhat more complex than that of adults, for the notions of guilt and seriousness are both dependent upon the attributes of criminal capacity and responsibility projected by the law. In the case of juveniles, these have often been influenced in their construction by external knowledge. For example, the chronological age of the child is a matter of enormous significance in criminal law. It determines: (a) whether or not the child enters the legal arena; (b) the nature of the proceedings; (c) the test applied in court to decide the child's capacity to commit offences, and (d) the nature and severity of the punishment to be inflicted upon the guilty child.

## 1   Constructing the culpable child

Clearly law is not unique among modern social institutions in categorizing the capacity of children in terms of their chronological age. In Western societies, education, medicine and even religion place great emphasis on date of birth, but in law the age divisions tend to be closed and rigid. This is necessary if the courts are to avoid long, intricate empirical arguments about the capacities of individual children, which would lead inevitably to dependence upon scientific expertise and the loss of law's validity. In other words, the very use of age categories has been a strategic legal response to external knowledge concerning the probable moral, intellectual and emotional capacities of children at various stages in their development. By solidifying these stages into fixed aged categories, law is able to reconstruct such knowledge on its own terms.

An example of this reconstruction taken from English law is that a child under the age of 10 is presumed incapable of criminal responsibility. All other Western industrialized countries have a similar presumption, although the age at which this presumption may be rebutted varies from jurisdiction to jurisdiction.[6] The law, therefore, is not concerned with examining the state of mind which inspired a particular very young child to break the law; rather, the law perceives the child as 'innocent'. This is a statement of legal reality, which may or may not correspond with the reality created by other discourses, such as religion or psychology. It could well be that another discourse would see the child as evil or as quite capable of harbouring a desire to harm others or to profit from ill-gotten gains.

Once law deems the child 'capable' (according to its 'knowledge' and procedures for determining maturity) of committing crimes, there is an increasing concentration on the nature and frequency of offences. This occurs whether the young person's age falls within a category where knowledge of right and wrong has to be 'proved', or is taken for granted. Once a young offender is adjudged 'capable', the law employs the same range of concepts for dealing with him or her as it does with adult offenders. In the UK, the trial and conviction, in 1993, of two young boys for the murder of James Bulger revealed these elements very clearly. They were held responsible and culpable, allowing them to be labelled by society as 'criminal', and justifying their fate of many years of incarceration.

As a result, within the legal discourse, juvenile offenders cannot be defined as mischievous, hot-tempered, or hyperactive youngsters, but only as the alleged perpetrators of specific crimes, such as burglary, theft, criminal damage and assault. Although information about the circumstances of each offence will be given in court, the item against the child's name on the court list or dossier, and subsequently in that child's criminal record, will simply be the formal offence (and, in some cases, the value of the property involved). So shoplifting becomes 'theft', breaking into the school building becomes 'burglary' and a successful attempt by a 12-year-old to extort sweets from a smaller child in the school playground would enter the records as 'robbery'.

## 2   Reconstructing information about the offender

Once a minor is known by the law as 'an offender', the law usually puts in motion wide-sweeping enquiries into his or her family, school behaviour, motivation and problems – all triggered by 'the offence'. In common law adversary systems, the 'moral evaluations' which result from these enquiries will, together with the child's present offence and past criminal record, determine the decision of the court.[7] Whilst the offence is the 'trigger', it is still important to analyse what is triggered. How does the law conduct these enquiries? How does it respond to the externally generated information?

Information about the offender, whether adult or child, has not always been deemed relevant, and to a large extent its collection for adults has been the result of the introduction by legislatures of non-custodial disposals[8] which have necessitated the provision to the courts of details about the offender's non-criminal activities. The opportunity to provide such details has led to the introduction in the legal arena, by both advocates and social workers, of knowledge external to law's constructions of offenders. This has led to a situation which Feeley (1979, p.284) has summarized thus:

> On the one hand the court is a legal tribunal bound by rules, principles and procedures which seek to protect the rights of the individual. At the same time, it is encouraged to provide 'individualized justice' which de-emphasizes the strictly legal proceedings and purposefully expands its inquiry beyond and away from the provoking incident in order to determine the root of the child's trouble . . . (quoted in Morris and Giller, 1987, p.198)

The apparent dichotomy, providing the basis for the clash of welfare and justice ideologies surveyed in Chapter 1, has often been perceived as unsatisfactory and its source analysed in terms of the 'confused theoretical foundations' of the juvenile court (Morris and Giller, 1987). However, if we follow the approach that Teubner advocates, a very different analysis of the Children's or Youth Courts becomes available. The confusion which Morris and Giller (among others) have described arises, according to Teubner, not primarily from uneasy compromises between different philosophical approaches, but, more fundamentally, from the attempt to merge 'truths' from different social systems and reconcile incompatible procedures for constructing truth.

The Lord Advocate, when introducing in Parliament the bill which set up the Juvenile Court system in England and Wales in 1908, saw the courts as combining law and science, and thus providing an enlightened form of justice:

> Many high-minded men and women, and many philanthropic societies, have been working upon this subject, and of recent years one is glad to note a large development of scientific knowledge. All these facts . . . have made out a case for this Bill. (Shaw, Lord Advocate, quoted in *Hansard*, 1908, Vol.186, cols. 1,251–2)

Yet, whilst the introduction of separate courts for young offenders was a response to 'scientific knowledge', there is little evidence that such knowledge significantly altered the *legal* criteria for reality construction being used on both sides of the Atlantic, despite successive alterations to the structure and personnel of such courts.[9] As Sutton says, reviewing research on the development of Juvenile Courts in various states of the USA, 'The juvenile court allowed the legal system to appear responsive to demands for individualized, therapeutic justice without any real alteration in routine decision-making practices and allowed juvenile justice agencies to maintain their ideology . . .' (1985, p.110).

The confusion within juvenile justice does not, therefore, arise from any failure to combine the professional endeavours of social workers and probation officers on the one hand and judges, magistrates and lawyers on the other. This merging has been successfully achieved in, for example, the compiling and presentation of social enquiry reports, where social workers or probation officers provide information about the young offender's personality, lifestyle, home and school circumstances, using procedures designed for the purpose of assessing that young person and evaluating the likely effectiveness of different courses of action in altering his or her behaviour. Studies of English Juvenile Courts have found, however, that, despite all this scientific knowledge, age, offence and previous record – criteria derived from law's own discourse – are the 'key determinants in disposition outcomes'.[10]

Even where highly qualified psychiatric experts are charged with the diagnosis of child offenders' problems and the offering of a solution to these problems, the dominant discourse remains that of law. Robert Emerson, describing in 1969 the work of psychiatrists within a US Juvenile Court clinic, writes:

> Gradual educative influence through continuing co-operation with court personnel assumed importance in clinic members' perception of their function.

Court-determined issues framed the diagnostic effort, and commendations were usually drawn from the alternatives posed by court personnel. Hence psychiatrists coming into the court clinic had to understand the court's concerns in particular cases and the alternative courses of action considered within the realm of possibility. (1969, p.25)

According to Emerson, it was not merely that individual psychiatrists became imbued with the court's logic, but that psychiatry itself was subjugated by legal considerations:

while the clinic represented the psychiatric approach to delinquency within the juvenile court, it did so primarily through the role of technician and consultant. In this way, the psychiatric approach remained somewhat marginal to the court's day-to-day operations, which basically proceeded in more traditional terms. This is not to say that the clinic's role in these operations was not important, but rather that it was *not made in terms of the framework and logic of psychiatry*. The juvenile court retained a distinctly legal focus, with *psychiatry functioning to help primarily legal goals rather than working to realize explicitly therapeutic goals*. (1969, p.26, our emphasis)

What we have again, therefore, is 'science-within-law' which we identified in Chapter 3, where the objectives of scientific enquiry are determined by the social discourse in which it is conducted and by the specific demands in this case of the law. However, our own approach would suggest that what is happening is that factors which might be relevant for child welfare decisions have been incorporated into the social enquiry reports of social workers and probation officers and into the decisions of Juvenile Court magistrates in ways that make perfect sense to those concerned with the management of juvenile crime. The problem is, therefore, that legal communications and child welfare communications co-exist within the legal process, and that this combining of discourses has been achieved through the law's enslavement of the knowledge of the agents of child welfare science which, when existing outside the legal discourse, constructs children's deviant behaviour in ways which are quite different from (and indeed incompatible with) the constructions of the law.

## 3   The response of non-legal professionals

Resistance to over-zealous or inappropriate application of legal principles is only possible if welfare professionals and scientific experts are prepared to renounce any epistemic authority derived from child welfare science and abandon any attempt to persuade the courts to apply a scientific approach in their decision-making. An example of such resistance comes from the strategies recently employed by social workers in England. Firstly, in some areas of the country they have refused to provide social enquiry reports on first- or second-time offenders, or they restrict their accounts strictly to the circumstances of the offence itself.[11] While this may have avoided interference, the price to be paid has been the adoption by social workers of a legal discourse which 'thinks' of children and young people purely in terms of their lawbreaking activities.

A second strategy involves social workers publicly renouncing any claim to epistemic authority for the discourse of child welfare science, and their agreeing to work within a knowledge framework provided by the legal discourse. This takes the form of directing the attention of judicial decision-makers to non-custodial programmes, and providing them with detailed accounts of the operation of these programmes (referred to on pages 116–120).[12]

Paradoxically, interference between, or confusion of, discourses obliges those welfare professionals who are intent on remaining within the scientific discourse to engage lawyers and the judiciary at their own game, accepting the rules and truth-validating criteria of the legal discourse, and the conceptual notion of the child as offender requiring punishment and/or control, in order that they may influence the form of such punishment and control – community, rather than custodial. The extent to which social workers are now willing to enter into the legal fray is evidenced by their concurrence in the use of appeals against sentence as a deliberate strategy against custodial sentences, with the aim, not of changing the discourse or the semantic notion of the child as offender, but rather of securing a non-custodial outcome for the child as an end in itself.[13] So the very notion of a separate discourse is abandoned in favour of political objectives which become ends in themselves, regardless of any scientific confirmation of their validity.

However, in some jurisdictions there have been different kinds of response to the 'problem' of juvenile crime. Two examples are the French and Scottish systems, which we discuss in the next section. Analysing these developments according to the Teubner/Luhmann theoretical scheme draws attention to the confusion that may occur in juvenile justice systems once they depart from applying the law's legal/illegal or lawful/unlawful code.

## III   Child welfare in place of law

Where interference occurs, neither the formal title of professionals nor the name of the decision-making body necessarily provide an accurate indication of the dominant discourse. Indeed, some professionals who are called 'judges' and some organizations which operate under the title of 'courts' might, at first sight, appear not to be operating within the legal discourse. In France, where the inquisitorial system operates, the response to external welfare considerations is via a process of 'dematerialization' of the child's offence. This concentration by the children's judge (*juge des enfants*) on the child's personality and the functioning of the family[14] rather than on the facts of crimes as indicative of 'the appropriate action' to be taken may start as soon as he or she enters the legal arena, even before any formal finding of guilt,[15] and may well be undertaken in the hope that no formal finding of guilt will be necessary. As a result, the role of the *juge des enfants* has been described as trying 'to find solutions to [family] disfunctions, to put these into operation and manage the contradictions in each situation. This involves evaluating the current risks (to which the clients are exposed) and establishing with each client a plan . . .' (Duprez, 1987, p.136). As Ely and Stanley write, it is a perspective 'which does not particularly differentiate delinquents from other children . . . Its focus is the personal development of the minors within it' (1990, p.45). The discourse, therefore, incorporates several of the principles which we identified on page 105 as defining the child welfare science discourse.

This is not to say that the French system is free of interference between law and welfare science. Ambiguity and confusion clearly exist, both at the initial stage of defining which young lawbreakers should go before the *juge des enfants* and which should be constructed as 'criminals', and also in the construction of those guilty of more serious offences, who are treated as 'dangerous' and brought before the *tribunal pour enfants* or the *assize des mineurs*. However, for the majority of young people who are apprehended for lawbreaking, it is the discourse of child welfare science which, via the *enquêtes sociales* of the court-based social workers (*éducateurs*), reconstructs the offending as problems to be investigated, analysed and solved through work with the child and family.

In Scotland there has been a different type of institutional response to the procedural and conceptual dominance of the legal discourse over young people who break the law. The Kilbrandon Report of 1964[16] advocated the separation of legal issues of guilt, responsibility and punishment, which were considered the concern of courts, from issues of child welfare, which, the report concluded, were more effectively dealt with in an informal setting by non-judicial adjudicators without the presence of lawyers. The Social Work (Scotland) Act 1968 created, therefore, in Children's Hearings, a decision-making forum to decide what should happen to young offenders who had already admitted committing a criminal offence. In 1969, therefore, the management of juvenile offenders was, with certain narrow exceptions, taken out of the courts and vested in a network of Children's Panels.[17] The Children's Hearings do not, therefore, have to concern themselves with determining guilt or hearing evidence about the offence, but concentrate their attention on assessment, treatment and reappraisal. The hearings take place before three members of the Children's Panel, which consists of lay people selected for their willingness to adopt a child welfare approach and trained in social work principles (May, 1977). The underlying philosophy of the hearing system is 'Help for tomorrow, not punishment for today', the child being constructed essentially as a member of a family, a pupil at a school, and a recipient of assistance and supervision from Social Services. This 'rhetoric of the system', according to one commentator, represents a 'marked contrast to legal intervention . . . the anticipated consequences of the different available disposals are the overriding criteria in all decisions made on behalf of children' (Adler, 1985, p.77).

Like the French system, therefore, the prevailing discourse corresponds closely to what we have called 'child welfare science'. However, as in France, there is interference at the earlier stage in the process, when the Reporter and Procurator Fiscal decide, according to a mixture of legal and child welfare considerations, which children should be treated as 'criminals' requiring punishment from the court, and which of them may be labelled 'clients' and go before the hearing in order to receive help.

Critics of the Scottish system (for example, Adler, 1985; May, 1977) complain that the reality is somewhat different from the rhetoric. Unlike French judges, who are served by a team of social workers and who liaise on a daily basis with social work agencies and children's homes, the power of Scottish Children's Panel members actually to help children is very limited. They may neither direct social workers as to how the child's problems may be solved, nor do they have any access to resources to assist the child and/or the family. Like English magistrates in their child protection capacity, they may do little more than authorize social work intervention. Their only choices are to allow the child to remain in the home under supervision, remove the child from home to a residential school or wait to see how things develop. If the discourse is that of child welfare science, the practical solutions available to the hearings preclude the sort of experimentation, empirical testing and observation that one would associate with scientific endeavours.

While this may not be 'welfare-within-law', with the discourse of child welfare science being reconstructed within the legal discourse, it is clearly a very narrow, individualized version of child welfare science which can accommodate only limited decisions directed at the particular child. If wider intervention is called for, such as activities to keep the child occupied and interested during school holidays, or the provision of housing for the family, this is left entirely to the discretion of social agencies beyond the reach of the Children's Panel.

Given the absence of any powers for Children's Panel members to control in any detail what assistance should be offered to the child or family, it is not surprising that a study observing 301 Children's Hearings reached the conclusion that:

> A good deal of the dialogue did not appear to reflect any systematic search for the specific etiology of the child's behaviour nor did it reasonably indicate any consideration of the implications of various possible dispositions. Panel members . . . did not appear to make use of a coherent framework of ideas concerning the causes of delinquency . . . (Martin et al., 1981)

This lack of a coherent discourse of its own leaves Children's Hearings vulnerable to interference from the legal discourse, so that information about the child and family, accumulated and offered with child welfare science objectives in mind, is reconstructed and interpreted in terms of the nature of the offence, legal responsibility and dangerousness. Adler (1985, p.81) gives an example of a case where this occurred:

Subject:              Boy. 15 years old
Grounds of referral:  Multiple thefts
Decision:             Continuation of supervision in a secure unit
Reasons:              That Gregory has repeatedly absconded from a number of residential placements and that he persists in committing serious offences and therefore needs to be contained in a locked unit.

A severe critic of the Scottish system sees this confusion of discourses as evidence that treatment does not afford a workable model for organizing juvenile justice, and must sooner or later give way to alternative solutions (May, 1977). He sees as the most likely alternative solution a reversion to a 'court' model. This interpretation ignores, however, the distinction between discourse and domain, and the possibility that the same decision-makers may change the discursive framework in which they are operating according to what they see as the demands of the situation. If one applies a discourse analysis to Children's Hearings, what appears to be happening is that it is only in those cases where the child is perceived as being 'dangerous' that the Children's Panel reverts to a legal discourse. In all other cases, the dominant discourse and procedures for constructing reality are those of child welfare science, but Children's Panel members, like social workers, are subject to political and economic forces which oblige them to operate within a confused mixture of discourses (see Chapter 3).

# IV   Informal justice: mediation and law

It would seem, therefore, that legal communications may operate in decision-making arenas outside formal legal institutions. Indeed, in the

USA some of the alternatives-to-court schemes set up under the heading of 'diversion' have become very similar in their procedures to the courts.[18] However, there are schemes on both sides of the Atlantic which have sought to avoid the adjudicatory trap by setting up quite different procedures for 'settling' criminal matters, notably by the use of mediation. In the UK, such mediation is usually of the outcome of a criminal matter in terms of reparation, though in the USA some community mediation schemes mediate the issue of guilt and innocence, and many of the US schemes also often contain a threat of prosecution if there is no settlement of the issue at mediation.[19]

In many respects, however, these US schemes are little different from Juvenile Courts in the UK, which are staffed by lay magistrates operating within semi-formal Juvenile Courts. Indeed, analyses of mediation schemes, not only in North America but also in Australia and New Zealand, suggest that schemes have been 'hijacked' by a rhetoric of community and consensual justice that masks the lack of any real change.[20]

> Thus the symbol of consensual justice is being redefined from a voluntary decision to participate to a consensual decision-making process where participation has been mandated. Consent by the parties still plays an important role in mobilising support for community mediation, but now is talked about as embedded in the mediation interaction and decision-making process and not necessary at the point of referral. (Harrington and Merry, 1988, p.721)

In the UK, mediation schemes have generally been designed only to mediate an agreement about victim–offender reparation. While the formal institutions of criminal justice retain control over decisions of guilt or innocence (either through courts or bodies empowered to make cautioning decisions), the process of mediation determines the outcome for the offender. Most of these reparation/mediation schemes have been set up with one of two objectives: either 'to divert the offender from prosecution or to provide some basis for the court to impose a lesser penalty than it would otherwise have done' (Davis et al., 1988, p.128). Some researchers have concluded that reparation in the UK has been 'moulded' to achieve these aims, in such a way that the benefits of reparation have been subordinated to them. As regards pre-prosecution schemes, Davis et al. conclude that, 'for them, "reparation" now forms but one part of an extremely complex pre-prosecution tariff'[21] because 'diversion needs to be sold according to the values which are espoused within our predominately retributive criminal justice system. It needs to be demonstrated (or at least suggested) that the offender has suffered and/or that she is reformed. Hence reparation' (1988, p.128).

In other words, the very concepts of mediation and reparation are reconstructed to fit in with law's truth-validating procedures and categorizations: 'It has meant that the current attempts to promote reparation in this country are half-baked; some are frankly injurious; and all are disappointing' (Davis et al., 1988, p.128). In some schemes the victim has little to gain except via the satisfaction of helping 'their' offender.[22] In other schemes, especially those pre-sentence schemes where the offender is referred from court,[23] the lack of 'true' consent to mediation and reparation is obvious to both victim and offender.[24] Neither is happy with mediation under these circumstances: the only benefit can be in terms of a lesser sentence, not the mutual emotional and practical benefits of reparation as proposed by its originators within a non-law communication system.

# V  Intermediate Treatment as 'interference'

There is a major problem for all involved in decisions about, or guidance or assistance to, young offenders who wish to carry out their work within the communicative realm of child welfare science. The problem is how to resist slipping into a legal discourse, where the child or adolescent is viewed primarily in terms of the offence and the need to demonstrate that something is being done about the offending. This problem may be as troublesome to 'liberal' magistrates and judges as it is to probation officers and social workers.

The history of Intermediate Treatment (IT) programmes in England provides a striking example of the way in which activities designed for the benefit of young people are likely to be colonized and the child welfare science discourse enslaved by becoming part of the legal apparatus. IT originally functioned within a scientific discourse which made no distinction between the child offender and children 'at risk' in other ways. Rather, it 'thought' of children in terms of their social and psychological disadvantages and the ways that these could be remedied through social work intervention. This problem-solving approach was clearly set out in the official government publication describing how IT was to be used (White Paper, 1968). This saw IT as falling into two categories. The aim of the first was 'to bring the young person into contact with a new environment and to secure his participation in some constructive activity' (para.26). The second type of treatment would 'be available for use where the basic need is for help and supervision in the home, but a short period away from home also seems desirable'. It would, for example, 'enable a child or young person to be placed in a home or hostel, or with relatives while help is offered in remedying a difficult family situation' (para.27).

According to Teubner's theoretical account, there were clear difficulties for the law in 'thinking' in this way about young people who break the law.

To begin with, the relation between 'treatment' and the offence was tenuous. Secondly, poor performance on the programme did not necessarily result in the imposition of a more severe sanction or even in a return to court for breach of the supervision order. The expectation that punishment would follow the crime was often confounded in the first instance by the imposition of a 'treatment' order, and a second time by the absence of any sanctions should the treatment fail, because of the indolence or lack of co-operation of the offender. However, political changes in the early 1980s and consequent changes in government policy were to have a rapid and dramatic impact on the nature of IT. In 1983 a £15 million programme was announced to fund IT schemes for a three-year period. This money could only be applied to schemes which offered 'alternatives to custody or to the removal of children into care'. By August 1986, 110 such schemes had been approved (Morris and Giller, 1987, p.132). For many of these new schemes, the objective was no longer the task of helping young persons to overcome handicap and disadvantage, but rather to offer the courts an alternative to incarceration (Rutherford, 1992, pp.18–24 and 112–20).

While the number of offenders under 17 years old receiving a custodial sentence fell substantially by the mid-1980s, *Intensive* Intermediate Treatment (IIT), as it has come to be known, sucked in an increasing number of social workers from the public and voluntary sectors, to work, if not within the legal system itself, then very much within a conceptual framework determined by the legal discourse. It was not simply that supervision with a condition of IIT occupied a higher position in the court's tariff of punishments, but that the very nature of the programmes had undergone a major transformation. The offence had become the central focus. The 'high-intensity' programmes intended as an alternative to custody and the 'medium-intensity' programmes intended to replace high-tariff non-custodial sentences (such as those offered by the Woodlands Centre in Basingstoke)[25] aimed at confronting the offender with his or her crime and its consequences. They were designed to instil a sense of responsibility, and they used behavioural techniques to raise the offender's resistance to temptation.[26] The resulting 'offence-focused package', or corrective curriculum, now usually takes the form of individual discussions with key workers, group discussions with fellow offenders, the use of role play about offending, talks from visiting speakers, and the making of life-history books (sometimes taking cartoon form)[27] about the young person's offending. The Junction Project in the London Borough of Lambeth is another example of these IIT schemes; opening in the same year as the Woodlands Centre, and also specifically as an alternative to custody or care, it saw its 'working approach' as being 'To . . . encourage each youngster to identify the salient factors leading to delinquency in his/her case and construct a programme setting targets for effecting change in these areas' (Interim Report, November 1982). This is very similar to the first aim of the Woodlands Centre: 'To identify rational behaviour responsible for the offences which might then be modified to produce behavioural change' (Rutherford, 1992, p.113). Furthermore, it was clear from the start that the success of this and all similar projects depended upon winning the approval of the magistrates. It was not sufficient simply to appoint local magistrates to serve on the management committee. If the project was to be seen and used as a real alternative to custody, magistrates involved in sentencing decisions would have to know precisely what would happen to an offender whom they referred to the project. To quote from a recent book written by one such magistrate, 'In projecting these programmes and convincing courts of the validity of its approach, the Centre clearly has to make sure that the courts understand what takes place in the various sessions which are named' (Curtis, 1989, p.35).

In addition, if a judge or magistrate is to have confidence in an IIT scheme, there must be proper arrangements to deal with breaches of the work programme which the court has approved. According to the same magistrate, commenting on the case of a serious persistent offender called Jim:

> It is crucial to explain what will happen if such a detailed schedule as Jim's is breached. What if he is rude to his supervisor on placement or leaves an untidy mess behind him in the garden of the old person whom he is supposed to be helping? . . . The Centre is swift and tough in its reaction, bringing the young person back to court. What at first blush is surprising is that by bringing the breaches back to court the Centre is sure *it strengthens the confidence of the magistrates in its work*. (Curtis, 1989, p.35, our emphasis)

For court referrals to the Junction Project, deferred sentences are the preferred course of action. This device enables the court to keep a close control over the offender's progress. Having deferred sentence for up to six months:

> The court gives its reasons for deferment and makes clear what it expects will happen during the period. The agreement is that if the offender does what is expected – it might be 'to keep out of trouble and to attend the Junction Project, bringing good reports back to court' – the disposal at the end of the period will not be severe. (Curtis, 1989, p.67)

Other projects in the UK have used the mechanism of a supervision order with a specified activities component.[28] Again the court knows what will happen to the youngster, and the legal enshrinement of such specifications allows the imposition of legal sanctions for any breach.

At the level of functional operation, therefore, the enslavement is total. Judges and magistrates approve or disapprove of schemes on the basis of their ability to deal with the 'real' problem – that is, the offending. Progress is assessed by the participant's good behaviour on the project, which, as in prison, is judged by obedience to the rules, politeness to staff, and not reoffending, and breaches in the rules are dealt with by some punitive measure. Knowledge about the child or young person is focused on his or her offending, whether in terms of the criminal law or in relation to the rules and programme laid down for his or her conduct within the project.

At the level of practice, however, the dominance of the legal discourse may be less than total. The fact that many of the workers in IT still prefer to communicate about children and adolescents in the language of child welfare science is likely to result in interference rather than total enslavement of the knowledge of this discourse. While IIT programmes may be dressed up to appeal to magistrates and judges, through an emphasis on the corrective curriculum, there are indications of some discomfort with a narrow, legal conceptualization of young people as offenders. Contrast, for example, the following two paragraphs taken from the brochure of one such project:

> Philosophy: the programme is based on a justice model of juvenile justice which emphasizes the young person's own responsibility for the offences they have committed. Consequently *the core elements of the programme are directly offence related*.

> The P.A.C.E. model also incorporated *a view of each young person as having a unique set of strengths, needs, aspirations and difficulties that require an individualized assessment and response.* (our emphasis)[29]

A similar juxtaposition is evident in Rutherford's argument that, 'Although the Woodlands Centre is closely aligned to the courts, its approach bears little resemblance to the punishment approach . . . In Programme terms, Woodlands is consistent with the developmental approach' (1992, p.119).

# VI  'Systemic' justice

## 1  The management approach

As we have noted, the legal discourse is not confined by courtroom doors or prison gates, and judges and lawyers are not the only professionals who apply law's procedures and criteria for constructing reality: to suggest otherwise is to confuse 'discourse' and 'domain'. Even outside the confines of the courts, where young people are sentenced to some form of psycho-social intervention, legal concepts, criteria and procedures, aimed at determining lawfulness and unlawfulness, while not always dominating communications and decision-making, cause, as we have shown, confusion and ambiguity – the symptoms of Teubner's 'interference'.

The possibility of such interference has been increased by a recent addition – an economic discourse – to the legal and welfare scientific discourses operating within juvenile justice. This new component organizes information around managerial concepts which promote improved functioning and co-ordination of the various institutions of juvenile justice as leading to 'better' juvenile justice:

> there has to be a rationalization of service delivery: greater co-ordination of the work of the respective agencies involved to ensure cohesion and efficiency, unified policies and strategies and the like . . . Such tendencies will no doubt continue: there will be further attempts to provide technology to eliminate operational malfunctions that empirical research has so far revealed (see e.g. Landau, 1981; Mott, 1983). (Pratt, 1986, p.213)

As a speaker at a conference in the UK commented, 'If we are to succeed in effectively managing the problem of juvenile offending, then it must be effectively organized' (Locke, 1988, p.1). Management had become the main task within juvenile justice.[30]

This new emphasis rests on a construction of the total domain of juvenile justice as a *system*. Attempts by organizational analysts to portray the courts as but one institution among others, all of which affect outcomes for the young offender, serve to emphasize this.[31] Indeed, a paper at the conference quoted above began with the statement: 'I am sure that no one these days can be in doubt about the *systemic* nature of juvenile justice' (Britton et al., 1988, p.12). Management of this system is seen as necessary because its development has been pragmatic and unco-ordinated. According to Lerman, 'There has emerged in an unplanned fashion a new youth-in-trouble system that includes old and new institutions from . . . juvenile correction, child welfare . . . mental health' (1980, p.282).

Determining the epistemic nature of this system is difficult. Texts are often unhelpful, in that management is presented as an end in itself: 'It is now increasingly acknowledged that a collective strategy is required in order to address the problems inherent in the fragmentation of the juvenile justice system and to increase the effectiveness of each of the agencies involved in that system at a local level' (Locke, 1988, p.4). Such statements are rarely followed by a discussion of how efficiency and effectiveness are to be measured. Indeed, the statement that, 'One of the most crucial ideas to emerge from our growing understanding of juvenile justice is the key role of systems management. An essential means of managing a system is through policy development' (Britton et al., 1988, p.vii) could be seen as explicit recognition that universal yardsticks might not exist, and that

management aims at constructing a policy by which successful management may be judged!

The escape from this circularity is in the acceptance that participants
have internalized very general goals of diversion from crime, court and
custody, so that effectiveness can only be in terms of an economic use of
resources to achieve diversion to non-court and non-custodial sections of
the system which are seen to offer a greater chance of reducing
reoffending. In selecting the relevant information and in determining the
strategy for a co-ordinated, resource-targeting approach to young people
who have broken the legal rules, therefore, the common currency is not
primarily the happiness, fulfilment or wellbeing of the young person, but
the avoidance of re-arrest and the consequent impact of the criminal justice
system upon repeated offenders. Scientific knowledge about the negative
effects of the criminal justice system on the life-chances of young people
has therefore been translated into practical efforts to keep young offenders
out of the courts. In Luhmann's terms, this avoidance of law could be seen
as representing a serious challenge to the effective operation of society. Yet
the pronouncement of the unlawfulness of a criminal act need not
necessarily take place in a court of law for the legal system to be performing
its function effectively.

For our own analysis, the current preoccupation with managing the
system serves to highlight a tacit acceptance of those yardsticks promoted
by law in its emphasis on offending history, and to raise questions which
can be answered only by an analysis of the constituent parts of the system.
Given an overall desire not to duplicate work, and to prevent young
offenders from entering the 'wrong' part of the system, attention must still
focus upon the procedures used by the diversionary schemes which are
part of that system.

## 2   Diversion from law to law?

As we have seen in Chapter 5, the law has in other areas been obliged to
confront knowledge from an external discourse which states that courts
and the legal system may cause harm to children. A similar challenge to the
criminal law originated in the 1960s and 1970s, when social scientists
deployed labelling theory to attack through empirical evidence the efficacy
of the law. They claimed that secondary deviance and subsequent criminal
careers could be caused by inappropriate responses – notably prosecution
and custodial sentencing – of the criminal justice system to relatively minor
misbehaviour by young people. Social scientists have since modified their
theories of labelling,[32] but there is still strong belief in the supposed
negative effects of the criminal justice system, and the need for 'minimum
intervention'.[33] However, this challenge is greater than that to family law.

Unlike the case of informal dispute-resolution of inter-parental disputes which leaves law's authority intact, the avoidance of the criminal law strikes at the very heart of law's credibility as society's moral entrepreneur. To allow 'criminals' to evade the law would be, as we have noted, to destabilize congruent expectations, and undermine the authority of the legal discourse.

The obvious solution for law was to extend the legal discourse beyond the borders of the courts, so that legal communications could be produced in non-judicial settings where labelling was assumed not to occur. On both sides of the Atlantic, therefore, decision-making bodies have been set up outside the traditional criminal justice system. These are composed of individuals from both within and outside criminal justice, notably social workers, probation officers, police, and education department officials. In the UK the first developments were from the 1960s onwards, in the form of police juvenile bureaux, where police officers seconded to the bureaux collected information about the young offender preparatory to a senior police officer making the decision whether or not to prosecute. The major development was that of Cautioning Councils, which in some cases developed out of police juvenile bureaux.[34] These multi-agency bodies had the function of making or recommending a decision in regard to the cautioning decision – that is, whether or not to prosecute, caution (issue a formal warning by the police) or take no further action. Some of these bodies have more recently taken on board another function, that of making a decision for a particular form of diversion other than cautioning. This is sometimes referred to as *cautioning plus*, in that activities, training or help may be recommended in addition to a caution.[35]

In the USA, a procedure similar to cautioning plus is that of *informal adjustment*, which is common in most states, and encouraged by the juvenile codes of those states which provide for the formal process to be halted or suspended while the youth is handled informally. As with cautioning, the juvenile must admit to the criminal act and voluntarily agree with the informal disposition. If the child and family agree to informal adjustment, and if the child has admitted the offence, then the various outcomes which may be selected include referral to mental health services for counselling, supervision by a probation officer, or monetary restitution. In at least six cities a new procedure under this system is that of youth juries, whereby a peer jury of five to nine young people of secondary school age make recommendations relating to the disposition of a first offender for minor offences.[36]

For the purposes of our analysis, however, these represent merely the different organizational forms in which decisions are increasingly made about young offenders. Research in Scotland and the United States in the early 1970s, which found that first-time and minor offenders were more likely to be cautioned,[37] would indicate an organization of knowledge deriving from a legal rather than child welfare discourse. This is supported by more recent research in England, showing the police and Crown Prosecution Service to be using an almost identical 'operational philosophy' when making decisions about juveniles (Gelsthorpe and Giller, 1990). Since that time, legal principles have found their way into the cautioning criteria issued by the UK Home Office. These state that the juvenile must admit the offence, that the parents must agree to cautioning, that the evidence must be sufficient to support a prosecution (Home Office Circular 70/1978), and that the evidence should be strong enough to make 'a conviction more likely that an acquittal' (Home Office Circular 14/1985).[38] This latter circular also constituted the cautioning of a minor in England and Wales as a piece of official legal knowledge, in that it can be cited in court if he or she is found guilty by the court of a subsequent offence.[39] It would appear, therefore, that, in terms of its epistemic roots, police cautioning, even where conducted as the consequence of a decision of a Cautioning Council, is part of communication determining illegality or unlawfulness.[40]

This may be an obvious conclusion to draw where the caution involves no more than an official warning, but when one looks in detail at the procedures and criteria used by 'cautioning plus' councils – those juvenile justice bodies which have a wider range of options to recommend for the young offender, which may include referral to supervised activities, mediation or reparation – a remarkably similar conclusion emerges: legal criteria are being used to construct the child primarily as 'offender', for whom any intervention must be justified and legitimized in terms of controlling his or her illegal behaviour. A paper by a co-ordinator of one such body gives clear evidence of the domination of this particular project by legal procedures, indicated, for instance, by the reference to cautioning as a 'disposal' (Veevers, 1989). This project devised a range of diversionary measures, including informal and formal warnings, cautions, mediation and reparation. The language and criteria are those of the courts in making their sentencing decisions.

> The next step on the *tariff* is prosecution. Reparation can be considered in conjunction with an official caution or higher on the tariff as an alternative to court; but it should not generally be considered when a person is being cautioned for the *first time unless the offence is appropriate* and this course of action is thought beneficial to the accused. (Veevers, 1989, p.71, our emphasis)

The initial decision to consider mediation as an option also stems from a categorization in terms of the 'seriousness of the offence' – another concept from legal communications: 'In addition to using mediation in cases of assault the team uses it in cases of theft, criminal damage and minor burglaries, by way of personal apologies to individuals . . . plus, occasionally, some form of voluntary compensation' (Veevers, 1989, pp.73 and 75). When mediation is recommended, using the criteria for cautioning, a secondary justification – that mediation is 'good for the child' – also focuses on offending: 'youngsters will probably benefit from mediation in that it will be a positive experience for them in terms of *prevention of a recurrence*' (p.73, our emphasis).

One significant feature in relation to these procedures is the ease by which young offenders are fed back into the courts by these diversionary bodies. Another is the way in which, in recent years, the legal system has itself been responsible for extending the boundaries of its own discourse. In one judicial review decision, for example, a decision by police and prosecutors to prosecute a young offender in spite of a recommendation to the contrary by a multi-agency panel was upheld by the court.[41] Interesting, too, is the way in which legal categorization is constantly being used in the first place as a criterion for the provision of welfare assistance. In some areas, for example, cautioning plus may be considered only where the young person has already been cautioned at least twice. Secondly, the notion of 'failure' is, in some schemes, that derived from the law. As we saw in the case of Intermediate Treatment, young offenders who absent themselves or break the rules on the treatment part of cautioning plus are liable to be sent to court.[42] Programmes in the USA[43] and Holland[44] show the same characteristics.

# VII   Policy concerns

While what happens to young people outside the criminal justice system may be less dramatic than subjection to the procedures and penalties of the Juvenile Court, to suggest that these informal processes provide a distinct alternative to the law is, in most cases, to misrepresent what are, in fact, satellites of the legal discourse. Their initial construction of children and adolescents essentially as offenders requiring control and deterrence ensures that all future assessments and interpretations of their behaviour will be in identical terms to those applied by the courts. In this way, continuity between court procedures and those of diversionary decision-making is ensured, through constructions of knowledge about young people which remain virtually identical from the social work office to the courtroom door.

One practical effect of this extension of the legal discourse is that a large number of people whose training and ambition were directed towards improving the lives of the young through the application of child welfare science find themselves increasingly operating within a decision-making environment where the only difference from the courts lies in the type and scope of disposals available to the decision-makers. The 'interference' caused by this confusion of discourses leads inevitably to more confusion, with social workers, for example, claiming credit for and making a virtue of 'successes' such as lower prosecution, custody and recidivism rates, which are, in effect, often the result of policy changes within the legal system. Yet once these criteria of success have been adopted by agencies for the application of child welfare science, they tend to supplant any ambitions to improve the lives of the young. In extending the boundaries of its formal communications, law has inflicted harm on other social institutions.

The extent of this harm is difficult to measure, but one indication is the extent to which scarce resources are diverted away from programmes and projects which aim to enrich and improve the lives of young people to those with the much narrower aims of avoiding prosecution, custodial sentences or recidivism. Such diversion of resources has certainly been a feature of youth policy in the UK in recent years.[45]

This is not to suggest that schemes for keeping children out of courts are in any way wrong. On the contrary, these schemes may be valuable and constructive in avoiding the stigmatization and contamination that the criminal justice system seems to generate. What it does suggest, however, is that 'interference', confusion and enslavement could be avoided if such projects were recognized as extensions of the legal discourse, to be staffed by people whose skills and knowledge were appropriate for the task they were asked to perform. The Halt Project in Rotterdam[46] is one example where an informal mediation and compensation scheme is seen very clearly as an adjunct of criminal justice, and not as social work. The staff consists of those who are skilled in communicating and negotiating with young people.

As far as the deployment of resources is concerned, the political linking of crime reduction with social science knowledge and practice has admittedly provided a rich seam for social workers to mine and exploit. Yet, as the French crime prevention programmes have shown, this may be done within a political discourse without subjecting child welfare science to the reality constructions of law.[47] Here schemes and projects aimed at helping *all* disadvantaged children and young people by enriching their lives and providing them with a positive self-image have been operating outside the ambit of juvenile justice and without the dominance of the police in determining the criteria for admissibility and success. The claims made to link these programmes with crime reduction are usually of a vague and general nature. There is no attempt to use local crime or court statistics as the criteria for success or failure of specific projects.[48]

# Notes

1   See Stein (1984, Ch. 5) for a historical review of the political reasons for the civil/criminal distinctions in selected jurisdictions throughout history.

2   For example, Stein (1984) gives the example of the Romans of the early Republic who were reluctant to develop a criminal jurisdiction because they did not wish to give the power of prosecution to officials, in case such officials became too powerful. On the other hand, in Imperial China the attitude was that 'any action by a man that was "antisocial" was also a violation of the total cosmic order' (1984, p.56), and therefore the law was exclusively penal.

3   This is not to imply that this analysis applies only to those legal systems which operate under a 'just deserts' rationale. Such a philosophy necessitates that punishment must be proportionate to the amount of culpability. Legal systems incorporating utilitarian philosophies still focus on culpability, though the decision-making on outcomes includes communications from non-law discourses.

4   Teubner, personal communication, 28 November 1989.

5   See, for example, McKittrick and Eysenck (1984) and Blomberg (1983).

6   The age of criminal responsibility varies greatly internationally, from no minimum age in Luxemburg, to 10 in the Netherlands, 15 in Sweden and 18 (with exceptions) in Belgium. There is also no clear correspondence between the age of criminal responsibility and the age at which offenders are treated as adults. See Prison Reform Trust (1987).

7   See, for example, Morris and Giller (1987, p.175) and Emerson (1969).

8   See Shapland (1981), who argues that in England and Wales the speech in mitigation was the only opportunity for most offenders to provide such information, and this was little more than a plea for mercy.

9   See, for example, Parsloe (1978), especially pp.140–4, where she discusses the legislation enacted in England and Wales subsequent to the Children Act 1908. This covered such issues as the selection of juvenile court magistrates, the use of different buildings or rooms from the rest of the criminal court, and the non-admittance of the public.

10   See Morris and Giller (1987, p.201), citing Priestly et al. (1977) and Parker et al. (1981).

11   See Morris and Giller (1987, p.217) and Tutt and Giller (1984b).

12   In Essex, for example, the Juvenile Justice Centres developed from a Resources Panel established in 1981 were originally intended to provide supervisors and select projects for youngsters referred by the court. Now these centres are linked more specifically to particular court disposals. In some areas they are referred to as 'Intermediate Treatment Panels', because they provide information to the courts about IT schemes proposed for a particular juvenile offender. A similar body is the Referral Panel or 'Service Area' set up by the Social Services Department of the London Borough of Hammersmith and Fulham.

13   See NACRO's account of appeals against the court's failure to respect the provisions of the 1982 and 1988 Criminal Justice Acts restricting the use of custody for young offenders (NACRO Briefing, 1990).

14   For an account of the work of the French *juge des enfants*, see Ely and Stanley (1990); King (1983) and King and Petit (1985).

15   Donzelot (1979, pp.110–11). See also King (1983) and King and Petit (1985) for an account of the French juvenile justice system.

16    *Report on Children and Young Persons* (1964) London. HMSO, Cmnd. 2,306.
17    The Social Work (Scotland) Act 1968. For discussions of the reforms and the operation of the Children's Hearings, see Grant, (1976).
18    For example, a community arbitration project in Maryland, based at Arundel – one of several similar projects in Maryland starting in 1976 – has a courtroom atmosphere and uses salaried lawyers to arbitrate and provide legal representation: see Law Enforcement Assistance Administration: *The Community Arbitration Project*, Washington DC: US Department of Justice (discussed in Marshall, 1985). Similarly, the Bronx New York Forum uses a panel of two or three volunteer residents of the area, and, although there is no legal representation, a juvenile is assigned an advocate from his or her own neighbourhood for counselling and practical help. Just over half the cases referred reach a hearing out of the approximate annual caseload of 700 (Sarri, 1983).
19    This may account for the surprising statistics of, for example, the Bronx New York Forum, where 60 per cent of the cases were settled at mediation, with a 90 per cent compliance rate with the settlement: see Marshall (1985). The US Bar Association in 1980 estimated that there were 180 mediation schemes in the US by the end of the 1970s, though details were available for only a minority of these schemes, and some of these schemes, for example, the Arundel schemes, are not strictly mediation schemes.
20    Harrington and Merry (1988); Adler et al. (1988).
21    Part of the research of Davis et al. (1988) was based on the Exeter scheme. Harding (1989) has drawn attention to the acknowledged development of this scheme 'to the point that reparation is more appropriately focussed on second and third time juvenile offenders who are more in danger of prosecution', p.30.
22    For example, the reparation and mediation scheme at Leeds approached victims on the basis that 'prison doesn't work: we want the offender to change; can you help us?' (a member of the management committee, quoted in Davis et al., 1988, p.130).
23    See, for example, an account of the Coventry Reparation Scheme – one of four experimental schemes in the UK funded by the Home Office 1985–87 – by Ruddick, in Wright and Galaway (1989).
24    See Davis et al. (1988, p.130) and Young (1989, p.467) for research material. Young concludes: 'The most striking finding to emerge from the 49 interviews conducted with offenders was that nearly twice as many were against the link with sentencing as supported the idea. Offenders saw the major problem as being that people in their position would take part purely in the hope of gaining some advantage for themselves or that they would be perceived to be motivated in this way' (1989, p.470).
25    This centre opened in 1981: see Rutherford (1992, pp.113–18).
26    See, for example, Ely et al. (1987) for a discussion of the Medway Close Support Unit, and Curtis (1989) for a description in Ch. 3 of the Junction Project, Lambeth.
27    See Rutherford (1992, pp.115–17) for examples of such cartoons.
28    At one such project, the Tendring Juvenile Justice Centre in Essex, the specified activity component is an offence-focused programme, whereby the young person must attend four compulsory sessions per week, three of which are individual sessions with a supervisor, talking about offending. Each group writes a script about the committing of one of their offences, the group acts it out, the play is videoed and the video forms the basis of further group

discussion (*Second Annual Report of the Tendring J.J.C.*, 1986, Essex County Council Social Services Committee, pp.5–6.).

29   Taken from the publicity brochure of the PACE Project in Coventry, England (PACE (Project for Alternative Community Experience), The Children's Society/City of Coventry, text N. PS 112832).

30   Another paper at this conference pointed out that 'it is no coincidence that economic evaluation and economic consideration entered the social care world during a period when resources became markedly constrained in public service provision' (Knapp, in Britton et al., 1988, p.7).

31   See, for example, Moxon (1985) which includes a discussion of a UK Home Office Research programme to apply dynamic modelling techniques to juvenile justice.

32   See, for example, the discussion of social control theory, in Hirsch (1972) and Junger-Tas and Block (1988).

33   'Minimum intervention is a key concept in work with juvenile offenders. This is accepted by the Government as an important underlying principle in policy formation. Most juveniles commit offences during their adolesence (how many of us did not?) and most grow out of it. They need help to grow through that difficult period without being confirmed in their delinquent behaviour . . . it is of central importance that our response to delinquent acts does not serve to drive a wayward youngster into becoming a career criminal' (Graham Sutton, of the Criminal Policy Department at the Home Office, London, in Britton et al., 1988, p.26).

34   See Rutter and Giller (1983, p.20) for a review of the literature.

35   An example of such a project is that of the Juvenile Liaison Bureaux in Northamptonshire, developed by the Northampton police force, whereby at a weekly meeting attended by senior representatives of police, Social Services and the Probation Service (all seconded full-time) every juvenile offender brought to the notice of the police was discussed, and details of possible alternative 'treatment packages' acquired. Research over a sample period when 45 cases were dealt with at one of the bureaux has showed that in 12 cases there was financial restitution; in 10 practical restitution; in 31, apologies were made to the victim and in 12, the young offender took part in Community Service (Marshall, 1985; Bowden and Stevens, 1986).

36   See Seyfrit et al. (1987) for a detailed discription of the organization of the Columbia (Georgia) County Peer Jury, which began operation in January 1980.

37   See Ritchie and Mack (1974).

38   While in the past the implementation of such official criteria has varied considerably, there is evidence to suggest that they are now widely adhered to. This is not to say that there has not been until recently major concern about 'justice by geography' stemming from varying cautioning policies in different police areas. The 1992 figures show the cautioning rate for 10–16-year-old males varies between 63 and 93 per cent, with an average rate of 78 per cent for all police force areas (source: NACRO).

39   A caution does not rank as a conviction, but records are kept of them for at least three years and they may be cited in court, on a subsequent conviction, as evidence of the offender's character (see Home Office Circular 14/1985). They may also affect subsequent decisions to prosecute (see Home Office Circular 18/ 1994).

40   Circulars 59/1990 and 18/94 have not changed the situation. Indeed, the latest circular imposes more rigid, offence-focused criteria.

41　*R* v. *Chief Constable of Kent and Another, ex parte L* [1991] Crim LR 841. See also Uglow et al. (1992).

42　For instance, one project in the UK, the West Midlands Juvenile Liaison Scheme, developed a procedure informally known as a 'deferred caution', whereby the giving of a caution depends on the performance of reparation to the victim; otherwise the case is sent for prosecution.

43　For example, the Bronx Neighbourhood Youth Diversion Programme, started in 1971 and dealing with youths between 12 and 15 years of age, holds its own formal hearings to determine what the outcome should be, but, if the performance of the young offenders on the programme is not satisfactory, the case would be referred back to formal court proceedings (Sarri, 1983, p.63).

44　For example, the Halt Project in Rotterdam (Junger-Tas, 1988).

45　See, for example, King (1989).

46　See Junger-Tas (1988).

47　See King (1988).

48　See King (1989).

# 7 The law's response and the responsiveness of law

## I Introduction

Our task in this book has been to explore and develop within the territory of legal decision-making about children some of the theoretical ideas that Gunther Teubner has expounded concerning law and its relationship with other social discourses. We have not set out to test these theories in any scientific way. Nor have we engaged in the sorts of arguments about principles in which legal scholars are so expert. We could, with some justification, be accused of exploiting and manhandling some of Teubner's ideas, at times stretching them to encompass the specific issue that concerns us, and at other times filling in, with some trepidation, gaps which appear to exist in the original theoretical model, in order to give it the coherence necessary for application to this area of law and social policy.

If we have done no more than to offer an unfamiliar way of looking at familiar phenomena, we shall at least have achieved the first of our objectives in writing this book. If our account of the way that the law thinks about children and the way that this 'thinking' affects other social institutions has proved convincing, then we shall also have achieved our second objective. To put Teubner's ideas about reflexive law and the partial withdrawal of epistemic authority to the test in any systematic way would, as we stated in Chapter 2, require some pilot schemes where 'reflexive law' could be seen to work in direct comparison with the 'responsive' or 'substantive' law model which at present characterizes the law's attempts to promote the welfare of children through legal decision-making. What we *are* able to do in this chapter is to list and discuss the conceptual problems implicit in the responsive law approach.

In 1916 the US jurist Roscoe Pound, in his article, 'The Limits of Effective Legal Action', drew attention to the inability and inappropriateness of the law to achieve such intangible objectives as the development or restoration of emotional bonds. Clearly there are differences between Pound's perspective and our own, in that Pound was concerned with the operation of the courts and legal system, while our analysis has, up to now, been in terms of cognitive discourses. Yet, drawing upon our application of Teubner's theoretical account to children's issues, our intention in this chapter is to identify and discuss those limitations of the legal discourse which may be relevant to its appropriateness to promote the wellbeing of children.

Up to this point we have not engaged in any direct comparisons between the value of different discourses. Instead, we have deliberately tried to maintain a neutrality by stating, for example, on several occasions, that the fact that different discourses produce different reality constructions does not necessarily imply that one is superior to the other. There are, however, times when Teubner himself appears to be claiming superiority for science over law in the ability of the former to deal directly with reality as experienced through learning, as, for example, in his definition of law as 'second-order autopoiesis'.

> The autonomy of modern law refers primarily to its normative operations that become independent from moral or political normativity; and secondarily, autonomy refers to law's cognitive operations that – under the pressure of normative operations – *construct idiosyncratic images of reality and move them away from the world constructions of everyday life and from those of scientific discourses.* (Teubner, 1989, p.742, our emphasis)

In an earlier article he went even further, claiming that social science writers have 'closer access to social reality' (1986). Our argument is not that science is superior in any absolute terms, but rather that, while law's truths may be effective within law's own normative domain, their idiosyncratic nature and dependence upon normative operations may make them highly inappropriate as a basis for reality construction in the types of issues that concern the wellbeing of children. If law as an epistemic discourse has such severe limitations as we suggest, those characteristics which restrict law's appropriateness to deal with such issues need to be recognized.

## II  The limits of law in securing children's wellbeing

### 1  Law simplifies, reducing the social world to manageable concepts

Many critics of law have made the point that the legal process is ill-equipped to deal with the complexities of human social relationships.

What Teubner and Luhmann tell us is somewhat different. Their message is that law, in order to perform its social function effectively, has no choice but to simplify and reduce. The previous pages provide some examples of this process by identifying the semantic constructs which law uses to make sense of the morass of emotional responses, scientific evidence and moral precepts that are associated in our society with the concepts of children and childhood: the child as witness, the child as innocent victim, the child as a bundle of needs, the child as the bearer of rights, the child as young offender.

This does not mean that law is in any way unique as a social discourse. All discourses simplify and reduce to a greater or lesser degree. The issue is not whether or not law promotes selective, simplistic and reductionist accounts of reality, but rather whether these accounts select, reduce and simplify in ways that are appropriate for the proper performance of the social roles that the courts, as an institution, are performing in relation to children.

The corollary of Teubner's message is that those who are critical of the problem-solving capacities of law in children's cases will not improve matters by trying to change its reductionist tendencies by bringing about reforms to make law more responsive and more sensitive to the particular demands of these issues. The autopoietic nature of law precludes any fundamental changes, both in the procedures for reality construction and in the epistemic framework within which law's semantic artifacts are produced and reproduced. All that change are the accounts of people and relationships within law's social world constructions. These new accounts are constructed in ways that enable them to fit easily into the pre-existing categories and classifications that law provides.

## 2   Law individualizes

Law's reality constructions, where children and families are concerned, place the individual firmly in the centre of the wheel of causality. In child care and protection cases this pivotal role for the individual is filled by the child's immediate adult carers – in most cases, the parents – those who are 'responsible' for the child. The statute law and proceedings in the courts have their sights on the target of the parent–child relationship. They focus upon the removal of the child from its parents, the granting and relinquishment of parental rights, the supervision of parents, and the continued contact or restrictions on the contact between the child and its parents. While the law's official concern is the welfare or best interests of the child, in practice its autopoietic nature brings it back to play a mediatory role, balancing the claims of individual parents to possess and exercise exclusive power over their children, and the rights of individual children to be free from the clutches of parents who are causing or likely to cause them harm. Even where the judge's role consists in part of supervisor of the child's welfare, such supervision takes the form of exhorting parents and bringing pressure on them to accept and perform their parental responsibilities.

There have been, and no doubt there will continue to be, brave attempts to substitute for this mediatory role a scientific enquiry into a child's welfare. These attempts cannot fully succeed as long as the law continues to 'think' about children's issues in terms of individualized relationships between children and parents, and our previous analysis suggests that, at least within modern society, the law cannot think about children in any other way. Whatever changes are made to the criteria for state intervention, to the rules of evidence and procedure and to definitions of the legal relationships between parents and children, the legal discourse and the semantic artifacts it produces seem always to be rooted in normative notions of individual morality and responsibility. In disputes between parents, therefore, the law 'thinks' about children's needs in relation only to the acceptability to a social environment ordered by law of the competing alternative solutions offered by each parent. The legal decision-making is framed by the offers, bids and counter-offers of the individual parents. Even where extended family, such as grandparents, are brought into the arena, it is as individuals competing in the normative arena to provide socially acceptable arrangements for the child.

In criminal proceedings, the law shifts its attention to the moral responsibility of the individual child. The law may make some allowances for age, and excuse from the burden of individual responsibility young children who fail to understand the difference between right and wrong. However, in general, children who commit crimes are deemed to do so through failings within themselves which can be remedied through some appropriate punishment or 'treatment' decreed by the law. Crime may not always be seen as a voluntary act on the part of the child, but, where it is perceived as involuntary, its cause is deemed to be some pathological functioning within the child or within the family, which, given the right level of motivation, is remediable through treatment. Often, the legal and social response to serious crimes committed by children wavers between these two accounts of causality.[1] Individual responsibility may from time to time give way to individual pathology, but only in ways that allow the law to re-impose the burden of responsibility in the form of 'failure to co-operate' or 'failure to respond to treatment'.

It could be argued that, in societies whose dominant culture champions the individual and sees people as controllers of their fate, it is only right that the law should reflect these values. This may well be so. However, such an analysis ignores the diversity of discourses within post-modern societies. Even within the institutions of these societies, the notions of collective responsibility and community action are not entirely absent. Determinism and the idea that people may be caught up in cycles of deprivation are to be found in current political and religious beliefs. Many sociological theories attempt to identify those social factors which affect people's lives and over which, as individuals, they have no direct control. According to some sociological evidence, for example, a person's race is likely to be a far greater determinant of social and economic status than any individual qualities that individual may possess.[2] Furthermore, psycho-analytic theory, while concentrating attention on the individual, attributes the cause of attitudes and behaviour to the unconscious, which, by definition, is not subject to the control of that individual.

In practice, the law's autopoietic function of 'stabilizing congruent expectations' (see pages 29–30) takes the form, in modern society, of excluding such dissonant interpretations of causality from its consider-ations. Law must continue to place individuals in the centre of the epistemic stage, and any attempt to remove them from that position is doomed to failure.

## 3   Law excludes

A repeated theme of our enquiry has been the way in which law selects from a multiplicity of factors which could have affected the child's present condition and which could affect his or her future welfare. These may be psychological, environmental, biological or economic. Within the limits of what is accepted by society as rational and believable, one may take one's pick as to what factor or combination of factors led to the child's 'problems'. The remedy prescribed for these problems will depend upon the prior identification of causes. Law, in its decision-making, generally concen-trates upon the dynamics of the dyadic relationships – child and mother, child and father – and excludes factors seen as irrelevant to these relationships. We have shown in Chapter 3 how law – through its procedures, its rules of evidence and relevance, and its designation of expertise – may, therefore, rule out versions of causality which it is unable to handle, or can handle only with extreme difficulty through its coding of lawful/unlawful. We have also examined in Chapter 5 the implications of this necessary concentration on the dyadic relationship for the develop-ment of new legal or quasi-legal structures.

## 4   Law encourages distortion and exaggeration

This is a well-documented subject concerning the adversary contests in the courts, where parties to legal actions are forced into polarized positions, if only to defend themselves against exaggerated attacks from the other side. This is likely to occur in any courtroom contest where the parties are pitted against one another, and the stakes are high, regardless of whether the proceedings take place within a nominally adversarial or inquisitorial legal system. The fact that care proceedings in England and Wales are officially deemed to be an enquiry into the future welfare of the child is of little consequence when often, in reality, social workers and parents are engaged in a fierce adversary contest over whether or not the child should return home to the parents' care.

## 5    Law compartmentalizes

Inevitably, law deals with cases involving children's welfare according to its own categorization of the matter as a legal issue. The cases of children of divorcing parents are, for example, in most jurisdictions, administered in different courts and according to different rules than those involving children believed to be in need of protection. Although there is usually some possibility of 'cross-over', so that delinquency and divorce matters cases may turn into protection cases, such transformations are difficult to achieve once the legal action has begun. Legal classifications may be justified according to the logic of the law, but their effects verge on the absurd when different rules as to what is and what is not admissible as information apply according to the type of court in which the action was started, or whether the case has reached the interim or final stage in the same proceedings (see pages 73–77).

Another, not so obvious, example concerns the child as witness. Where the child is categorized as a victim (for example, in sex abuse cases) there is much concern about the trauma of the courtroom experience, and much ingenuity directed towards devising ways of easing the burden of giving evidence.[3] No such concern or ingenuity is applied to those young children who give evidence as defendants in criminal cases. The only matter of concern here is the possible labelling and alienating effect of the criminal process.

## 6    Law enslaves child welfare science

Much of our work in this book has been concerned with the relationship between the epistemic world constructions of law and child welfare science. We have given many examples of the 'reconstruction' of science within law. Law has been seen to select for admission only those theoretical perspectives which it is able to incorporate within its own meanings, and to require radical transformations of, or exclude altogether, other theoretical accounts. Law and child psychology and law and child psychiatry are not, as some would have us believe, the merging of disciplines, but rather the admission into the legal forum of certain accounts of behaviour from psychology and psychiatry which advance and legitimize for public consumption the law's search for right and wrong, or for rights and wrongs.[4]

The adoption by some US jurisdictions of the concept of 'the psychological parent', as conceived by Goldstein et al. (1973), is a good example of this process (see pages 55–58). Another example is the attempt by law to impose parental duties on spouses after divorce or separation so as to encourage continuing contact between the child and non-custodial parent (see pages 51–52). Psychological concepts which make good sense as research findings within a scientific discourse thus become reconstructed and emerge in law as simple rules of thumb or normative dictates to parents.

In a similar manner, 'psy' experts, whether giving evidence in court or operating within Juvenile Court clinics, find, in Emerson's terms,[5] that court-determined issues frame their diagnostic efforts, and their recommendations are restricted to 'those alternatives posed by court personnel'. The price to be paid for power and influence in court decisions, it seems, is a loss of identity, and assimilation within the dominant legal paradigm.

Those accounts of reality which can find no common ground with law's quest may continue to exist as theoretical perspectives, organizing knowledge outside the confines of the law in, for example, marriage guidance bureaux, mediation services and child guidance clinics, but they take no part in joint epistemic ventures with law. Those 'psy' concepts which do gain admittance to law are suitably adapted and reconstructed so as to make sense in legal contexts.

For Teubner, however, the loss of authority does not appear so one-sided. While extra-legal discourses may suffer reconstruction within law, the process also diminishes law's own epistemic authority. The law may continue to dominate the issues to be addressed and the choices to be made, but individualized child welfare science may make important gains in formulating law's semantic artifacts concerning 'children' and 'childhood', and simultaneously displacing law's traditional (and now no longer socially acceptable) artifacts. Moreover, communications of 'psy' scientists within legal contexts may, according to Teubner's model, still retain their scientific meaning as separate and distinct from the meaning imposed by law on these communications. The problem with enslavement and interference is not so much that it creates a subservient scientific race, but that it produces confused, and at times contradictory, statements which diminish the epistemic authority of both law and science.

So far as social work is concerned, these difficulties are compounded by the lack of a firm epistemic base. Social work may, as we have seen, enter into total legal servitude in, for example, the 'treatment' of young offenders,[6] or as in child abuse detection.[7] On the other hand, much of social work activity takes place outside the law's domain, in areas where interference and domination is more likely to come from the political system. While the natural epistemological home for social work may be a scientific/medical discourse, the most publicly visible roles that social workers are obliged to play, at least in Anglo-American jurisdictions, lie within those hybrid discourses dominated by law.

## III   Beyond autopoiesis: the law's response to children

For Teubner, law's self-referential nature, in combination with its tendency to colonize and do violence to other social institutions, precludes any real transformations within law to enable it to deal effectively with the problems thrown up by other social institutions. Where it attempts to be 'responsive', it succeeds only in enslaving other discourses or in creating unsatisfactory hybrids. However, a selective reading of Teubner's theoretical account does not lead to such a pessimistic conclusion. Indeed, many of the insights that his theoretical approach offers may allow us to make some progress in our conceptualization of the issues, and eventually to devise solutions to the problems created by law's autopoietic tendencies. It is possible, for example, that law's need to defer to other discourses, such as science, may provide a restraint on law's reality constructions and framing of substantive issues. This, in turn, may affect the law's semantic constructs of children and childhood in ways which alter the treatment of children by the courts. Teubner's objections to hybrid discourses may make good epistemological sense. Yet, as long as the nature of the legal discourse and the dangers of legal reconstructions of child welfare science are acknowledged and, as far as possible, avoided, the continued involvement of social workers and 'psy' scientists may offer important restraints to the often insensitive and heavy-handed operation of the legal system and reduce the negative impact of that process upon children.

A more optimistic interpretation of Teubner's account of the epistemic trap would be to interpret the interference between law and other discourses as a transitional stage at which recognition is given to the potential harm caused to children by involvement in legal proceedings. One direction which this transition may take is 'reflexivity', and the 'liberation' of non-legal discourses from the reality constructions of law, and their subjection only to law's procedural controls (see pages 35–37). Although any such 'liberation', and the precise form it takes, may depend upon local conditions, the account of the development of out-of-court mediation in England[8] provides some evidence for this interpretation.

Another possibility, which we have discussed during the course of our book, is to recognize that part of Teubner's scheme, which he derives from Luhmann's theory of autopoiesis, as operating at the level of legal communications. This means that other communications may and do occur within court settings. In other words, the boundaries of any communicative system are not drawn by geographical location, but by the system's coding of its environment. It is then possible to escape from the confines of having to define all that happens in court buildings as legal operations. Clearly, courts, in their decisions, produce law (legal communications) and nothing but law, and these communications are functional for society in their stabilizing of congruent expectations. It is also the case that much of what occurs before the legal decision takes place within the communicative framework which law provides – the bargaining within the shadow of the law. However, this does not exclude the possibility of communications taking place *within* courts or court buildings, but which are external to law's communicative system.

A book which was concerned solely with the application of Gunther Teubner's ideas about law and law's relationships with other discourses would end here with this thin ray of guarded optimism on an otherwise dark and bleak horizon. Yet to close the story at this point would be to ignore a whole range of variations within and between legal systems which, at Teubner's level of abstract generality, are studiously avoided. Like John Fowles in *The French Lieutenant's Woman* (1969), we offer an alternative ending which, rather than avoiding these variations, examines them in some detail in the search for decision-making processes which do not do violence to children and their emotional environment. In doing so, however, we shall not abandon Teubner entirely, but merely put some distance between his pessimism and our own limited optimism.

In our alternative ending we wish to retain Teubner's important principle (derived from Foucault) of concentrating analytical attention on the reality constructions of institutions, rather than upon the values and characteristics of those actors who perform their roles within these institutions. This, we recognize, is in direct contradiction with much of the recent and current research on legal issues, where the analytical approach, very much in the legal realist tradition, is to subject to critical scrutiny the individual and collective characteristics of judges, magistrates, police officers, lawyers, probation officers, social workers and court clerks.[9] In many of these studies, class bias or prejudicial attitudes towards racial minorities or women are identified as causes of injustice or of projecting an inaccurate or damaging image of ethnic minorities or the nature of women. While such analyses may be useful in 'deconstructing' the law into its political and ideological components, the frequently-made assumption that the very nature of the legal system would change fundamentally if there were, for example, more working-class, black or female judges would seem to us to be mistaken. If one recognizes law as a social institution which 'thinks' independently of its members, one is forced to accept that such analyses can offer only a partial explanation of legal decision-making, and the solutions that researchers adopting that approach propose are unlikely on their own to provide the changes which they are seeking to achieve. To use Teubner's vocabulary, one is left with the uncomfortable conclusion that, rather than constructing law, these judges, magistrates, lawyers, etc. are semantic artifacts constructed by law, so that, for example, black lawyers and women judges communicate, and will continue to communicate, *as lawyers* within a system of communications which is characterized by its legal coding of the external environment. Despite their avowed feminism or anti-racism, they are unable to transform law into a political discourse which promotes the interests of women or black people.

To return, however, to our previous discussion, we do not accept Teubner's implicit conclusion that lawyers and judges, as semantic artifacts are uniformly produced across all legal systems.[10] On the contrary, we recognize that there are considerable variations in the conceptions of the lawyers' or judges' role, depending upon local, cultural traditions, and in the distribution of definitional and interpretive power among professional groups.[11] In the same way, semantic artifacts of children and childhood produced by law, far from being uniform, may vary considerably. These variations are, we would argue, expressed in the procedures and styles in which particular legal systems deal with cases concerning children's welfare. For this reason we end our book with a comparative account of the decision-making of different legal systems on issues concerning children's welfare. In doing so we deliberately go beyond the limits of Teubner's general theory in an attempt to define and identify 'child responsiveness' as a measure of comparison between different systems.

# Notes

1   The confusion caused by the abduction and murder of James Bulger by two 11-year-old boys was ultimately resolved by the law's imposition of criminal responsibility and the subsequent use by the Home Secretary, in response to public concern, of the legal notions of guilt and responsibility in deciding that the boys should not be released for at least fifteen years. The possibility that the boys might be cured of their 'pathological functioning' long before that period apparently played no part in his decisions.
2   See, for example, Rose (1969) and Smith (1977).
3   See, for example, Glaser and Spencer (1990).
4   See Freeman (1983).
5   See pages 110–111.

6 See pages 117–120.
7 See King (1994 and 1995).
8 See Chapter 5.
9 Seminal research was that of Karl Llewellyn in the USA in the 1920s and 1930s: see, for example, Llewellyn (1930). For more recent research in that tradition, analysing the English judiciary, see Griffith (1977).
10 While Teubner, unlike Luhmann, does admit the notion of cognitive 'closure' as a distinguishing feature of different forms of law, when we examined the application of this distinction (see pages 29–39), we found that it is only in 'archaic societies' that law is not 'closed'. In modern societies, whatever the form legal institutions take, law is always 'closed'. Luhmann (1988b, p.18) writes that an autopoietic system is 'recursively' closed, in so far as it 'can neither derive its operations from its environment nor pass them onto that environment'.
11 See King and Garapon (1987).

# 8 Child-responsive legal systems

As a preface to our alternative ending, we accept for our hermeneutic purposes Teubner's general statements about the nature of law as a social discourse and its implications for law as a decision-making institution. Now we need to go on from this point and ask what operational concept or concepts would best reflect Gunther Teubner's theoretical concerns and allow some of the lessons learnt from Teubner's analysis to be given practical expression.

## I From children's rights to child-responsiveness

### 1 Rights for children

When we examined earlier the concept of rights, we remarked upon its individualizing and reductionist application within law, the way that it was applied effectively to transform complex moral and social policy concerns into issues of legally right and legally wrong, to identify villains and victims, the rights-transgressors and the rights-transgressed. Outside the legal context, however, the notion of rights may be used to denote something much broader and more profound: in the case of human rights as the claim to be respected as a human being, for example, or as a separate racial, ethnic, cultural or religious group, or, in the case of animal rights, as creatures with feelings and dignity. Seen in this way, children's rights may be defined as the claim of children to be regarded as people with particular attributes, qualities, sensibilities and vulnerabilities which make them different from adults. This broad version of children's rights tends to become reconstructed within law, however, into something much narrower – as

143

either the right to be treated in approximately the same way as an adult,[1] or the right to be seen as belonging to a parent, to parents or to a family, and thus not normally to be removed from that setting.

Social institutions wishing to respond to the broader version of children's rights would have to adapt themselves in ways which not only treated children as different from adults, but which allowed them to understand and respond to these differences so as to minimize the harm caused to children and, wherever possible, to promote their interests. Such institutions would, in Foucault's terms, produce semantic constructs of children and childhood and, in Teubner's terms, think about children and childhood in ways which reflect the sensitivities, vulnerabilities and complexities which we have mentioned. There are social institutions which are well suited to adapt in this way. Education is one such institution; medicine may be another.[2] However, the notion of law as a social institution bearing heavy moral, normative burdens does not support the view that law may be changed in fundamental ways. The evidence from our survey of law's thinking about children gives some support to this pessimism. Children's interests do indeed become reduced to legal decisions; they do become submerged by the conflicts between adults to the point where they sometimes disappear altogether. Children are at times reified and at other times treated as if they were little adults without child-like characteristics. The complexities and sensitivities of their emotional, physical and intellectual development do become simplified into legal precepts and rules of thumb which guide decision-making. Moreover, even if the law makes the promotion of children's welfare its rhetorical objective, it is impossible for it to ignore other, often more pressing, claims for its attention, such as protection of the social order and the management of conflicts.

If we want decision-making institutions which are responsive to the broad concept of children's rights, then we have to look for them outside the legal system. The law may play its reflexive role within these institutions in laying down the 'norms of procedure, organization and competence' (see pages 35–37) for decision-making, but it should not be permitted to colonize them by destroying or enslaving their rules and procedures for reality construction and substituting its own. Teubner may well be right. Ideally, from a purist intellectual perspective, it is probably right, wherever possible, to keep complex issues involving children's welfare away from the operations of the legal system.

However, any suggestion that law should abdicate epistemic authority (either totally or partially) has to contend with the important questions of principle of a moral and constitutional nature. These may, for example, involve issues of parental or state authority. Furthermore, intransigent conflicts which arise from time to time within these non-legal institutions will require resolution by some independent authority – a role which modern societies often assign to the law. In such cases it is difficult to see how the law could make such decisions without imposing its own version of reality, constructed according to its rules and procedures for producing truth. However hard one tries to avoid the law, therefore, it would seem that ultimately, in the absence of some alternative higher authority, one would need to return to it for these 'difficult cases'.

If law, as Luhmann suggests, has the function in modern societies of maintaining and stabilizing normative expectations and so avoiding the need to learn from experience, it would be ill-advised to ask the legal system to renounce totally its epistemic authority. Moreover, if children's rights as human beings are to be respected, the problematic nature of the legal system in handling children's cases cannot simply be avoided by assigning to other more appropriate institutions the decisions for which, traditionally, law has been responsible. We would suggest, however, that this dilemma should be put in somewhat different terms than those of 'rights', 'responsibilities' and 'duties' which legal scholars and statutory draughtsmen have traditionally employed. Furthermore, it is unrealistic for reformers to attempt to transform the legal system into an institution ideally suited to deal with children's cases, for it can never be this. What needs to be done, rather, is to restrain and restrict the self-reproducing regularities of law in ways which allow the special nature of children, as developing human beings who respond to the environment and are affected by that environment differently to adults, to be addressed and accommodated. In a similar vein, while accepting that all versions of the social world are constructions, law needs procedures which allow and encourage the complexities and uncertainties of child development to enter the decision-making process, rather than being denied altogether, or reduced and simplified by that process to the point of total distortion. While law's constructions, and that of any institution, must necessarily be selective and reductionist, there are degrees of selectivity and reduction-ism, and, therefore, the effectiveness of any legal system to handle children's issues may be judged in part by its success in restraining these tendencies.

## 2   Child-responsive law

Buildings may be judged for their child-responsiveness by assessing how well architects and designers have restrained their tendencies to design with only adults users and adult activities in mind. Door handles and light switches could, for example, be fixed at a height where they do not impede the mobility and independence of a child of 7 or older. Safety measures, such as thick carpeting and stair gates, may be provided to protect very young children, and opaque safety glass be used in doors for active older children. In the same way, child-responsive criteria may usefully be applied to different legal systems.

The final chapter of our book makes a preliminary attempt to do just this. This attempt does not aim at comprehensiveness, either in terms of possible child-responsive criteria or different legal systems. What we are concerned to do, rather, is to provide some examples of 'good practice' and 'bad practice'. Moreover, it should not be imagined that we are so naïve as to believe that those legal systems which have achieved a high level of child-responsiveness are necessarily *better* in any absolute terms than those lower down the league table. It may be inevitable, for example, that, in being more responsive to children, a system will be less fair to adults. It may also be that the stringent procedural protections that apply, for example, in the criminal prosecutions of adults will detract from the child-responsiveness of criminal prosecutions of children. These matters clearly raise important social policy issues, but if, as we propose, social policy should be based upon the broad notion of children's rights that we have defined, then restraint of those aspects of legal systems which actually or potentially cause harm to children must be the first and overriding objective. Of course, one may, in some situations, be left with a difficult choice between different types of harm. Here, the solution must be to apply to each individual case existing child welfare science knowledge concerning the nature and seriousness of these different harms, and choose the course of action which, in the light of this knowledge, is likely to cause the least damage to the child.

Another way of approaching the same issue would be to restrict the application of legal operations to the task of endorsing or rejecting, purely on legal grounds, decisions made according to child welfare criteria, following the procedures of child welfare science. Rather than engaging in the confusing process of using legal procedures to determine what is best for the child's interests, the courts would leave this task to those institutions which could be relied upon to undertake the investigation and decision-making in ways that were least disruptive to the child and family. The task of the legal system would be confined to ensuring that minimum safeguards against unfairness and intrusiveness were respected, and, where appropriate, to give legal authority to any decision made.

The perennial problem of 'tyranny by experts' could be avoided by the involvement in the process of independent non-experts (but not lawyers), and by the courts having a duty to promote co-operation and consent between those to be affected by the decision, including the child.

The alternative, and more optimistic, ending to our book takes the form, therefore, of an examination of different legal systems in order to identify those procedural features and conceptual approaches which allow the law to incorporate and apply the knowledge of child welfare science in ways which do not risk harming the very children and adolescents which it seeks to protect and whose welfare it seeks to promote.

## II A comparative account

### 1 Contest or enquiry: the great divide

'Inquisitorial' and 'adversarial' are the usual terms employed by lawyers to describe the differences that exist between the legal systems which follow the European tradition of civil law and those which derive their traditions from the English common law. The adversarial way of proceeding supposedly takes the form of a contest or dispute, where the contestants engage one another according to the legal rules of procedure before the judge, a passive arbiter, whose sole task is to reach a decision. In the inquisitorial mode, by contrast, proceedings are supposedly structured as an official enquiry where officials of the court perform most of the activities.

At this point, critics of the Anglo-American style of justice could well point out how inappropriate and lacking in child-responsiveness is a system which turns problems into contests and individuals seeking solutions to problems into disputants. How much better a system that conducts matters in the spirit of an enquiry. However, as Damaska (1986) points out, one frequently finds adversarial features in supposedly inquisitorial systems, and inquisitorial features in adversarial systems. We have already mentioned, for example, that care proceedings in English Magistrate's Courts have been characterized by the Appeal Court as 'objective inquiries'.

According to Damaska, therefore, this dichotomy between adversarial and inquisitorial is at best useful in the way that architectural styles are useful rough-and-ready classifications of buildings, but:

> If narrow and sterile constructs are to be avoided, the background against which lawyers oppose, contest and inquest, official and party control, and similar principles of the legal process must be explored. Moreover vain attempts to express by the core of the contrast between continental and Anglo-American administration of justice by juxtaposing such concepts [*as inquisitorial and adversarial*] must also be abandoned. Most features that constitute the essential contrast cannot be captured by them, especially if one's vision extends beyond the narrow area of criminal procedure. (1986, p.9, original emphasis)

To see the issue of child-responsiveness in terms of adversarial versus inquisitorial procedures, with all the positive elements being on the side of the inquisitorial, is too simple an analysis. Similarly, those who propose the adoption of an inquisitorial process as the solution to the difficulties of Anglo-American jurisdictions are likely to be disappointed with the results. Whatever the nature of the legal procedures, the antagonistic nature of the confrontation of interests that the law projects and reproduces will continue to exist and affect the degree to which children may be harmed by the legal process.[3]

Take, for example, the role of lawyers, who, despite their involvement in a process designed to promote the child's welfare and secure the child's best interests, still talk about 'winning' and 'losing'. Success in the legal profession tends to be judged not according to how good a lawyer is at improving the lives of children, but how effectively that lawyer secures the best outcome for their client. The powerful clients are those who return repeatedly to the courts with new cases. In cases concerning children's welfare, these are public bodies such as social services, education and health departments of local authorities.

The operation of the Divorce Courts in France, working within a wholly inquisitorial system, serves to illustrate the problem of changing the lawyers' role, even in a system which is not adversarial in nature and in cases where there are no powerful public bodies as clients. The changes that occurred in the French law towards the end of the 1970s attempted to confer upon lawyers the role of reconcilers and conciliators. Yet, as a psychiatrist commenting on these changes wrote: 'one must not under-estimate the combative force of any divorce procedure which obliges a lawyer to identify with the cause he is representing.'[4] She went on to state with certainty that numerous French lawyers were in no way ready to take on this role of mediator.[5]

An inquisitorial procedure on its own, therefore, does not necessarily remove the antagonistic element from legal cases concerning the welfare of children. One needs to search more deeply for those positive elements which help to restrain the potentially harmful tendencies of the law. This conclusion clearly played a part in the introduction in France of a new cadre of specialist judges to deal with the problems created for the law by the large increase in divorce in the 1960s and 1970s and, in particular, by the numbers of children affected by the involvement of their parents in divorce proceedings. Thus:

> the draughtsmen of the law of 1975 intended that the *juge aux affaires matrimoniales* should be present at *every stage* in *all* the proceedings relating to a divorce, because his presence offers a warranty of efficiency and security. In order to achieve this objective a specialist category of judges would be introduced who are trained in the unusual complexities of these procedures – complexities which are no more than legal projections of emotional situations which are even more complex and entangled. (Lienhard, 1985, p.188, original emphasis)

The law, according to this view, does not create the emotional chaos which characterizes many divorces, but it was possible for the legal process within the European Continental tradition to structure these emotions by providing specialist judges and continuity in decision-making. This tradition allowed the image of the judge to be conceived in quasi-administrative terms. The judge becomes almost a trustee of the divorce, a guarantor that the child's interests will be protected. While lawyers in French divorce proceedings continue to represent their clients' interests, both in and out of court, the judges, more than the lawyers, shape the proceedings and frame the issues which need to be decided.

Seen in Teubner's terms, the attempt by the French divorce law to react in a 'responsive' way to emotional complexities cannot achieve satisfactory results, for it can only augment the confusion of discourses and structures. The fact, for example, that a much higher proportion of divorces in France than in the UK are contested[6] may indicate the continued dominance of the legal discourse, despite the specialized judiciary and the continuity they offer. It is possible that the obligatory representation by lawyers of parties to divorce proceedings guarantees the continuance of this domination. Moreover, largely as a result of the deliberate policy to make the legal system more responsive rather than provide alternatives to the legal process, the out-of-court mediation movement which has flourished in the USA (and, more recently, in the UK) is much less developed in France. Many would argue that these alternative dispute-resolution forums may be more effective than the legal process in protecting the rights of children, and that the best way to restrain the harmful impact of the law is to remove the issues of parental contact with children and the residence of children from the legal arena entirely.

If child-responsiveness is difficult enough to achieve in a Continental European system, how much more so in the Anglo-American tradition of generalist judges, appointed for their reputation as lawyers, and where the legal profession rather than the judiciary frame the issues and present the arguments for the court to decide. Under these conditions, the attempt by policy-makers to protect children's interests by imposing inquisitorial procedures seems a hopelessly inadequate gesture.

If the ideal conditions for child-responsiveness can exist only outside the legal system, how does one explain the apparent successful operation of the French *juge des enfants*, which, while operating within the court structure, nevertheless seems to contain all the features that one would require of a child-responsive system? One interpretation would be that there is, in fact, very little of the legal coding of lawful/unlawful in evidence. If one concentrates on child protection cases, almost all decisions are made following informal discussions in the judge's room. Lawyers hardly ever attend these discussions. The children, even quite young children, are present and able to talk directly with the judge. The law merely sets out the principles for the decision-making process. It does not offer any substantive case law as to what is lawful or unlawful behaviour on the part of parents, or under what conditions children should be removed from the family. Many decisions follow the advice and recommendations of the court social workers (*éducateurs*), who work with the judge, or of psychiatric or psychological experts. Indeed, all that links this process to the legal system is the physical location of the judge's room within the law courts, and the fact that the decision-maker is a judge, albeit a judge who in most instances will not have worked on any other type of case than those involving children. It would not be too far-fetched, therefore, to see the jurisdiction of the *juge des enfants* as one where reflexive rather than substantive law operates, and where the dominant discourse is not law, but child welfare science.

## 2   Written and live testimony

At a later stage in his book, Damaska (1986, p.61) identifies as one of the principal features that has distinguished Continental and English admin-istration of justice the fact that the former relies for evidence upon records in the file and the latter on oral communication. While in common law countries documents have assumed an increasing importance, 'no real counterpart', Damaska tells us, 'has emerged of the official file as the chief repository of information on which adjudicators can predicate their judgement'. Since common law countries still rely to a high degree upon the 'day-in-court trial', the differences between the two traditions may have serious implications for children's interests.

The evidence of young children, as we have seen, may pose problems of enormous proportions for common law jurisdictions. Elaborate video links and the screening off of child witnesses have to be brought into play in order to enable children to give evidence which could be crucial to the outcome of the proceedings. Many allegations of sexual abuse in England and Wales never reach the courts,[7] simply because any proceedings, whether civil or criminal, depend for their success upon the oral evidence of a young child, and those officials responsible for initiating proceedings believe that the child would not be able to give evidence in open court, or that the ordeal of involvement in court proceedings would cause unnecessary harm to the child.

The day-in-court trial, where the written information available to the decision-makers is severely restricted by rules of evidence, may, in some cases, result in outcomes for the child which would have been very different had a particular witness been willing and available to give oral evidence: 'The disappearance of a single witness can ruin even a carefully prepared case' (Damaska, 1986, p.61). This strict interpretation of the primary evidence rule may well have some justification in criminal trials where the court has the power to send an accused person to prison for a long period, as in child sex-abuse trials,[8] or where a person's reputation and livelihood is at stake. It is hardly appropriate where the declared objective of the court is to protect a child or find a solution to a pressing problem concerning that child's welfare. The rule also prevents one witness giving information about what another person may have said. This may cause particular problems where child care agencies wish to provide information to the court concerning the relationship between parents and children over a long period and staff changes have made it difficult or impossible to trace all social workers who have been involved in the case.

Even where there are no restrictions on the admissibility of evidence, legal systems may differentially establish, for fact-finding purposes, a hierarchy of reliability. The word of a psychiatrist may, for example, carry more weight than that of a social worker, even where the social worker is much more familiar with the child and family (see pages 53–55). That social worker, in turn, may be treated as a more credible, more authoritative witness than a member of the child's family. As David Nelken puts it: 'Establishing the truth of events may . . . depend upon finding people with the appropriate reputation and authority to bear witness rather than discovering a witness to the event' (Nelken, 1990, p.25).

The main argument in favour of retaining strict rules of evidence is that it is dangerous to allow all information to be available where the decision-makers are not sufficiently trained or experienced to give the appropriate weight to different types of information and, in particular, to treat such potentially prejudicial evidence as a defendant's previous criminal record with appropriate caution. This explains why, in the hierarchy of English and many Commonwealth courts, hearsay is admitted in the higher courts, where the decision-makers are experienced professional judges, but excluded in the lower courts, where lay magistrates decide cases. This problem does not arise in Continental countries, where the use of lay people in the legal system is tightly restricted and controlled by the professional judiciary.[9] This admission of part-time lay decision-makers, therefore, marks an important difference between Continental and Anglo-American systems – a difference, moreover, which has several repercussions for the ways in which children's cases are handled in the courts.

## 3  Lay people or professionals

Clearly, there are strong arguments in favour of lay participation in the legal process, the most important of which being to prevent professionals adopting an inward-looking, cloistered perspective and developing values which are remote from those of 'ordinary people'. The question that we need to ask in the context of children's issues is not, therefore, 'Should there be lay participation?', but rather, 'How may lay people participate without affecting the legal process in ways which potentially cause harm to children?'

We have already examined the 'potential harm' to children that may be caused by rules which are designed to assist inexperienced lay people in assessing the evidence before them. A far greater harm may be caused, however, by the organization of cases in ways which are amenable to part-time lay participation. Ideally, cases that fall to lay decision-makers should occur within a continuous time block, preferably over a period of no longer than one day. In this way the working lives and other extra-judicial activities of the ordinary men and women who sit in the courts is not unduly interrupted. Thus the petty criminal cases that were assigned to English lay magistrates for verdicts and sentencing decisions were perfect for this purpose. The problems begin, however, when the cases to be heard by lay people stretch over several days. This may occur where the decision-making is of an episodic nature rather than a one-off nature. This may happen where an immediate decision has to be made to deal with an emergency that has arisen, then further intermediate decisions are required until all the evidence has been accumulated and marshalled for the final court hearing. It may also occur where, instead of being completed in a single time block, the case spills over, so that the lay decision-makers are forced to disrupt their extra-judicial lives.

In practice, there are two ways of resolving such problems. The first is to arrange for different lay decision-makers to be involved at the different stages, so that the episodes come to resemble separate, isolated 'stories'.[10] The other is to retain the same lay decision-makers throughout, but to organize the hearings of the case in ways that are compatible with their part-time participation. If, for example, the lay decision-makers are able to attend court on one day of the week only, hearings will be adjourned from one week to the next until the case has finally been decided.

These factors affecting the organization of hearings are less of a problem in those systems which allow much of the evidence to take the form of written statements and reports. Here the lay participants may, literally, take the evidence home with them and consider it outside court hours. The hearings in such jurisdictions are likely to be short, as they will consist of clarifications of any ambiguities in the evidence, and submissions of arguments and discussions among the decision-makers themselves as to the appropriate outcome.

If we accept that legal systems will, for reasons unrelated to the welfare of children, continue to include lay people in one capacity or another in decision-making, the criterion of child-responsiveness would require certain restraints to be exercised in those cases where children's interests are at stake. These include, firstly, removing all restrictions on the kind of information that might be presented, so long as it is relevant to the child's situation; secondly, abolishing rules of evidence which tend to prolong court cases, such as those which restrict documentary and insist upon live testimony, in so far as this can be done without detracting from the reliability of such evidence; thirdly, insisting that, whatever may be the practice in other types of case, where children's interests are concerned, decision-makers who are familiar with the facts of the child's life and with the various people likely to affect the child's development continue to act in that capacity rather than handing over to strangers to the case, and fourthly, avoiding the likelihood of situations arising where decisions are delayed because of the unavailability of decision-makers.

It is possible that these restraints will not be achievable in some jurisdictions except by relegating lay decision-makers to a relatively minor role. Indeed, it is only by restricting lay participation in this way that the systems operating, for example, in France and Holland are able to provide a structure which is able to meet these criteria.[11] However, Scottish Children's Panels (see pages 113–115), which consist entirely of part-time lay people, are able to go a long way towards meeting these ideals. This has been achieved by accepting for lay decision-making only those cases where there is agreement over the facts, and by introducing the professional Reporter to collect these facts and present them to the panel members in a form which provides a framework for rapid decision-making. Continuity between panels making decisions at different times about the same child is attempted in Scotland by a rule which states that at least one Children's Panel member from the panel of three which originally heard the case should be present at all subsequent hearings.

The system which, in our experience, fails entirely to meet these child-responsive requirements is that operating in English Magistrate's Courts. These courts combine lay decision-makers (usually three) with day-in-court hearings. The complexities of cases often mean that there are several preliminary hearings before the final trial, often including a long interim hearing. The bench of magistrates may be different for each of these hearings, and there is no guarantee that those magistrates adjudicating the trial will have had any prior knowledge of the child or his or her situation. Indeed, the criminal court ethic which pervades child care proceedings prefers that the trial bench should come to the case afresh, so that the magistrates are not prejudiced by past information that they may have received about the case.[12]

Adherence for the most part to oral evidence to be presented in full, cross-examined and re-examined, means that cases where the need for care and protection is contested by parents may continue over several days.

Given the extra-judicial commitments of the lay magistrates, these days are unlikely to be consecutive, but may continue over several weeks. Although, once the trial has begun, every effort is made to ensure continuity, it is sometimes the case that the bench changes its membership during the course of the trial. Regardless of the qualities of individual magistrates or the worthy attempts to provide them with specialist training, the structure of the court organization is such that it is difficult to conceive a system of justice which is less child-responsive than that operating in English Magistrate's Courts, where the broad rights of children receive less consideration than the need to maintain the court's organizational structure.

Moreover, the legal result – which of the lawyer's arguments wins the day, which version of 'the facts' is accepted, and why – may become something of an irrelevance where harm has been caused to the child's prospects through the uncertainty and insecurity caused by delays and the insistence of the court upon procedural niceties.

This potential for harm is both diminished and increased by the recent introduction of the guardian *ad litem*[13] – an independent social worker whose task it is to advise the magistrates on the child's wishes and interests. This in some way compensates for the lack of expertise and continuity among judicial decision-makers. Ideally, it also provides the child with an advocate who will not see issues in terms of fairness to the parents or punishing them for their villainy, but concentrate on the best arrangements to promote that child's welfare. However, the price to be paid is long delays, for the guardian *ad litem* cannot be appointed until after proceedings have been begun, and the investigations are often long and complex. Unlike the French children's judges, the English magistrates cannot deal with issues concerning the child's future welfare until the case has been heard in full. They cannot, for example, adjourn the case indefinitely on an interim order in the hope that there will be no need for the matter to go to a full hearing.

## 4   Episodic intervention versus continuous process

The issue of continuity deserves further development, since it both epitomizes an essential difference between Continental European and Anglo-American systems and, at the same time, has important repercussions for children's cases. Clearly, it is not simply a question of judicial style, with lay part-time judges favouring the day-in-court trial while professional full-time judges prefer a more continuous process. Even where professional judges decide cases in the Anglo-American system, it is only rarely that they make an effort to retain some judicial supervision of the child and family. Even in English wardship proceedings, where the child actually remains a ward of court and the court has to be consulted before any major decision can be made affecting that child's life, it is only when the judge specifically asks for all future matters to be referred to him or her personally that any continuity of decision-maker is maintained. Where supervision orders are made by magistrates or judges in civil or criminal proceedings in England, further referrals to the court for revocation of the order or breach of the conditions of subversion will often mean that the case comes before a judge or bench of magistrates who have no prior knowledge of the child or family. Contrast this with the French *juge des enfants* or the Dutch Juvenile Court judge, who retain the dossiers of particular children or whole families within their personal jurisdiction until the file is closed or the judge moves to another post.

Damaska relates the Continental legal process to the hierarchical organization of legal officialdom in these countries:

> because hierarchy is multilayered, proceedings must consist of several stages. And because this apparatus is also partial to functional specialization, it is normal to expect that the stages be assigned methodical subtasks. One stage can be devoted to the gathering and organization of relevant material, another to the initial decision, still another to hierarchical review and so on . . . (1986, pp.47–8)

Kafka's hero, 'K', therefore, was not 'tried' as such; he was 'implicated in proceedings', the original German title of the book being *Der Prozess.*

Lawyers trained in the Anglo-American tradition often find it shocking, however, that judges in Continental jurisdictions exercise wide powers of intervention in the lives of children under provisional orders before any formal finding of child abuse or criminal guilt, and that these provisional orders may take effect immediately, even where there are no arrangements made for a final hearing. Unlike in Anglo-American jursidictions, if no further offences are committed, or the child continues in care, the child's case is typically reviewed by the judge at regular intervals. For Continental jurists, however, these measures present no problems. The process is a continuous one. It may be prolonged at any stage where this is considered necessary in the child's interests, or to see how the child responds to the treatment ordered or to a period of residence in a particular family situation. In fact, many cases, both criminal and civil, under this system never reach the stage of formal hearing in open court, but are dealt with by provisional measures.[14]

In delinquency cases, the tendency is at its most extreme in jurisdictions which systematically prosecute young people who commit crimes, rather than dealing with them as being in need of protection, and which see children in terms of specific acts or episodes. If it is possible to inhibit or remove altogether the tendency of the law to concentrate on single acts, and see lawbreaking by children as part of a lengthy maturing and socializing process, then the necessary structures may be erected to allow decision-makers to reflect in their decisions the rapidly changing nature of childhood by, for example, permitting them to try out different measures and, if unsuccessful, adjust them accordingly. Such adjustments are not possible in a system which intervenes from time to time, and allows decisions to be made by people who see no more than an episodic glimpse of events in the child's life.

One must, however, be cautious before reaching such a seemingly obvious conclusion. If Teubner's ideas are to be taken seriously, the reconstruction of the child and its problems by the law is not necessarily a good thing. It may well be preferable for some other institution to take responsibility for formulating the substantive issues concerning the child's welfare, referring matters to the law only in exceptional circumstances. This is what some Anglo-American jurisdictions have sought to achieve, but have found considerable difficulty in sustaining, when faced with pressure from legalistic rights campaigners, complaining of the tyranny of experts, the absence of formal procedures and the dangers of informal resolution of disputes and extolling the wisdom of judicial decision-making.[15] The result has been a hybrid system which, after the initial 'final' decision, offers judicial intervention at the behest of a parent, the child or a state's prosecution or child protection agency, but gives no guarantee that the decision-makers at subsequent hearings will be acquainted with the child's history, except in so far as this is brought before them as evidence in the new proceedings. Each new application before the court is treated, therefore, as if the only valid knowledge before the court is that set out in past court orders. These orders apart, the slate is clean and the parties must start afresh.

One argument in favour of this fresh start every time the parties go to the courts concerns certainty and finality. It may well be, in some cases, where there is no chance of rehabilitation of a child in its family, that a final, irrevocable decision to end contact between child and parents and allow substitute parents to commit themselves to the child and for the child to feel secure with them may be preferable to a system in which such finality is difficult to achieve. In France, for example, adoptions without parental agreement, or orders disqualifying parental rights, are rare compared to Anglo-American countries.[16] There is certainly a strong case to be made out against delays and procrastinations where the welfare of children is concerned.[17] Yet this is a far cry, we would suggest, from advocating a system which treats decision-making about children's continuing relationships with adults as if they were isolated problems, confined and defined by the label which the legal system applies to them.

One final matter in favour of continuity concerns not the welfare of individual children, but the knowledge and expertise of the decision-makers. Any decision-making organization, if it is to be effective, needs information on the results of its decisions. A general criticism of judicial decision-making, particularly in criminal cases, is that, where the judges see the results of their decisions, these results are almost entirely negative; in other words, they see only the failures. Those offenders who stay out of trouble do not return to the court. In cases where the court's objective is to promote the welfare of children, this flow of information concerning the outcome of decisions is of particular importance if judges are to learn from experience. Conversely, where no such information is available or only negative outcomes are referred back to the judge, the system is likely to encourage judges either to fall back on their commonsense notions of what is good for children in their choice of measures, or to develop a total cynicism about the effectiveness of any judicial action. This does not mean to say that all judges become bigots or cynics. Many obtain general information about outcomes through other sources, such as training courses. Others, such as part-time lay people, may have acquired such knowledge through their extra-judicial work. What it does mean, however, is that, where the organization of the legal system concerned with children's issues is of the episodic type, the extent to which decision-makers can improve their performance through learning 'on the job' is severely limited. They may learn how to conduct themselves in court; they may learn what the law and rules of evidence of procedure say on particular issues, but they are unlikely to learn much about the effect of their decisions upon the children and families who appear before them.

In some jurisdictions, particularly those in Continental countries which use specialist children's judges, continuity, achieved through assigning particular children and families to specific judges, is assured.[18] Of course, this is no guarantee of decision-making quality, but the conditions for learning by experiences are at least present. The same can hardly be said to be true in some of the lower courts in Anglo-American countries.

## III  Child-responsive specialists

To see the legal system as driven by the people who work in the law is at odds with the theoretical perspective we have adopted in this book. This emphasizes, rather, the law as an institution generating legal communications giving rise to roles and tasks which are filled and fulfilled by people whose attributes answer law's demands for further legal communications. Historically, the legal tradition has sought out decision-makers whose attributes include impartiality, detachment, an extensive and detailed knowledge of the law, the ability to absorb and extract relevant issues from large amounts of information, and a desire to exercise power. Not surprisingly, 'child-responsiveness' or any attributes that one might associate with responsiveness to children and their rights, broadly defined, does not appear on this list. However, most Western industrialized countries have, in the past forty years, been moving some way towards the specialization of children's issues. In some jurisdictions this has involved the development of a specialist children's judiciary or specialist advocates to handle children's issues.

# 1   The judiciary

Of all the Continental countries, France has probably gone further than others down the road of creating a specialist children's judiciary in the form of the *juge des enfants* (see pages 113 and 149–150) who handles all child protection and juvenile delinquency cases which reach the courts. Most, though not all, French *juges des enfants* have made a positive decision to specialize in children's issues.[19] Those who remain *juges des enfants* for more than two years do so because this is the work they wish to do. This self-selection, together with the highly discretionary nature of the decision-making and the continuous daily contact with social workers and child care experts, has tended to generate a role identity and role requirements which are very different from those traditionally associated with the judiciary.[20] These include a working knowledge of child development, family systems theory, skills of communication with children, familiarity with recent research by child specialists concerning the types of issues which frequently arise in the cases before them, and an acquaintance with the range of facilities offered within their own jurisdiction which aim to help children with particular problems. The *juge des enfants* will, therefore, attend lectures and conferences, will go on courses and receive training in these areas of knowledge. This education and training is seen as part of the job, and is subsidized and promoted by the French Ministry of Justice. *Juges des enfants*, for example, are encouraged to attend courses and conferences on child psychology and family dynamics.[21]

This notion that children need specialist judges has also found favour in several other European countries, including Holland, Germany, Spain and Belgium. Furthermore, several European countries have also introduced specialist branches of the police and specialist prosecutors to handle child abuse and neglect cases, as well as prosecutions against children.[22]

The inherent tendency towards specialization of Continental legal systems, combined with the existence of professional career judges, most of whom are recruited in their mid-to-late twenties, has made it relatively easy for these systems to develop a child-responsive judiciary. In Anglo-American countries, however, the same favourable conditions do not exist. Obstacles include, firstly, the fact that judges are usually appointed from among the ranks of practising lawyers, for whom child-responsiveness is not a highly prized attribute; in some jurisdictions they are even elected or appointed on a 'political ticket'. Secondly, the nature of the adversary system is such that, unlike their Continental counterparts, they often have little control over the way in which the issues are defined in court. Finally, the generalist tradition of the common law has demanded judges who may handle criminal trials and civil disputes with equal competence, and who make no distinction between the general principles involved in determining financial and property matters and those which concern delicate human relationships.

Within the Anglo-American tradition, the move towards specialization has tended to take the form less of creating a child-responsive judiciary than of bringing together all issues concerning the family under one judicial roof – the Family Court. These family matters are likely to include finances and property, divorce and judicial separation, and violence between spouses. They are not thus confined to children's cases. Some (for example, New York) classify juvenile crime as a family matter, to be dealt with by the Family Court judge, while most (for example, England and Wales, the state of Victoria, the Republic of Ireland and many North American jurisdictions) have specialized Juvenile or Children's Courts for this purpose. While in most of these arrangements judges are specialized in the sense that they work only within these courts, rarely are they specially trained in or selected for child-responsive attributes.

Given the difficulties within the Anglo-American tradition of creating a professional, specialist children's judiciary, the alternative strategy of seeking part-time lay people to fill this specialist role has sometimes been adopted.[23] The Scottish Children's Panel members are one example.[24] These panel members are truly specialists, being selected, trained and appointed exclusively to handle child welfare and juvenile delinquency decisions to determine the child's best interests. Moving south to England and Wales, the lay magistracy also offers specialism in the Family Proceedings or Youth Courts. Here, however, the magistrates sitting in these courts are originally appointed to the adult Criminal Court, where they are required to spend a period before becoming eligible for election to the specialist panels.[25] Moreover, they continue to sit in the adult court in addition to carrying out their Family Proceedings and Youth Court duties. The ideal of generalism, or at least that the magistrates should have 'a good grounding' and continue to maintain their skills in traditional judicial decision-making, seems to be more important here than the development of child-responsive knowledge and skills.

The specialized judiciary that we have described so far is confined to the courts of first instance, or lower courts. In some jurisdictions, the specialist children's judge or magistrate may sit with other judges on appeals,[26] but as, a general rule, the higher one proceeds up the court hierarchy, the less the tendency towards specialization. A notable exception, however, is the Family Division in England, where High Court judges may, under their inherent powers of wardship, take cases without the earlier intervention of a lower court.[27] The specialization of these judges has developed through demand, rather than through any clear strategy to create child specialists at this level. They are few in number, so that it is frequently the case that deputy judges, who often have no experience or limited experience in handling children's issues, are called in to relieve their case load. It is worth, at this point, making the contrast with France, where it would be inconceivable for a Criminal Court judge to deputize for a *juge des enfants* in a child protection hearing.

The problems that Anglo-American courts have encountered recently when confronted with the need to take evidence from young child victims of sexual assaults has highlighted the extent to which the legal systems operating in many jurisdictions had, up to that point, either treated children as totally incompetent as witnesses, or competent only if they could behave like adults. The adjustments to procedures, such as video links[28] and the use of pre-recorded videos, represent an attempt to make these systems more child-responsive without any major changes either to the organization of the legal system or to the personnel who operate it. Some countries, as we have noted (see page 69), have introduced child psychologists to interview the child and to report to the court, both on what the child said happened and on their assessment of the reliability of the child's evidence. The strategy here, therefore, is one of 'importing' trained specialists in child-responsiveness, rather than attempting to change the traditional judicial attributes. It would seem that the law, in ways that Teubner's model would have predicted, prefers to hand over part of its decision-making function to 'scientific experts' rather than undergo any changes to its own traditions.[29]

The different functions of the judiciary in the Continental and in the Anglo-American systems may be put forward as a partial explanation for the failure of the latter to produce a specialist judiciary for children's issues. It could be argued that judges in the Anglo-American system are no more than impartial arbiters of the issues presented to them by the parties. Their role is not to question witnesses or to raise issues, but rather to allow the courtroom drama to unfold before them. Up to a point, this is true. Lay magistrates in English Juvenile Courts, for example, rarely ask questions or attempt to extract the issues which they consider important. However, the more extensive the use made of the courts for deciding issues of child welfare, the more the judge is placed in a position of having to walk onto the stage instead of just watching from the balcony. This is particularly so in those cases which are not strongly contested, or where the issue of a child's welfare is raised not by the parties, but by the court itself. Judges, for example, may request reports from experts, and may even formulate the questions that they wish these experts to answer. In the interpretation of these reports, child-responsive knowledge is likely to be of more use or of more benefit to the child's welfare than traditional legal knowledge. Having made this point, it must also be admitted that, in Anglo-American jursidictions, it is lawyers, not judges, who have responsibility for the collection or presentation of evidence. These are tasks where child-responsive skills, knowledge and attitudes should operate to restrain those wiles, strategies and antagonistic attitudes traditionally associated with litigation.

## 2 Child-responsive advocates

In the case of lawyers, the attributes that the law has tended to encourage and reward include the ability to express oneself cogently and persuasively to other adults in oral and written communications, the ability to communicate effectively with adult clients, negotiation skills and strategic skills in the deployment of arguments and in tactical manoeuvring to win cases or, at least, obtain the best possible outcome for their clients. Some of these attributes, it needs hardly be stated, are equally important for cases involving children's issues as they are for those where only adults are affected by the decisions. This is particularly true where older children are concerned. Here the children may be treated very much as if they were adults. Indeed, many will have reached physical and intellectual maturity, even if their emotional development and experience of the world may be limited. Others may not have reached such levels of maturity, and, in acting for them and for younger children, the traditional legal skills, knowledge and attitudes may need restraint and the substitution of different attributes.

Increasingly in many Anglo-American jurisdictions, the concept of the specialist children's rights' lawyer is emerging.[30] In England, for example, the Law Society, which is responsible for the training and validation of solicitors, has drawn up panels of solicitors who, it considers, are qualified to represent children in child care cases. These solicitors will have attended training courses on child law and on matters related to their role in court proceedings. They will also have had experience in appearing for children.

As we remarked earlier, this development is very much within the legal tradition of children's rights – that is, giving children the same procedural protections as are available for adults. It does not, so far, reflect the broader version of children's rights which would involve a very different breed of lawyer – whose role would include protecting their clients from the harm caused by insensitive legal intervention and the indifference to children's welfare of the traditional legal discourse. Those who are part of that intervention and who operate very much within that legal discourse can hardly be expected to protect children against their own functioning as lawyers. This would appear to be a major problem in any attempts to make lawyers more child-responsive, since true child-responsiveness, over and above the acquisition of superficial skills of communication, really demands that they stop being lawyers. Does this indeed happen when lawyers operate outside the confines of the courts?

To some extent we have already seen the answer to this question in Chapter 5, when we examined the problems that arise when lawyers are actively involved in the divorce conciliation or mediation process. As we saw, child welfare issues often become distorted or set to one side, so that the settlement or final court order comes to reflect the normative principles of the law and its general lack of concern for consequences. The involvement of lawyers and other purveyors of the legal discourse in child protection and juvenile justice has, we would suggest, similar problems. These are likely to exist, regardless of the good intentions of the legal profession and the 'understanding' that may appear to exist between legal and non-law professionals. This is certainly true wherever the legal discourse is allowed to dominate through the shadowy presence of the court or through the decision-making power of the legal professionals.

Even outside the confines of the formal courtroom or the court buildings, therefore, the active participation of lawyers, police, investigating magistrates, etc. in a child-responsive decision-making system risks the eventual colonization of that system by the legal discourse. Only where the power of the legal professional is severely restricted and where the ultimate adjudication is made according to child welfare science rather than legal principles is this colonization likely to be avoided.

The other development in child-responsive advocacy is for non-lawyers with the appropriate skills, training and experience to be appointed to represent children's interests in legal proceedings. Ideally, these advocates are not themselves a party to the proceedings in the sense that they would be personally affected by the outcome. The English system's guardian *ad litem*, who may appear in adoption and child protection cases, is an example of this type of advocate. The clinic staff attached to Victoria's Children's Courts who may be called upon to prepare an assessment of the issues and a recommendation for the child's future, and the Safeguarder in the Scottish system,[31] are other examples. This strategy would appear to us to be a preferable way of restraining the law and making it more responsive to children than that of trying to convert lawyers into social workers. Once again, however, it has the effect of reducing the decision-making authority of the judiciary. This is particularly true in the case of a lay part-time judiciary, who are likely to be under considerable pressure in many cases to defer to the opinion of a child advocate who is skilled and knowledgeable in matters concerning children's welfare.

# IV   Conclusion

We made it clear from the outset that our book is not directly concerned with reforming the law or improving legal systems relating to children. Our objectives started out as analytical and didactic, rather than political or polemic. However, it would be less than candid for us to deny that our application and development of Gunther Teubner's ideas on the relationship between discourses and reflexive and responsive law, together with our comparative analysis of different legal systems, have focused some of our pre-existing anxieties over legal decision-making concerning children's welfare. While our alternative ending has allowed us to apply theoretical concepts to existing problems concerning the law's involvement with children, it does not offer any easy solutions. What it has done is to draw attention to those aspects of different legal systems which encourage and those which inhibit or prevent altogether the development of *child-responsiveness*.

To summarize, we would identify the negative aspects as follows:

1   A litigious culture which sees taking proceedings in the courts as the first step in any dispute concerning children or any infringement of what the law has defined as the rights of adults or children, regardless of the ability of the law to resolve the issues satisfactorily or to enforce any orders that the courts may make.
2   The adversarial nature of the proceedings, with all the problems and limitations that we have described in the preceding pages, and in particular the day-in-court episodic nature of these proceedings.
3   The extensive use of lawyers to filter and define the issues in terms which reflect the interests of their adult clients, or according to narrow, individualized legal concepts. The inequalities created by any system that relies so heavily upon hired advocates, but does not ensure that all parties have equal access to the best legal representation and to the resources necessary for the preparation of cases for court.

4    The use of part-time, non-professional judges as the principal decision-makers at the first tier of legal proceedings, not only on account of their possible lack of understanding of complex psychological concepts, but also because of its distorting effects upon the decision-making process. Almost inevitably, this process becomes episodic rather than continuous, and the lack of confidence and expertise among decision-makers is likely to thwart any attempt to make the proceedings more inquisitorial. The potential for long delays is also increased considerably by the limited availability of these decision-makers.

5    The use in some jurisdictions of non-specialist judges to hear complex children's issues. More generally, the lack of accountability of the judiciary for decisions which damage children, and their ignorance about the likely effects of their decisions upon the children whose welfare they are trying to promote.

6    The emphasis placed upon the status and qualifications of providers of information, at the expense of the reliability of that information. We refer in particular to the preferential treatment often given to the court by those defined as 'experts', while others who have known the child intimately for long periods are either ignored entirely as credible sources of information, or little weight is given to the information which they offer.

Clearly, many of these disturbing aspects occur within Anglo-American common law systems, which are much more limited than Continental civil law systems in their ability to adapt in child-responsive ways.

As for the development of positive attributes – those which promote and encourage child-responsiveness – the following features of existing systems appear to us to offer the most promise:

1    Out-of-court mediation processes, which either involve lawyers in a very limited capacity only, or which work in close liaison with the legal profession.[32]

2    A decision-making forum where child welfare science is the dominant discourse, as is to be found in the French *juge des enfants* in the handling of child protection and minor criminal cases, the Dutch Child Protection Council, and, often, but not always, in the Scottish Children's Hearings. There are, of course, serious risks involved in giving unrestricted power to child welfare 'experts'. For this reason we find particularly attractive those systems in which law regulates the procedural fairness of the process, and offers appeals to a legal forum where the principles of due process or natural justice have not been respected. The Dutch combination of Child Protection Council and juvenile judge probably come closest to this ideal.

3   The provision of a children's representative in any formal decision-making forum and in any formal negotiation process concerning the future welfare of a child. We are convinced, however, that the use of lawyers in this role almost inevitably results in the narrowing and individualizing of issues that we have described. We would recommend, therefore, the guardian *ad litem* system operating in some English courts, but not the dominant legal discourse that these courts tend to impose upon all participants. Indeed, the role of the child representative should be not only to promote the child's welfare, but also to protect children's rights in the broad sense of the term, in particular from those harms arising from the legal process itself.

4   Systems which do not demand that children become 'little adults', but are able to adjust to the particular attributes and needs of those children and young people who become involved in legal processes. The Israeli system of youth examiners (see page 69) would appear to have much to recommend it as a method of providing courts with information from children, while at the same time retaining the protection of fair procedures in criminal cases. In Continental civil law countries, judges, prosecutors and police officers who specialize in children's cases are obviously an advantage.

Clearly, any resolution of these issues has to take account of the local conditions existing in each jurisdiction, and it is not our purpose to provide a detailed blueprint for reform for all countries in the world. We do not claim even that the introduction of more child-responsive processes will necessarily lead to the promotion of children's wellbeing, better protection for children, more responsible parenthood or a reduction in juvenile crime. These social policy objectives depend more upon political and economic factors, such as the availability and deployment of resources for improving education, health care and housing, than on decisions of courts and tribunals. However, child-responsiveness as an ideal should go some way to reducing much of the confusion that at present inhabits the law's decision-making apparatus in children's cases and inhibits any progress away from models of understanding that merely serve to rationalize and justify that confusion.

# Notes

1   One example would be laws which insist that children should be consulted before any decisions are made concerning their future welfare. Another example would be the provision of lawyers to represent children in court.

2   The changes in hospital policies over the past twenty years to allow parents to remain overnight in hospital with their sick children is an example of medicine's ability to adapt to children's needs.

3   The limited empirical evidence available indicates that children do poorly in cases of protracted, antagonistic mediation, such as is likely to occur where this is imposed by the courts on uncooperative couples. See Reece (1983, pp.775–83) and Johnston et al. (1985, pp.563–74).

4   Liberman (1984, p.197).

5   It is worth noting here that all parties to divorce proceedings in France are obliged to be represented by a lawyer.

6   In France in 1987, 4,172 (almost 3 per cent) of divorce and judicial separation petitions were rejected by the court. No statistics exist for the proportion of petitions which were contested and subsequently granted. (*Annuaire Statistique de la Justice*, 1987, Ministère de la Justice). In England and Wales, the proportion of divorces which were contested in court in 1988 was 0.1 per cent – 196 out of 173,917 petitions (*Judicial Statistics*, HMSO, 1989).

7   In England and Wales, the Home Office Advisory Group on Video Evidence (the Pigot Committee) was set up in order to recommend ways of improving the situation of child witnesses so that more prosecutions could be mounted. See Home Office (1990).

8   See King (1988); Davies (1988).

9   In France, for example, lay people sit with the judge as assessors in child care and delinquency cases, but only for the final hearing of the case. They play no part in the earlier, often very important, provisional decisions made by the judge. In Holland there are lay representatives on the Child Protection Council, but their responsiblity rarely extends to making important decisions in individual cases, and, where it does, the decisons are made with the advice of professional lawyers and social workers.

10   See Bennett and Feldman (1981).

11   In France two *assesseurs* sitting with the judge in *tribunaux pour enfants* will often be guided by the judge's advice. They do not participate at all in the decisions taken by the judge in chambers. Child Protection Councils in Holland consist of lay people, but their role is similar to that of a management committee, with all the operational decisions being made by professionals.

12   See King (1984).

13   Now subject to ss.42–3 of the Children Act 1989.

14   We are aware that provisions for deferred or delayed sentences exist in Anglo-American jurisdictions, but these are used relatively rarely, and cannot be deployed until after the accused has been convicted.

15   See, for example, Morris et al. (1980); Taylor et al. (1979).

16   In France there can generally be no adoption of a child without parental consent or without a court having pronounced a *declaration d'abandon*. In 1988 only 442 such declarations were made (*Annuaires Statistiques*).

17   See Goldstein et al. (1973).

18   France and Holland are examples.

19   The selection process is complicated, but it is possible for some judges to be assigned for their first post to a Children's Court. Those judges who are unhappy in this role will usually move elsewhere in the legal system after two years.

20   For accounts in English on the selection, training and working practices of the *juges des enfants*, see King and Petit (1985) and Ely and Stanley (1990).

21   These usually take place at the Centre de Recherche Interdisciplinaire de Vaucresson, which is part-financed by the Ministry of Justice.

22   For example, the *Brigade des Mineurs* in France, which operates in most of the major cities.

23   In France, part-time, lay *assesseurs* are selected to serve in the *tribunaux pour enfants*, but their role is limited by the fact that only the most serious cases reach this court, the majority being disposed of by the *juge des enfants* in chambers, and by the presence of this judge to guide and advise them during their deliberations.

24   We are aware that many Scottish lawyers would argue that their system does not fall within the Anglo-American tradition, but, where the appointment and deployment of the judiciary is concerned, it is not so very different from the English model.

25   An exception is London, where magistrates may be appointed directly to the juvenile bench.

26   England and France are examples of this.

27   This has now been changed by the Children Act 1989, which restricts the use of wardship to cases which do not involve disputes concerning children in local authority care.

28   Pigot (1989).

29   We should add that, in Continental countries, children's evidence does not pose these problems, because the investigating magistrates have always had the option of interviewing the child outside the courtroom and informing the court of their view of the reliability of the child's evidence.

30   A similar development is occurring in some Continental countries – for example, France and Holland.

31   See Curran (1982).

32   See Walker et al. (1994) for research on the five pilot projects of comprehensive mediation organized by National Family Mediation in the UK.

# Bibliography

Adler, P., Lovaas, K. and Milner, N. (1988) 'The Ideologies of Mediation: The Movement's Own Story', *Law and Policy*, Vol.10, No.4, pp.316–39.

Adler, R.M. (1985) *Taking Juvenile Justice Seriously*, Edinburgh: Scottish Academic Press.

Allen, F. (1964) *The Borderland of Criminal Justice*, University of Chicago Press.

Almodovar, J. (1988) 'Le "Psy", le juge et l'enfant', in Bailleau, F. and Gueissaz, M. (eds) *'De quel droit? De l'intérêt aux droits de l'enfant'*, *Cahiers du CRIV*, 4, pp.63–72.

Alston, P., Parker, S. and Seymour, J. (1992) *Children, Rights and the Law*, Oxford: Clarendon.

Apel, S. (1989) 'Custodial Parents, Child Sexual Abuse and the Legal System: Beyond Contempt', *Am.U.L.*, Vol. 38, p.491.

Aries, P. (1973) *Centuries of Childhood*, Harmondsworth: Penguin.

Asquith, S. (1983) 'Justice, Retribution and Children' in Morris, A. and Giller, H. (eds) *Providing Criminal Justice for Children*, London: Edward Arnold.

Backett, K. (1982) *Mothers and Fathers*, London: Macmillan.

Badinter, E. (1981) *L'amour en plus*, Paris: Flammarion.

Ball, C. (1992) 'Young Offenders and the Youth Court', *Criminal Law Review*, p.277.

Barker, D.L. and Allen, S. (eds) (1976) *Sexual Divisions in Society: Process and Change*, London: Tavistock.

Barnes, G. (1982) 'Pattern and Intervention', in Bentovim, A., et al. (eds) *Family Therapy*, London: Academic Press.

Baxter, L. (1987) 'Family Welfare and the Courts', *Canadian Bar Review*, Vol.56, pp.37–48.

Beirne, P. and Quinney, R. (eds) (1982) *Marxism and Law*, New York: Wiley.

Bennett, W. and Feldman, H. (1981) *Reconstructing Reality in the Courtroom*, London: Tavistock.

Berger, P.L. and Luckmann, T. (1967) *The Social Construction of Reality: A Treatise in the Sociology of Knowledge*, Harmondsworth: Penguin.

Berliner, L. and Barbieri, M. (1984) 'The Testimony of the Child Victim of Sexual Assault', *Journal of Social Issues*, Vol.40, No.2, pp.155–63.

Blankenberg, E. (1984) 'The Poverty of Evolutionism: A Critique of Teubner's Case for Reflexive Law', *Law and Society Review*, Vol.18, p.273.

Blomberg, T. (1983) 'Diversion's Disparate Results and Unresolved Questions: An Integrative Evaluation Perspective', *Journal of Research in Crime and Delinquency*, January, p.24.

Bowden, J. and Stevens, M. (1986) 'Justice for Juveniles – A Corporate Strategy in Northampton', *Justice of the Peace*, 24 May.

Bowlby, J. (1988) *A Secure Base*, London: Routledge.

Brandt, R.B. (1976) 'The Concept of Welfare', in Timms, N. and Watson, D. (eds) *Talking About Welfare*, London: Routledge and Kegan Paul.

Britton, B., Hope, B., Locke, T. and Wainman, L. (1988) *Policy and Information in Juvenile Justice Systems*, London: NACRO/Save the Children Fund.

Brophy, J. (1985) 'Child Care and the Growth of Power: The Status of Mothers in Child Custody Disputes', in Brophy, J. and Smart, C. (eds) *Women in Law*, London: Routledge and Kegan Paul.

Brophy, J. and Smart, C. (eds) (1985) *Women in Law*, London: Routledge and Kegan Paul.

Bruch, C. (1988) 'And How are the Children? The Effects of Ideology and Mediation on Child Custody Law and Children's Wellbeing in the United States', *International Journal of Law and the Family*, Vol.2, pp.106–26.

Cameron, J. (1988) 'Community Mediation in New Zealand: A Pilot Project', *Journal of Social Welfare Law*, Vol.5, p.284.

Carney, T. (1989) 'Voluntary Care Arrangements: Responsive Welfare Entitlements? Or Coercive Intervention Revisited?', *Australian Journal of Family Law*.

Central Statistical Office (1985) *Social Trends*, 15, London: HMSO.

*The Child, the Family and the Young Offender* (1965) Cmnd 2742, London: HMSO.

Clarke, A.M. and Clarke, A.D. (1978) 'The Child's Social World', in Lerner, R. and Spanier, G. (eds) *Child Influences on Marital and Family Interaction*, New York: Academic Press.

Cohen, L.J. (1977) *The Probable and the Provable*, Oxford: Clarendon.

Conciliation Project Unit (1989) *Report to the Lord Chancellor on the Costs and Effectiveness of Conciliation in England and Wales*, University of Newcastle upon Tyne.

Coogler, O. (1978) *Structured Mediation in Divorce Settlement*, Lexington, Mass.: Lexington Books.

Cooper, D. (1971) *The Death of the Family*, London: Allen Lane.

Corlyon, J. (1993) 'Violent Allegations', *Family Mediation*, Vol.3, No.2, pp.14–15.

Cotterrell, R. (1984) *The Sociology of Law: An Introduction*, London: Butterworth.

Cotterrell, R. (1986) 'Law and Sociology: Notes on the Constitution and Confrontation of Disciplines', *Journal of Law and Society*, Vol.13, p.9.

Crewdson, J. (1988) *By Silence Betrayed: Sexual Abuse of Children in America*, Boston, Mass.: Little, Brown.

Curran, J.H. (1982) 'Safeguarders in the Children's Hearings', *Scottish Office Research Paper*, Edinburgh: Scottish Office Central Research Unit.

Curtis, S. (1989) *Juvenile Offending: Prevention through Intermediate Treatment*, London: Batsford.

Damaska, M.R. (1986) *The Faces of Justice and State Authority*, New Haven, Conn. and London: Yale University Press.

Davies, G. (1988) 'The Use of Videos in Child Abuse Trials', *The Psychologist*, Vol.1, No.1.

Davies, G. and Drinkwater, J. (1988) *The Child Witness: Do the Courts Abuse Children*, British Psychological Society Pamphlet, Issues in Criminological and Legal Psychology Series, No.13, Leicester: British Psychological Society.

Davis, G. (1982) 'Conciliation: A Dilemma for the Divorce Court Welfare Service', *Probation Journal*, Vol.29, No.4, pp.123–8.

Davis, G. (1983) 'Conciliation and the Professions', *Family Law*, Vol.13, No.1, pp.6–13.

Davis, G. (1985) 'The Theft of Conciliation', *Probation Journal*, Vol.32, No.1, pp.7–10.

Davis, G. (1988a) 'The Halls of Justice and Justice in the Halls', in Dingwall, R. and Eekelaar, J. (eds) *Divorce Mediation and the Legal Process*, Oxford: Clarendon.

Davis, G. (1988b) *Partisans and Mediators: The Resolution of Divorce Disputes*, Oxford: Clarendon.

Davis, G. and Bader, K. (1985a) 'In–court Mediation: The Consumer View, I', *Family Law*, Vol.15, pp.42–9.

Davis, G. and Bader, K. (1985b) 'In–court Mediation: The Consumer View, II', *Family Law*, Vol.15, pp.82–6.

Davis, G., Boucherat, J. and Watson, D. (1988) 'Reparation in the Service of Diversion', *Howard Journal*, Vol.27, pp.127–33.

Davis, G., Stephenson-Robb, Y. and Flin, R. (1986) 'The Reliability of Children's Testimony', *International Legal Practitioner*, pp.95–103.

Davis, P. (1987) 'There is a Book Out . . .: An Analysis of Judicial Absorbtion of Legislative Facts', *Harvard Law Review*, Vol.100, pp. 1,539–603.

Dingwall, R., (1986) 'Reports of Committees: The Jasmine Beckford Affair', *Modern Law Review*, Vol.49, pp.489–507.

Dingwall, R. and Eekelaar, J. (1984) 'Rethinking Child Protection', in Freeman, M.D.A. (ed.) *State, Law and the Family*, London: Tavistock.

Dingwall, R. and Eekelaar, J. (eds) (1988) *Divorce Mediation and the Legal Process*, Oxford: Clarendon.

Donzelot, J. (1979) *The Policing of Families*, London: Hutchinson.

Douglas, G. and Willmore, C. (1987) 'Diagnostic Interviews as Evidence in Cases of Child Sexual Abuse', *Family Law*, Vol.17, pp.151–4.

Drake, M. (1985) 'Conciliation: The Australian Experience', *Family Law*, Vol.15, pp.65–8.

Dreitzel, P. (1973) 'Childhood and Socialisation', *Recent Sociology*, No.5, New York: Macmillan.

Duprez, D. (1987) *Prevention de la delinquance et protection judiciaire de la jeunesse*, Centre Lillois d'Etudes et de Recherches Sociologiques et Economiques.

Eastman, N. (1992) 'Psychiatric, Psychological and Legal Models of Man', *International Journal of Law and Psychiatry*, Vol.15, pp.157–69.

Eekelaar, J. and Clive, (1977) *Custody after Divorce: Family Law Studies*, 1, Oxford: Economic and Social Research Council.

Ehrlich, E. (1936) *Fundamental Principles of the Sociology of Law* (transl. by W. Moll), New York: Amo Press.

Elliott, J. and Richards, M.P.M. (1991) 'Children in Divorce: Educational Performance and Behaviour Before and After Parental Separation', *International Journal of Law and the Family*, Vol.5, pp.258–76.

Elster, J. (1983) *Explaining Technical Change*, Cambridge University Press.

Elster, J. (1985) *The Multiple Self*, Cambridge University Press.

Ely, P., et al. (1987) *The Medway Close Support Unit*, Edinburgh: Scottish Academic Press.

Ely, S. and Stanley, C. (1990) *The French Alternative: Delinquency Prevention and Child Protection in France*, London: NACRO.

Emerson, R. (1969) *Judging Delinquents*, Chicago, Il.: Aldine Press.

Enright, S. (1989) 'Dolls as an Aid to Interviewing: A Legal View', in Levy, A. (ed.) *Focus on Child Abuse*, London: Hawksmere.

Erlanger, H., Chambliss, E. and Melli, M. (1987) 'Participation and Flexibility in Informal Processes: Cautions from the Divorce Court Context', *Law and Society Review*, Vol.21, No.4, pp.585–604.

Faigman, D. (1989) 'To Have and Have Not: Assessing the Value of Social Science to the Law as Science and Policy', *Emory Law Journal*, Vol.38, No.4, pp.1,005–95.

Farrell, B.A. (1981) *The Standing of Psychoanalysis*, Oxford University Press.

Feeley, M. (1979) *The Process is the Punishment*, New York: Russell Sage.

Felstiner, W. and Sarat, A. (1988) 'Negotiations between Lawyer and Client in an American Divorce', in Dingwall, R. and Eekelaar, J. (eds) *Divorce Mediation and the Legal Process*, Oxford: Clarendon.

Feyerabend, P. (1975) *Against Method: Outline of an Anarchistic Theory of Knowledge*, London: NLB.

Fine, B., et al. (eds) (1979) *Capitalism and the Rule of Law*, London: Hutchinson.

Fineman, M. (1988) 'Dominant Discourse, Professional Language and Legal Change in Child Custody Decision-making', *Harvard Law Review*, Vol.101, No.4, p.727.

Finer Report (1974) *One Parent Families*, Cmnd 5629, London: HMSO.

Fisher, T. (1994) 'Listening to the Voice of the Child, Consulting Children – Resolving a Conceptual Impasse', *Family Mediation*, Vol.4, No.1, pp.13–15.

Foucault, M. (1972) *The Archaeology of Knowledge*, London: Tavistock.

Foucault, M. (1974) *The Order of Things: An Archaeology of the Human Sciences*, London: Tavistock.

Foucault, M. (1977) *Discipline and Punishment*, London: Allen Lane.

Foucault, M. (1979) *The History of Sexuality Volume 1: An Introduction*, London: Allen Lane.

Foucault, M. (1982) 'The Subject and Power', in Dreyfus, H. and Rubinow, P. (eds) *Michel Foucault: Beyond Structuralism and Hermeneutics*, University of Chicago Press.

Fowles, J. (1969) *The French Lieutenant's Woman*, London: Granada.

Francis, P. (1989) *Family Conciliation and Mediation*, Social Work Monograph, Norwich: University of East Anglia.

Freeman, M.D.A (1983) *The Rights and Wrongs of Children*, London: Pinter.

Freeman, M.D.A. (ed.) (1984) *The State, the Law and the Family: Critical Perspectives*, London: Tavistock.

Freeman, M. and Veerman, P. (1992) *The Ideologies of Children's Rights*, Dordrecht, The Netherlands: Martinus Nijhoff.

Fricker, N. and Coates, L. (1989) 'Conciliation and a Conciliatory Approach in Welfare Reporting', *Family Law*, Vol.19, pp.56–60.

Frost, N. and Stein, M. (1989) *The Politics of Child Welfare*, Hemel Hempstead: Harvester Wheatsheaf.

Furniss, T. (1991) *Handbook of Child Sexual Abuse: Integrated Management, Therapy and Legal Intervention*, London: Routledge.

Garapon, A. (1989) 'Modèle garantiste et modèle paternaliste dans les systèmes de justice de mineurs', *Actes*, No.66, pp.19–24.

Geach, H. and Schwed, E. (1983) *Providing Civil Justice for Children*, London: Edward Arnold.

Gee, I. (1992) 'The Mediation Process', *Family Law*, Vol.22, pp.91–2.

Gelsthorpe, L. and Giller, H. (1990) 'More Justice for Juveniles: Does More Mean Better?', *Criminal Law Review*, pp.153–64.

Glaser, D. and Spencer, J. R. (1990) 'Sentencing, Children's Evidence and Children's Trauma', *Criminal Law Review*, p.371.

Goldstein, J., Freud, A. and Solnit, J. (1973) *Beyond the Best Interests of the Child*, New York: Free Press.

Goodman, J. and Jones, P.H. (1988) 'The Emotional Effects of Criminal Court Testimony on Child Sexual Abuse Victims: A Preliminary Report', in Davies, G. and Drinkwater, J. (eds) *The Child Witness: Do the Courts Abuse Children?*, Leicester: British Psychological Society.

Graham Hall, J. (1973) *Proposal for a Family Court*, London: National Council for the Unmarried Mother and Her Child.

Graham Hall, J. and Martin, D. (1993) *Child Abuse, Procedure and Evidence in Juvenile Courts*, (3rd edn), Chichester: Barry Rose.

Grant, J. (1976) 'Protecting the Rights of Children', in Martin, F. and Murray, K. (eds) *Children's Hearings*, Edinburgh: Scottish Academic Press.

Greatbatch, D. and Dingwall, R. (1989) 'Selective Facilitation: Some Preliminary Observations on a Strategy used by Divorce Mediators', *Law and Society Review*, Vol.23, pp.613–41.

Greer, R. 'Child Witness in Court', unpublished MA dissertation, Uxbridge: Brunel University.

Griffith, J.A.G. (1977) *The Politics of the Judiciary*, London: Fontana.

Grillo, T. (1991) 'The Mediation Alternative: Process Dangers for Women', *Yale Law Journal*, Vol.100, pp.1,545–610.

Gypps, G. (1983) 'Matrimonial Negotiations', *Litigation*, Vol.3, No.1, p.21.

Habermas, J. (1971) *Knowledge and Human Interest*, Boston, Mass.: Beacon.

Habermas, J. (1973) 'Wahreitstheorien', in Fahrenbach, H. (ed.) *Wirklichkeit und Reflexion*, Pfullingen: Neske.211.

Habermas, J. (1984) *The Theory of Communicative Action*, Vol.1, *Reason and the Rationalization of Society*, Boston, Mass.: Beacon.

Habermas, J. (1985) 'Law as Medium and Law as Institution', in Teubner, G. (ed.) *Dilemmas of Law in the Welfare State*, Berlin: De Gruyter.

Haines, H.H. (1979) 'Cognitive Claims-making, Enclosure and the Depoliticization of Social Problems', *Sociological Quarterly*, Vol.20.

Hallett, C. (1989) 'Child Abuse Inquiries and Public Policy', in Stevenson, O. (ed.) *Child Abuse: Public Policy and Professional Practice*, Hemel Hempstead: Harvester Wheatsheaf.

Harding, J. (1989) 'Reconciling Mediation with Criminal Justice', in Wright, M. and Galaway, B. (eds) *Mediation and Criminal Justice*, London: Sage.

Harrington, C. and Merry, S. (1988) 'Ideological Production: The Making of Community Mediation', *Law and Society Review*, Vol.22, No.4, p.70.

Harris, R. (1985) 'Towards Just Welfare', *British Journal of Criminology*, Vol.25, No.1, pp.31–45.

Harris, R. and Webb, D. (1987) *Welfare, Power and Juvenile Justice*, London: Tavistock.

Hayek, F.A. (1944) *The Road to Serfdom*, London: Routledge.

Haynes, J. (1978) *Divorce Mediation*, New York: Springer.

Hess, R. and Comara, K. (1979) 'Post-divorce Family Relationships as a Mediating Factor in the Consequences of Divorce for Children', *Journal of Social Issues*, Vol.35, No.4, p.26.

Hesse, M. (1980) *Revolutions and Reconstructions in the Philosophy of Science*, Brighton, UK: Harvester.

Hetherington, E., Cox, M. and Cox, R. (1979) 'Play and Social Interaction in Children Following Divorce', *Journal of Social Issues*, Vol.35, No.4, p.79.

Hipgrave, T., French, D. and Baroness Faithfull, L. (1989) 'The Way Forward', *Family Law*, Vol.19, pp.264–7.

Hirsch, T. (1972) *Causes of Delinquency*, Berkeley, Ca.: University of California Press.

Holman, R. (1978) *Poverty, Explanations of Social Deprivation*, London: Martin Robertson.

Holman, R. (1988) *Putting Families First*, Basingstoke: Macmillan.

Home Office (1990) *Report of the Advisory Group on Video Evidence*, London: HMSO.

Home Office and Department of Health (1992) *Memorandum of Good Practice*, London: HMSO.

Howard, J. and Shepherd, G. (1987) *Conciliation, Children and Divorce: A Family Systems Approach*, London: Batsford/BAAF.

Institute for Judicial Administration and the American Bar Association (1977) *Juvenile Justice Standards Project*, Cambridge, Mass.: Gallenger.

James, A. (1988) 'Civil Work in the Probation Service', in Dingwall, R. and Eekelaar, J. (eds) *Divorce Mediation and the Legal Process*, Oxford: Clarendon.

James, A. (1992) 'An Open or Shut Case? Law as an Autopoietic System', *Journal of Law and Society*, Vol.19, No.2, pp.271–83.

James, A. and Hay, W. (1993) *Court Welfare in Action*, Hemel Hempstead: Harvester Wheatsheaf.

Johnston, J.R., et al. (1985) 'Latency Children in Post-separation and Divorce Disputes', *Journal of American Academic Child Psychiatry*, Vol.24, pp.563–74.

Junger-Tas, J. (1988) 'Strategies against Vandalism in the Netherlands', paper given at the Conference on Crime Prevention, Münster, Germany, September.

Junger-Tas, J. and Block, R. (1988) *Juvenile Delinquency in the Netherlands*, Amsterdam: Kugler.

Kaganas, F. and Piper, C. (1990) 'Grandparents and the Limits of Law', *International Journal of Law and the Family*, Vol.4, pp.27-51.

Kaganas, F. and Piper, C. (1994a) 'Joint Parenting Under the Children Act 1989', in Lockton, D. (ed.) *Children and the Law*, London: Cavendish.

Kaganas, F. and Piper, C. (1994b) 'Domestic Violence and Divorce Mediation', *Journal of Social Welfare and Family Law*, No.3, pp.265–78.

Kennedy, D. (1986) 'Freedom and Constraint in Adjudication: A Critical Phenomenology', *Journal of Legal Education*, Vol.36, p.518.

King, M. (1981) 'Welfare and Justice', in King, M. (ed.) *Childhood, Welfare and Justice*, London: Batsford.

King, M. (1983) 'Children's Justice French Style', *Social Work Today*, 13 December.

King, M. (1984) 'Child Protection and the Search for Justice for Parents and Families in England and France', in Freeman, M.D.A. (ed.) *The State, the Law and the Family*, London: Tavistock.

King, M. (1986) *Psychology in and out of Court: A Critical Examination of Legal Psychology*, Oxford: Pergamon.

King, M. (1987a) 'Playing the Symbols – Custody and the Law Commission', *Family Law*, Vol.17, pp.186–91.

King, M. (1987b) 'Crime Prevention in France', *Home Office Research and Planning Bulletin*, November.

King, M. (1988) *The French Experience: How to Make Social Crime Prevention Work*, London: NACRO.

King, M. (1989) 'Social Crime Prevention à la Thatcher', *Howard Journal*, Vol.28, No.4, pp.291–331.

King, M. (1991a) 'Child Welfare Within Law: The Emergence of a Hybrid Discourse', *Journal of Law and Society*, Vol.18, No.3, pp.303–22.

King, M. (1991b) 'Children and the Legal Process: The View from a Mental Health Clinic', *Journal of Social Welfare and Family Law*, No.4, pp.269–84.

King, M. (1993) 'The "Truth" about Autopoiesis', *Journal of Law and Society*, Vol.20, No.2, pp.1–19.

King, M. (1994) 'Children's Rights as Communication: Reflections on Autopoietic Theory and the United Nations Convention', *Modern Law Review*, Vol.57, No.3, pp.385–401.

King, M. (1995) 'Law's Healing of Children's Hearings. The Paradox Moves North', *Journal of Social Policy*, in press.

King, M. and Garapon, A. (1987) 'Judges and Experts in England and Wales and in France: Developing a Comparative Socio-legal Analysis', *Journal of Law and Society*, Vol.14, No.4, pp.459–73.

King, M. and Garapon, A. (1988) 'Le juge, l'expert et le contrôle de la réalité dans les juridictions de la jeunesse en France et en Angleterre', *Droit et Société*, No.10, pp.425–43.

King, M. and Petit, M. (1985) 'Thin Stick and Fat Carrot – The French Juvenile Justice System', *Youth and Policy*, No.15, pp.26–31.

King, M. and Piper, C. (1990) *How the Law Thinks About Children*, (1st edn), Aldershot: Gower.

King, M. and Schütz, A. (1994) 'The Ambitious Modesty of Niklas Luhmann', *Journal of Law and Society*, Vol.21, No.3, p.261.

King, M. and Trowell, J. (1992) *Children's Welfare and the Law: The Limits of Legal Intervention*, London: Sage.

Kuhn, T.N. (1962) *The Structure of Scientific Revolutions*, Princeton University Press.

Lakatos, I. (1970) 'Falsification and the Methodology of Scientific Research Programmes', in Lakatos, I. and Musgrave, A. *Criticism and the Growth of Knowledge*, Cambridge University Press.

Lamb, M.E. (ed.) (1981) *Non-traditional Families: Parenting and Child Development*, Hillside, New Jersey: Lawrence Erlbaum.

Landau, S. (1981) 'Juveniles and the Police: Who is Charged Immediately and Who is Referred to the Juvenile Bureau?', *British Journal of Criminology*, Vol.21, No.1, p.27.

Law Commission (1986) *Family Law Review of Child Law: Custody*, Working Paper No.96, London: HMSO.

Lee, C. (1980) 'Official Inquiries', in Carver, V. (ed.) *Child Abuse: A Study Text*, Milton Keynes: Open University Press.

Lees, S. (1989) 'Trial by Rape', *New Statesman*, 24 November, pp.10–13.

Lehner, L. (1994) 'Education for Parents Divorcing in California', *Family and Conciliation Courts Review*, Vol.32, No.1, pp.50–4.

Lempert, R. (1988) 'The Autonomy of Law: Two Visions Compared', in Teubner, G. (ed.) *Autopoietic Law: A New Approach to Law and Society*, Berlin: De Gruyter.

Lerman, P. (1980) 'Trends and Issues in Deinstitutionalization of Youths in Trouble', *Crime and Delinquency*, July, p.282.

Lerner, R. and Spanier, G. (eds) (1978) *Child Influences on Marital and Family Interaction*, New York: Academic Press.

Lewis, M. and Feiring, C. (1978) 'The Child's Social World', in Lerner, R. and Spanier, G. (eds) *Child Influences on Marital and Family Interaction*, New York: Academic Press.

Liberman, R. (1984) *Les enfants devant le divorce*, (2nd edn), Paris: Presses Universitaires de France.

Lienhard, C. (1985) *Le role du juge aux affaires matrimoniales*, Paris: Economica.

Llewellyn, K. (1930) 'A Realistic Jurisprudence: The Next Step', *Columbia Law Review*, Vol.30, pp.431–65.

Locke, T. (1988) 'Policy, Information and Monitoring Juvenile Crime and Justice', in Britton, B., Hope, B., Locke, T. and Wainman, L. *Policy and Information in Juvenile Justice Systems*, London: NACRO/Save the Children Fund.

Lord Chancellor's Department (1993) *Looking to the Future: Mediation and the Ground for Divorce*, Cm. 2424, London: HMSO.

Luhmann, N. (1972) *Rechtssoziologie*, Rowohlt: Reinbek.

Luhmann, N. (1974) *Rechtssystem und Rechtsdogmatik*, Stuttgart: Kohlhammer.

Luhmann, N. (1982) *The Differentiation of Society*, New York: Columbia University Press.

Luhmann, N. (1984) *Soziale Systeme: Grundriß Einer Allgemeinen Theorie*, Frankfurt: Suhrkamp.

Luhmann, N. (1985) *A Sociological Theory of Law* (transl. by King-Utz, E. and Wybrow, M.) London: Routledge and Kegan Paul.

Luhmann, N. (1986) 'The Autopoiesis of Social Systems', in Geyer, F. and Van der Zouwen, J. (eds) *Sociocybernetic Paradoxes: Observation, Control and Evolution of Self-steering Systems*, London/Beverly Hills: Sage.

Luhmann, N. (1988a) 'Closure and Openness: On Reality in the World of Law', in Teubner, G. (ed.) *Autopoietic Law: A New Approach to Law and Society*, Berlin: De Gruyter.

Luhmann, N. (1988b) 'The Unity of the Legal System', in Teubner, G. (ed.) *Autopoietic Law: A New Approach to Law and Society*, Berlin: De Gruyter.

Luhmann, N. (1989) 'Law as a Social System', *Northwestern University Law Review*, Vol.83, Nos 1 and 2, pp.136–50.

Luhmann, N. (1992) 'Some Problems with "Reflexive Law"', in Teubner, G. and Febbrajo, A. (eds) *European Yearbook of the Sociology of Law*, Milan: Guiffrè.

Lund, M. (1984) 'Research on Divorce and Children: Implications for Reforms in Divorce Procedure', *Family Law*, Vol.14.

Maclean, M. and Wadsworth, M.E.J. (1988) 'The Interests of Children after Parental Divorce', *International Journal of Law and the Family*, Vol.2, pp.155–66.

Maidment, S. (1984) *Child Custody and Divorce*, London: Croom Helm.

Manning, N.H. (1985) 'Constructing Social Problems', in Manning, N.H. (ed.) *Social Problems and Welfare Ideology*, Aldershot: Gower.

Marshall, J. (1966) *Law and Psychology in Conflict*, Indianapolis: Bobbs-Merrill.

Marshall, T.F. (1985) *Alternatives to Criminal Courts*, Aldershot: Gower.

Marshall, T.H. (1976) 'The Right to Welfare', in Timms, N. and Watson, D. (eds) *Talking about Welfare*, London: Routledge and Kegan Paul.

Martin, F.M., Fox, S.J. and Murray, K. (1981) *Children out of Court*, Edinburgh: Scottish Academic Press.

Matthews, R. (1988) *Informal Justice*, London: Sage.

Maturana, H. and Varela, F.J. (1980) *Autopoiesis and Cognition*, Boston, Mass.: Reidel.

May, D. (1977) 'Rhetoric and Reality: Ambiguity in the Children's Panel System', *British Journal of Criminology*, Vol.17, p.109.

McEwen, C., Maiman, R. and Mather, L. (1990) 'The Impact of Divorce Mediation on Legal Practice in Maine', paper presented to the Annual Conference of the Socio-Legal Association, Bristol, April.

McEwen, C., Mather, L. and Maiman, R. (1994) 'Lawyers, Mediators and the Management of Divorce Practice', *Law and Society Review*, Vol.28, No.1, pp.149–86.

McGregor, O.R. (1957) *Divorce in England*, London: Heinemann.

McIntyre, A. (1964) *Secularization and Moral Change*, London: Open University Press.

McIsaac, H. (1994) 'Orientation to Mediation in Portland, Oregon', *Family and Conciliation Courts Review*, Vol.32, No.1, pp.55–61.

McKittrick, N. and Eysenck, S. (1984) 'Diversion: A Big Fix', *Justice of the Peace*, Vol.8, pp.377 and 393.

McLaughlin, D. and Whitfield, R. (1984) 'Adolescents and their Experience of Parental Divorce', *Journal of Adolescence*, Vol.7, pp.155–70.

McLeod, M. and Saraga, E. (1988) 'Challenging the Orthodoxy: Towards a Feminist Theory and Practice', *Feminist Review*, No.28, pp.16–55.

Mead, G.H. (1934) *Mind, Self and Society: From the Standpoint of a Social Behaviourist*, edited with an introduction by Morris, C.W., University of Chicago Press.

Minuchin, S. (1974) *Families and Family Therapy*, London: Tavistock.

Mitchell, A. (1983) 'Adolescents' Experience of Parental Separation and Divorce', *Journal of Adolescence*, Vol.6, pp.175–87.

Mitchell, A. (1985) *Children in the Middle: Living through Divorce*, London: Tavistock.

Mitchell, G. (1989) 'Professional Decision-making in Child Abuse Cases: The Social Worker's Dilemma – Part 2', *Family Law*, Vol.19, pp.11–16.

Mnookin, R. and Kornhauser, L. (1979) 'Bargaining in the Shadow of the Law: The Case of Divorce', *Yale Law Journal*, Vol.88, pp.950–70.

Moncur, A. and Austin, D. (1989) *Margaret Thatcher's History of the World*, London: *Guardian*/Fourth Estate.

Morris, A. and Giller, H. (1983) *Providing Criminal Justice for Children*, London: Edward Arnold.

Morris, A. and Giller, H. (1987) *Understanding Juvenile Justice*, London: Croom Helm.

Morris, A., Giller, H. and Schwed, H. (1980) *Justice for Children*, London: Edward Arnold.

Mott, J. (1983) 'Police Decisions for Dealing with Juvenile Offenders', *British Journal of Criminology*, Vol.23, No.3, pp.249–62.

Moxon, D. (ed.) (1985) Managing Criminal Justice, Home Office Research and Planning Unit, London: HMSO.

Murch, M. (1980) *Justice and Welfare in Divorce*, London: Sweet and Maxwell.

Murch, M. and Hooper, D. (1992) *The Family Justice System*, Bristol: Family Law.

NACRO (1986) *Black People and the Criminal Justice System*, London: NACRO.

NACRO Briefing (1990) 'Criteria for Custody', No.69, London: NACRO.

Nelken, D. (1987) 'The Use of Contracts as a Social Work Technique', in Rideout, R. and Jowell, J. (eds) *Current Legal Problems*, London: Sweet and Maxwell.

Nelken, D. (1988a) 'Social Work Contracts and Social Control', in Matthews, R. (ed.) *Informal Justice*, London: Sage.

Nelken, D. (1988b) 'Changing Paradigms in the Sociology of Law', in Teubner, G. (ed.) *Autopoietic Law: A New Approach to Law and Society*, Berlin: De Gruyter.

Nelken, D. (1990) *The Truth about Law's Truth*, Working Paper No.7, Faculty of Law, University College London.

Nelson, A. (1984) 'Some Issues Surrounding the Reduction of Macroeconomics to Microeconomics', *Philosophy of Science*, Vol.51, p.537.

New, C. and David, M. (1985) *For the Children's Sake*, Harmondsworth: Penguin Books.

Nonet, P. and Selznick, P. (1978) *Law and Society in Transition: Toward Responsive Law*, New York: Octagen.

O'Donovan, K. (1993) *Family Law Matters*, London: Pluto.

Parker, D. and Parkinson, L. (1985) 'Solicitors and Family Conciliation Services – A Basis for Professional Cooperation', *Family Law*, Vol.15, pp.270–4.

Parker, H., Casburn, M. and Turnbull, D. (1981) *Reviewing Juvenile Justice*, Oxford: Blackwell.

Parkinson, L. (1986) *Conciliation in Separation and Divorce*, London: Croom Helm.

Parkinson, L. (1989) 'Co-mediation with a Lawyer Mediator', *Family Law*, Vol.19, pp.135–9.

Parsloe, P. (1978) *Juvenile Justice in Britain and the United States*, London: Routledge and Kegan Paul.

Parton, N. (1985) *The Politics of Child Abuse*, London: Macmillan.

Parton, N. (1986) 'The Beckford Report: A Critical Appraisal', *British Journal of Social Work*, Vol.16, pp.511–30.

Parton, N. (1991) *Governing the Family: Child Care, Child Protection and the State*, Basingstoke: Macmillan.

Pigot, Judge (1989) *Report of the Advisory Group on Video Evidence*, London: Home Office.

Piper, C. (1987) 'Divorce Conciliation: Who Decides About the Children?', unpublished PhD thesis, Uxbridge: Brunel University.

Piper, C. (1988a) *For the Sake of the Children: A Study of the Conciliation Process*, Brunel Socio-Legal Working Papers, Uxbridge: Brunel University Law Department.

Piper, C. (1988b) 'Divorce Conciliation in the UK: How Responsible are Parents?', *International Journal of the Sociology of Law*, Vol.16, pp.477–94.

Piper, C. (1993) *The Responsible Parent*, Hemel Hempstead: Harvester Wheatsheaf.

Piper, C. (1994a) 'Parental Responsibility and the Education Acts', *Family Law*, Vol.24.

Piper, C. (1994b) 'Looking to the Future for Children', *Journal of Child Law*, Vol.6, No.3, pp.98–104.

Popper, K. (1959) 'Philosophy of Science: A Personal Report', in Mace, C.A. (ed.) *British Philosophy in Mid-century*, London: Allen and Unwin.

Popper, K. (1965) *The Logic of Scientific Discovery*, New York: Harper.

Pound, R. (1916) 'The Limits of Effective Legal Action', *International Journal of Law and Ethics*, Vol.27, pp.150–1 and 161–7.

Pratt, J. (1986) 'Diversion from the Juvenile Court', *British Journal of Criminology*, Vol.26, No.3, p.212.

Pratt, J. (1989) 'Corporatism: The Third Model of Juvenile Justice', *British Journal of Criminology*, Vol.29, No.3, p.236.

Priest, J. and Whybrow, J. (1986) *Custody Law in Practice in the Divorce and Domestic Courts: Supplement to Law Commission Working Paper No.96*, London: HMSO.

Priestley, P., Fears, D. and Fuller, R. (1977) *Justice for Juveniles: The 1969 Children and Young Persons Act – A Case for Reform*, London: RKP.

Prison Reform Trust (1987) 'Comparisons in Juvenile Justice', *Juvenile Justice: Project Report*, No.1.

Pruhs, A. Paulsen, M. and Tysseling, W. (1984) 'Divorce Mediation: The Politics of Integrating Clinicians', *Social Casework*, Vol.65, No.9, pp.532–40.

Reder, P., Duncan, S. and Gray, M. (1993) *Beyond Blame*, London and New York: Routledge.

Reece, S.A. (1983) 'Joint Custody: A Cautious View', *University of California Davis Law Review*, Vol.16, pp.775–83.

Reifen, N. (1973) 'Court Procedures in Israel to Protect Child Victims of Sexual Assault', in Drapkin, I. and Viano, E. (eds) *Victimology: A New Focus*, Vol.3, Lexington, Mass.: Lexington Books.

Reisman, D. (1977) *Richard Titmuss: Welfare and Society*, London: Heinemann.

*Report of the Matrimonial Causes Procedures Committee* (1988), London: HMSO.

Richards, M. and Dyson, M. (1982) *Separation, Divorce and Development of Children: A Review*, Report for DHSS, London: HMSO.

Riley, D. (1983) *War in the Nursery: Theories of the Child and Mother*, London: Virago.

Ritchie, M. and Mack, J. (1974) *Police Warnings*, University of Glasgow.

Roberts, M. (1990) 'Systems or Selves? Some Ethical Issues in Family Mediation', *Journal of Social Welfare and Family Law*, No.1, pp.6–17.

Roberts, M. (1992) 'Who is in Charge? Reflections on Recent Research on the Role of the Mediator', *Journal of Social Welfare Law*, No.5, pp.372–87.

Roberts, S. (1983) 'Mediation in Family Disputes', *Modern Law Review*, Vol.46, No.5, p.537.

Roberts, S. (1988) 'Three Models of Family Mediation', in Dingwall, R. and Eekelaar, J. (eds) *Divorce Mediation and the Legal Process*, Oxford: Clarendon.

Rorty, R. (1982) *Philosophy and the Mirror of Nature*, Brighton: Harvester.

Rose, E. (1969) *Colour and Citizenship: A Report on British Race Relations*, Oxford University Press.

Rosenthal, R. (1963) 'On the Social Psychology of the Psychological Experiment: The Experimenter's Hypothesis as Determinant of Experimental Results', *American Scientist*, Vol.51, pp.268–83.

Rottleuthner, H. (1983) *Rechtssoziologische Studien zur Arbeitgerichtsbarkeit*, Baden-Baden: Nomos.

Rottleuthner, H. (1989) 'A Purified Sociology of Law: Niklas Luhmann on the Autonomy of the Legal System', *Law and Society Review*, Vol.23, No.5, pp.779–97.

Rustin, M. (1989) 'Observing Infants: Reflections on Methods', in Muller et al. (eds) *Closely Observed Infants*, London: Duckworth.

Rutherford, A. (1992) *Growing Out of Crime: The New Era*, (2nd edn), Winchester: Waterside.

Rutter, M. (1972) *Maternal Deprivation Reassessed*, Harmondsworth: Penguin.

Rutter, M. and Giller, H. (1983) *Juvenile Delinquency: Trends and Perspectives*, Harmondsworth: Penguin.

Sarat, A. and Felstiner, W. (1986) 'Law and Strategy in the Divorce Lawyers Office', *Law and Society Review*, Vol.21, No.1, p.93.

Sarri, R. (1983) 'Paradigms and Pitfalls in Juvenile Justice Diversion', in Morris, A. and Giller, H. (eds) *Providing Criminal Justice for Children*, London: Edward Arnold.

Searle, J. (1984) *Minds, Brains and Science*, London: Penguin.

Seeley, J.R. (1963) 'Social Science? Some Probative Problems', in Stein, M. and Vidich, A. (eds) *Sociology on Trial*, New York: Prentice-Hall.

Seyfrit, C., et al. (1987) 'Peer Juries', *Youth and Society*, Vol.18, No.3, p.302.

Shapland, J. (1981) *Between Conviction and Sentence, The Process of Mitigation*, London: Routledge.

Shepherd, G., Howard, J. and Tonkinson, J. (1984) 'Conciliation: Taking it Seriously?', *Probation Journal*, Vol.31, No.1, pp.21–4.

Sibley, S. (1981) 'Making Sense of the Lower Courts', *The Justice System Journal*, Vol.6, pp.13–27.

Silby, C. and Merry, S. (1988) 'The Making of Mediation', *Law and Society Review*, Vol.22, No.4, pp.709–35.

Simpson, R. (1991) 'The Children Act 1989 and the Voice of the Child in Family Mediation', *Family and Conciliation Courts Review*, Vol.29, No.4, pp.387–97.

Smart, C. (1989) *Feminism and the Power of Law*, London: Routledge.

Smith, D., Blagg, H. and Derricourt, N. (1988) 'Mediation in South Yorkshire', *British Journal of Criminology*, Vol.28, No.3, pp.378–95.

Smith D.J. (1977) *Racial Disadvantage in Britain*, Harmondsworth: Penguin.

Spencer, J. and Flin, R. (1990) *The Evidence of Children: The Law and the Psychology*, Oxford: Blackstone.

Stein, P. (1984) *Legal Institutions: The Development of Dispute Settlement*, London: Butterworth.

Stender, F. (1979) 'Les conflits entre parents pour la garde des enfants: quel rôle jouent les professionels?', *Revue Internationale de l'enfant*, No.41, June.

Stephenson, G.M. (1992) *The Psychology of Criminal Justice*, Oxford: Blackwell.

Stone, M. (1988) *Cross-examination in Criminal Trials*, London: Butterworth.

Stone, M. (1989) 'Giving the Lie to the Old Fashioned Hunch', *Independent*, 13 October.

Sutton, A. (1981) 'Science in Court', in King, M. (ed.) *Childhood, Welfare and Justice*, London: Batsford.

Sutton, J. (1985) 'The Juvenile Court and Social Welfare: Dynamics of Progressive Reform', *Law and Society Review*, Vol.19, No.1, p.107.

Taylor, L., Lacey, R. and Bracken, D. (1979) *In Whose Best Interests?*, London: Cobden Trust.

Teubner, G. (1983) 'Substantive and Reflexive Elements in Modern Law', *Law and Society Review*, Vol.17, No.2, p.239.

Teubner, G. (1985) 'After Legal Instrumentalism', in Teubner, G. (ed.) *Dilemmas of Law in the Welfare State*, Berlin: De Gruyter, p.299.

Teubner, G. (1986) 'Industrial Democracy through Law. Social Junctions of Law in Institutional Innovations', in Daintith, T. and Teubner, G. (eds) *Legal Analysis in the Light of Economic and Social Theory*, Berlin: De Gruyter, p.261.

Teubner, G. (ed.) (1988) *Autopoietic Law: A New Approach to Law Society*, Berlin/New York: De Gruyter.

Teubner, G. (1989) 'How the Law Thinks: Toward a Constructivist Epistemology of Law', *Law and Society Review*, Vol.23, No.5, pp.727–56.

Teubner, G. (1993) *Law as an Autopoietic System*, Oxford: Blackwell.

Thane, P. (1981) 'Childhood in History', in King, M. (ed.) *Childhood, Welfare and Justice*, London: Batsford.

Tims, N. and Watson, D. (eds) (1976) *Talking about Welfare*, London: Routledge and Kegan Paul.

Titmuss, R. (1950) *Problems of Social Policy*, Westport, Conn.: Greenwood.

Titmuss, R. (1970) *The Gift Relationship*, London: Allen and Unwin.

Tutt, N. and Giller, H. (1984) *Social Inquiry Reports*, Lancaster: Information Systems.

Twining, W. and Miers, D. (1985) *How to do Things with Rules*, London: Weidenfeld and Nicholson.

Uglow, S., Dart, A., Bottomley, A. and Hale, C. (1992) 'Cautioning Juveniles – Multi-agency Impotence', *Criminal Law Review*, pp.632–41.

Veevers, J. (1989) 'Pre-court Diversion for Juvenile Offenders', in Wright, M. and Galaway, B. *Mediation and Criminal Justice*, London: Sage.

Vizard, E. (1987) 'Interviewing Young Sexually Abused Children', *Family Law*, Vol.17, pp.28–33.

Walczak, Y. and Burns, S. (1984) *Divorce: The Child's Point of View*, London: Harper and Row.

Walker, H. and Beaumont, B. (1981) *Probation Work: Critical Theory and Social Practice*, Oxford: Blackwell.

Walker, J., McCarthy, P. and Timms, N. (1994) *Mediation: The Making and Remaking of Cooperative Relationships – An Evaluation of the Effectiveness of Comprehensive Mediation*, University of Newcastle, Relate Centre for Family Studies.

Wallerstein, J. and Kelly, J. (1981) *Surviving the Break-up*, London: Grant McIntyre.

Walrond-Skinner, S. (ed.) (1981) *Developments in Family Therapy*, London: Routledge and Kegan Paul.

Waterhouse, The Hon. Mr Justice (1989) 'Allegations of Child Abuse: The Court's Approach', in Levy, A. (ed.) *Focus on Child Abuse: Legal, Medical and Social Work Perspectives*, London: Hawkesmere.

Wattam, C. (1992) *Making a Case in Child Protection*, Harlow: NSPCC/ Longman.

Weintraub, E.R. (1979) *Microfoundations: The Compatibility of Microeconomics and Macroeconomics*, Cambridge University Press.

White Paper (1968) *Children in Trouble*, Cmnd 3601, London: HMSO.

Woody, J., et al. (1984) 'Child Adjustment to Parental Stress Following Divorce', *Journal of Contemporary Social Work*, Vol.65, No.7, p.405.

Wright, M. and Galaway, B. (1989) *Mediation and Criminal Justice*, London: Sage.

Young, R. (1989) 'Reparation as Mediation', *Criminal Law Review*, pp.463-72.

Zander, M. (1985) *The Law-making Process*, London: Weidenfeld and Nicholson.

Zolo, D. (1992) 'The Epistomological Status of the Theory of Autopoiesis and its Application to the Social Sciences', in Teubner, G. and Febbrajo, A. (eds) *State, Law, Economy as Autopoietic Systems: Regulation and Autonomy in a New Perspective*, Milan: Giuffrè.

# Index

Conciliation Project Unit, 90, 95
construction of truth, 22–6, 90–92
consumer information, 36
continuity, 154–7
Coogler, O., 88
Corlyon, J., 92
corporal punishment, 2
Cotterrell, R., 28–9
crime, children and, xi, 4–5, 7, 8, 70,
    77, 103–26, 134, 155–6
Critical Legal Studies, 63
Curtis, S., 119
custody issues, 56–8, 72–3

Damaska, M. R., 147, 150–51, 155
Davis, G., 9, 79, 89, 96, 97, 116–17
Davis, P., 56
de-differentiation, xiv–xv, 38
determinism, 135
diagnostic interviews, 71
diffusion, 33
Dingwall, R., 98
discourse
    legal, 28, 29–30, 31
    power and, 24
    theory of, 22–3
diversion schemes, 116–17, 122–5
divorce
    access/custody and, 52, 72–3
    law and, 83–100, 148–9
    mediation and, xi–xii, 6, 8–9, 87–100
    welfare/justice clash and, 5–6
documentary evidence, 150–51
domestic violence, xii
Donzelot, J., 11, 55
Douglas, G., 71
Duprez, D., 113
Dyson, M., 85

Eekelaar, J., 97, 98
Ely, S., 113
Emerson, R., 110–11
empiricism, 44, 45
Enright, S., 71
enslavement, notion of, xii, 50–51
epistemic trap, 31–2
    avoidance of, 32–7

Erlanger, H., 98
ethnic minorities, crime and, xi
evidence from children, 49–50, 67–72,
    75–6, 150–51, 160
experts, 53–5, 68, 69, 71–2, 73, 111–12,
    157–63

family
    changing attitudes to, 83–5
    mediation in, xi–xii, 6, 8–9, 87–100
    state power and, 2–3, 5
    systems theory of, 59, 84
Family Courts, 8–9, 10, 159
Family Law Act (Australia), 14–15
Farrell, B. A., 46
fathers *see* parents
Feeley, M., 4, 7, 109
Feiring, C., 85
Felstiner, W., 98
feminism, family mediation and, xi–xii
Fineman, M., 90
Foretich, E., 75
Foucault, M., 11, 24, 26, 37, 139,
    144
fragmentation, notion of, 26, 28
France, 10, 35, 53–4, 113, 126, 148–50,
    156, 158
Freud, A., 137
Freudianism, 55–6, 65
Furniss, T., 49–50

Garapon, A., 66
Gee, I., 89
Gelsthorpe, L., 124
Giller, H., 7, 109, 118, 124
Grillo, T., 91
Goldstein, J., 55–6, 84, 137
group dynamics, 84
guardian *ad litem*, 9, 154, 162
Gypps, G., 97

Habermas, J., 22–4, 25, 28, 37
Halt Project, 126
Harrington, C., 116
Harris, R., 7, 11
Hay, W., 35